D0025222

usic in Human Life

hropological Perspectives on Music

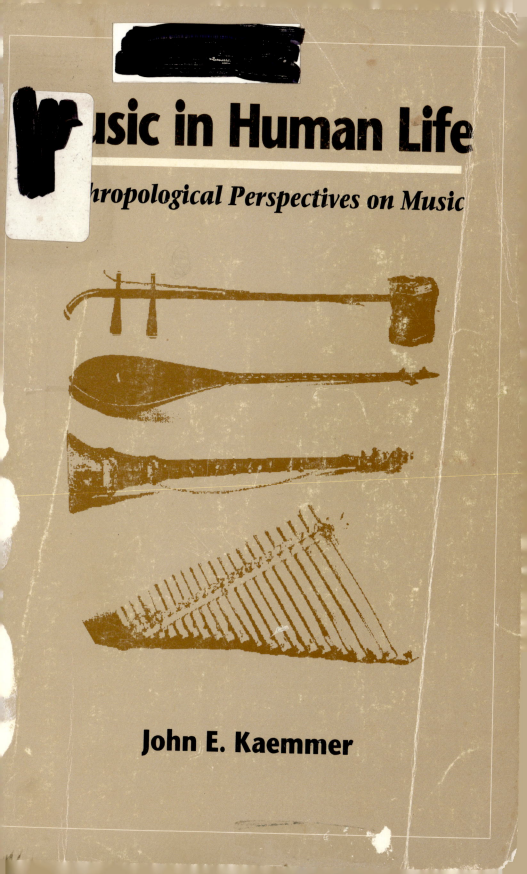

John E. Kaemmer

Music in Human Life

Texas Press Sourcebooks in Anthropology, No. 17

Music in Human Life

Anthropological
Perspectives on Music

JOHN E. KAEMMER

as Press, Austin

[WITHDRAWN

Thanks to the William Hammond Mathers Museum for permission
to use photographs by the author of instruments in their collection.
The following photographs are of instruments in that collection:
2.1, 3.1, 4.2–4.14, 4.16, 5.1, 5.2, 5.5, 7.2, and 7.3.

Copyright © 1993 by the University of Texas Press
All rights reserved
Printed in the United States of America
First edition, 1993

Requests for permission to reproduce material from this work
should be sent to Permissions, University of Texas Press, Box 7819,
Austin, TX 78713-7819.

⊗ The paper used in this publication meets the minimum requirements of American National Standard for Information Sciences—
Permanence of Paper for Printed Library Materials, ANSI Z39.48-1984.

Library of Congress Cataloging-in-Publication Data

Kaemmer, John E. (John Edmund), 1928–
    Music in human life : anthropological perspectives on music / John E. Kaemmer.
    — 1st ed.
        p.   cm. — (Texas Press sourcebooks in anthropology ; no. 17)
    Includes bibliographical references and index.
    ISBN 0-292-74313-0.—ISBN 0-292-74314-9 (pbk.)
    1. Music and society.   2. Music and anthropology.   3. Ethnomusicology.
    I. Title.   II. Series.
    ML3798.K33   1993
    306.4'84—dc20   92-14937
                                                                                CIP
                                                                                MN

To the memory of Alan P. Merriam,
who opened for me the doors to the anthropology of music,
and to
Mombo Manuhwe Nemasasi
and
Fellow Chagwambare,
who helped me pass through those doors

Contents

Preface and Acknowledgments

PEOPLE WHO STUDY MUSIC on a cross-cultural basis have never agreed on the role of anthropology in their field, but they are inclined to agree that it has something important to say. This book is intended to point out why many anthropologists feel that their perspective is important in understanding the place of music in human life. Thus it would be both incorrect and presumptuous to call this book an introduction to ethnomusicology. This book is not intended as an exhaustive presentation of the music of the world, a task which now requires many volumes; it is rather the presentation of a holistic framework for viewing music.

Although the enjoyment of music as performer and listener is more basic than talking or writing about it, the latter activities provide an understanding that should enable people to participate in music with more awareness of what they are doing. This book thus focuses on features of socially determined human motivation and behavior that produce music. It is assumed that musicians are capable of understanding the basic ideas of anthropology, and that anthropologists are capable of understanding the rudiments of music, but that neither group has the time to master the technical professional jargon of the other in its entirety. Viewing the social ramifications of music is intended to provide a broader perspective than musicians customarily achieve when concentrating on performance. Musicians should gain some insight into what music is—not merely in their own society, but as a part of the life of people everywhere. Persons whose interests lie in the social sciences should find here enough detail regarding music as sound that they can develop a clearer understanding of the musical resources used by musicians in various parts of the world. Nonmusical anthropologists will perhaps see that the study of music is not so formidable as the perspective of the highly specialized music profession makes it appear. This book, in short, is where musicians can turn when they want more information about anthropology, and where anthropologists can turn when they want more information regarding music.

The anthropological approach to music not only provides new perspectives on the subject, it has stimulated the discovery of extensive knowledge about the musical activities of humans all over the world. In 1964 Alan P. Merriam published his *Anthropology of Music*, urging anthropologists to take music more seriously and seeking to convince musicologists that consideration of the social background of music was essential to fully understanding it. Now, thirty years later, much research has resulted from Merriam's book, and this new volume includes a survey of the major findings of this research. Moreover, new theoretical approaches have developed since 1964, and they play an important part today in understanding musical behavior.

An important feature of the anthropological perspective is recognizing the importance of attitudes toward music. These attitudes are often the result of social forces of which we are unaware, and they color and perhaps limit our potential to enjoy music. Society is more important in determining attitudes than is the nature of the music itself.

In this day and age when rapid communication has the effect of making the world appear smaller, it is increasingly important to understand people in other societies. Understanding the ways people elsewhere make and use music will, one hopes, lead to a greater appreciation of them as human beings. Comprehending the music of the people of other societies involves not only making sense of the sounds, but also understanding how and why those sounds are formed.

The social forces influencing musical activity operate not only in exotic societies, but also in modern industrial states. An important aim of anthropology in general is to develop new perspectives on one's own society by increasing sensitivity to how people are living their lives in other societies. Relating this process to music is an important objective of this book.

The study of music, as of any other aspect of culture, involves four major features: form, meaning, use, and function. These four features are related to both musical sounds themselves and to the events at which music occurs. Focusing on these features means that the book is organized in terms of major topics rather than musical or cultural areas. Chapter 1 consists of an introduction to the study of music as the product of human behavior. Chapters 2 and 3 emphasize the role society plays in shaping musical behavior and musical forms. Chapter 2 deals with the forms assumed by the social organization of various societies. Chapter 3 concerns the forms of culturally determined concepts about music and their impact on the music itself. Chapter 4 treats the kinds of musical materials that humans customarily use, including a variety of musical forms and practices commonly found throughout the world. The fifth chapter concerns the question of meaning, or how various features of society and of music cause humans to react to music the way they do. Where Chapters 2–5 focus on the impact of a society and its norms on music, Chapter 6 explores how music serves human needs and influences the course of human events. Chapter 7 concerns the processes of change that occur in human musical activity, both in general terms and in relation to the development of a system of worldwide economic power. Chapter 8 serves as a conclusion to bring together the various ideas and probe their relationship to current forms of musical life.

The examples used throughout the text focus on a few societies from representative areas of the world. These groups are emphasized in order to avoid the confusion that can result from references to too many diverse groups. The book is accompanied by an audiocassette of recorded examples of selected materials. References to this tape are noted in the book as examples, as (Ex. 1.1). Illustrations are referred to as photos, as (Photo 1.1), and musical examples and diagrams are labeled figures, as (Figure 1.1).

Foreign words are *italicized* except when they are found in English dictionaries as borrowed words. This is the case with such terms as mbira, sitar, and koto, which will nevertheless be explained in the text. Many technical words in social science and music, as well as borrowed words, will be explained in the Glossary at the end of the book. **Boldface** is used to indicate terms that are likely to be of most importance for the person who goes on to read more detailed works on world music.

Describing this book as an "introduction" implies its use by students. Indeed, it was written with students in mind, but it will be found useful by anyone who is developing an interest in music of the rest of the world. The book does not pretend to exhaustively cover the wealth of information about world music; it does, however, seek to provide an understanding that will make the reading of additional literature more comprehensible and enjoyable. Even without further reading, one should find his or her appreciation of the musics of other societies enhanced.

This book developed through teaching one course in world music and, later, one on anthropology and the arts. I was stimulated to produce it by the lack of a comprehensive undergraduate text covering the anthropological approach to music. This book has been improved considerably by the creative suggestions of many students through the years, particularly those of the fall semesters of 1989 and 1990.

I owe a great deal to all the Shona musicians who helped me become involved in the music of another society, including the tedious recording sessions as well as the welcomes I received at personal, family, and community events. I could not have written this book without the opportunities for field research provided by the University of Zimbabwe, the National Endowment for the Humanities, and the Wenner-Gren Foundation. I am grateful to DePauw University for allowing time for writing, enabling me to travel in Eastern Europe and Japan, and providing funds for manuscript preparation. I especially appreciate all my colleagues in ethnomusicology whose work I used, and who were so generous in helping me with photographs and recordings. If I misconstrued any of their work it was my shortcoming and not theirs. I finally want to thank my wife, Gloria, and my children, Greta, David, and Marta, for putting up with my many absences from home and my preoccupation with this work as it progressed.

Music in Human Life

1	Aborigines	11	Kaluli
2	Afghanistan	12	Kpelle
3	Aymara	13	Macedonia
4	Bali	14	Mbuti
5	Blackfoot	15	Navajo
5	Flathead	16	Shona
6	India	17	Suya
7	Inuit	18	Tikopia
8	Japan	19	Tuareg
9	Java	20	Venda
10	Kalabari		

Location of groups given major attention in the text.

CHAPTER ONE

"Sciencing" about Music

ALTHOUGH IT HAS PROBABLY NEVER occurred to most people that music can be dangerous, it is sometimes viewed that way for several reasons. Modern parents in the 1990s are concerned about the messages contained in the song lyrics of rock groups, fearing that listening to such ideas through a powerful medium like music will have a negative effect upon the value system and behavior of their children. Earlier in the century a similar controversy was raging over jazz, but in that case it was not simply the lyrics that were criticized, but the "decadent" nature of the music itself. The Navajo people of the American Southwest consider the danger in music to be due to its supernatural power. Since the Navajo believe that music affects the forces guiding the universe, it is seen as dangerous in its own right. Therefore, music is performed only by the most competent individuals for fear that a mistake might cause disaster. Even children are discouraged from singing because inexperience might lead to a dangerous error. David P. McAllester, who has studied Navajo music for many years, compares it with electricity, saying that although it is very useful, it can be handled safely only by carefully trained adults (1954:64). The danger that is sometimes seen in music is only an indication of the various attitudes toward music existing in different societies. Music in some form exists in all human societies, but they vary greatly in the ways they use it and in the nature of the sounds which they appreciate.

Today the rapid expansion of communications throughout the world has enabled anyone to experience the music of distant places. Travelogues and documentaries on television, as well as many scenes in movies, can bring us immediately to the center of a market in India or a festival in Latin America. Exotic music may intrigue some people, strike others as unpleasant, or move the emotions of those who find it beautiful. Upon hearing such music, many people wonder how much it means to the people creating it and why they are performing it that way. Seeking answers to such questions is the purpose of this book. Finding such answers necessitates going beyond the sounds themselves to investigate the complex variety of concepts and behavior that produce the sounds.

People relate to music in a variety of ways. The most common and most important way is the practical, i.e., creating and listening to music. Another way is discourse, which includes talking and writing about music. The difference between discourse and practice is seen in the Oriental tradition that considers participating in music and verbalizing about it as separate "arts" (Hood 1971:227). Although the distinction usually considers practice to refer to performers, one should not forget that musical practice in this sense includes the listeners. People have engaged in discourse about music for several thousand years, yet everyone recognizes that discourse somehow is different from and inferior to participating in musical experiences. Not all peoples in the world have subjected music to extensive discourse, and many consider a largely practical knowledge of it quite sufficient.

The perspective taken by the people who formulate discourse about music affects the forms and results of any particular discourse. Much musical discourse is conducted by musicians as they try to make their music more enjoyable and interesting. They basically approach their discourse from the artistic perspective, which represents a major concern with the quality and effectiveness of the music as a means of self-expression.

Much musical discourse simply reflects the notions about music that are found in the commonly held beliefs of the people in a society. These culturally determined beliefs have been termed the commonsense perspective (Geertz 1973:111). What many people do not realize is that the way they have always viewed things is determined largely by their experiences while growing up in a particular society at a particular time. The commonsense perspective in a given society would lead people to believe that they are singing and dancing to influence the spirits, although an outsider might not view it that way. The significance of recognizing this type of perspective lies in the fact that people in various societies have different ideas of common sense, including the nature of a commonsense attitude toward music. Consequently, it is unlikely that any universal commonsense perspective on music is to be found. When the commonsense perspective dominates the attitudes of anyone confronting new and strange experiences, it becomes ethnocentrism. **Ethnocentrism** is the common tendency to view all human behavior from the value system of one's own society, often including the tendency to consider other practices inferior and misguided. The scholar must therefore avoid the commonsense perspective of his or her own society, and seek to understand other people's practices from their point of view. Every society has its own commonsense perspective, and part of the task of understanding music in other societies is to understand the commonsense perspective commonly held in those societies.

Other types of discourse are intended to place music within a framework of a general understanding of reality. The philosophical or aesthetic perspective is concerned with the value of music, particularly in regard to qualities of beauty and how they appear in various works of music. Another perspective, the historical, characterizes much of the scholarly study of music. This perspective seeks to explain musical styles as the result of historical developments. The historical perspective can be applied to musical behavior as well as to musical styles, but such approaches are only now being developed. Historical perspectives on music are often disconnected from the social factors that have influenced the creation of music over time. When that happens, the history of music becomes simply a description of consecutive musical styles or successive musical practices. The gap between social science and history is narrowing as social scientists recognize the importance of history, and historians are increasingly interested in the impact of social conditions on historical events.

Another perspective toward discourse is the scientific. Ultimately, the scientific perspective is less concerned with the problems of musical participation at any particular time and place than it is with the principles of musical behavior that operate throughout the world. Science has often been defined in terms of its subject matter—the natural world. Ideas of science changed in the late nineteenth century as the study of human beings came under its scrutiny. Instead of thinking of science exclusively as a way of dealing with the natural world, people came to see science as a special way of looking at anything, including humans and their creations. In order to emphasize this view of science, Leslie White, an anthropologist, used the word "science" as a verb (1949:3), describing his work as "sciencing" about culture. Discourse in this book will take the form of "sciencing" about music, with the hope that using the goals and methods of science will not only increase our understanding of music as a form of human experience but also enhance participation in it. Although the scientific view does not reveal everything that needs to be said about music, it does provide important information and insights that are lacking in other approaches.

The Goals of Science

The major goal of science is to explain things, rather than simply to describe or evaluate them. Describing things is basically a preliminary step to later classification and explanation of the data. Description is important because it clarifies the nature of the materials requiring explanation. Just as biologists in the eighteenth century were traveling throughout the world collecting, sketching, and writing descriptions of the exotic animals and plants they found, early musicologists were concerned with recording, notating, and describing the music they heard throughout the world. Because description of music through notation and analysis has been difficult and highly specialized, many scholars of music have not carried their investigations of music much further. The scientific perspective, however, sees the description of a musical style not as an end in itself, but as a means to gain further understanding of musical behavior.

An important task in scientific description of music is defining what it is. Cross-cultural study and comparison of musical practices requires clear definition to be sure that the same types of things are being compared. A problem arises because the definition of music varies widely from one society to another. This variation is shown by the variety of words used to refer to music, as well as by the fact that many languages do not have a word that can be translated as music. Many societies have separate verbs for singing, for playing an instrument, and for dancing, but lack a term that covers only the first two of these, as our word "music" does. Ancient Sanskrit in India, as well as many modern languages in Africa, utilize terms that include all three of the above forms of activity. The Blackfoot people of Montana consider music to be singing, and the things that go with it, including drumming and words, are secondary (Nettl 1989:87). The Shona of Zimbabwe and the Venda of South Africa consider drumming and shouting as forms of playing and singing simply because of the presence of rhythm, even though the singing voice is not used (Ex. 1.1). English speakers refer to the sounds of birds and whales as songs, but speakers of many other languages do not relate such sounds to music at all. The Macedonian people in Yugoslavia use the term *musika* for instrumental sounds, and *pesni* for singing. Dirges are not considered songs because they elicit sadness rather than pleasure (N. Sachs 1975:222, 225). Most researchers determine for themselves the types of sound that they will include in their study, both using their own definition of music and taking into account the local concepts.

Classification is another step toward explanation. By encouraging discussion in terms of types of things, a system of classification eliminates the cumbersome process of having to deal with each individual case separately. While a classification of materials necessarily follows a certain amount of comparison, it also facilitates further comparison. In biology, the formulation of the Linnaean classifications provided a system for achieving some order among the immense diversity of living organisms that had been found throughout the world. In the study of music, classifications have often been expressed in terms of **genre,** meaning the types of musical works or performances that occur in any society. Many different criteria distinguish one genre from another, including the way the music is used (lullabies, war songs, ritual songs), features of the performance (solo, chant, chorus), and the instruments used (koto, violin, percussion).

A major problem with determining genres on the basis of these factors is that the classifications vary from one society to another, making a universal classification rather elusive. When the concern of research is the relationship between a society and its music, the focus on the music itself is not particularly enlightening. Even in a single society a particular song can be classified in different ways depending on the situation, particularly as songs change in usage over time. For the Shona people of Zimbabwe, certain songs, known to old people as funeral songs, are viewed by younger people as ancestral spirit songs or even dance songs. John Blacking cites a case of a popular dance song among the Venda of South Africa being called a grinding song simply because someone had heard a woman singing it while grinding grain (1973:43). In rural India a genre of song called *sagun* is determined by the context where it is performed rather than by the text or the tune (Henry 1988:34). When focusing on the relationship between society and music, the most effective form of classification is based on the types of music events. These will be presented in the following chapter.

Explanation, as the ultimate goal of "sciencing," is concerned less with the forms assumed by the object of study than with the processes that lead to those forms. These processes are often termed laws. For example, the genetic principles discovered by Mendel and the more recent research in DNA have provided explanations for the diversity of living creatures found in biology. Social scientists have looked for such laws, but human behavior involves so many complex variables that meaningful laws have evaded formulation. The kind of generalizations about human action that serve as realistic goals of research in human behavior are more accurately termed **regularities,** i.e., basic principles used for explanation in spite of occasional exceptions. The goals of "sciencing" about music relate to finding regularities in the musical behavior of human beings throughout the world.

"Sciencing" does not include evaluation of music as one of its goals. Musicians customarily include as a part of their work the evaluation of various types of music or various presentations. Whereas the aesthetic approach is concerned with the question of whether certain types of music are good or bad, beautiful or medio-cre, the scientific approach is concerned with the question of whether or not music does what its performers intend. This ap-proach also considers how music evokes a response in human be-ings, and whether such forms of response are universal or deter-mined largely by factors involving particular societies and their norms. Although it is now recognized that truly value-free science is impossible, scientists still strive for as high a degree of objectivity as possible. This objectivity relies on several criteria which form the basis for the methods of science.

The Methods of Science

In defining science, the methods are as important as the goals. Knowledge of the methods used in science is important not only to the potential researcher, but to everyone. When presented with any set of facts or ideas, one should always ask how that material was obtained. Methods in science include more than simply gathering data. A first step is developing an underlying theoretical framework that clarifies goals and the ways of achieving those goals. When that framework is understood, the techniques of gathering data relevant to a particular research situation are not so difficult to develop.

The Holistic Approach

The underlying theoretical framework in anthropology is often called the **holistic** approach. The term holistic comes from the word "whole," and it emphasizes two major features of the scientific study of human behavior. First, the holistic approach is **inclusive,** which means that it does not exclude any known human society throughout the world. Although anthropology has traditionally spe-cialized in small-scale, isolated societies (those commonly called "primitive"), its goal has been to increase our understanding of man-kind as a whole by considering all the naturally occurring ways in which humans have organized themselves and wrested a living from the earth. This feature of the holistic approach adds significant dimensions to the study of human musical behavior. Limiting the study of music to the larger, literate societies not only eliminates intriguing types of musical behavior and musical sound, but also deprives researchers of new perspectives from which to view musical activity in their own societies. On the other hand, limiting a study to the small-scale societies customarily emphasized by anthropologists tends to restrict potential implications of the results.

The second feature of the holistic approach is its **integrative** quality, which results from seeking to understand how different aspects of society or culture are related to each other. This goal is based on the assumption that the relations between things are as important as the nature of the things themselves. In order to achieve a more complete understanding of the whole, the integrative approach links economics, politics, religion, language, and the arts. If the social aspects of music making are omitted and the study of music is limited to the sounds themselves, an illusion is created that music is an entity in itself and musicians need not be concerned with the world around them. Failure to appreciate how other aspects of society and culture influence musical behavior can lead to excessive elitist attitudes in music.

The integrative aspect of the holistic study of music is most apparent in the study of music as part of a sociocultural system. A sociocultural system is often called a society by sociologists and a culture by anthropologists, depending upon the emphasis they are giving to the parts within the system. The term **system** is used to refer to society and culture because it indicates a collection of phenomena that are so closely related to each other that a change in one of them will bring about changes in others. Social scientists formerly considered societies and cultures to be rather fixed and static. Today it is recognized that social and cultural institutions are constantly being re-created and re-formed to suit people's needs. These interrelated dynamics are the reason for referring to social and cultural realities as a type of system, although the degree of integration varies according to the time and place, as well as to the aspects of culture that are involved.

Although the sociocultural system is usually a well-integrated unit, it is more clearly analyzed when viewed as consisting of several rather distinct components, as shown in Figure 1.1. The first component is **material,** consisting of features related to the human requirements for food and shelter, as well as the tools for providing these things. Another component of the sociocultural system is **social,** and it concerns the need of human beings to relate somehow to the people around them. The social aspect of the sociocultural

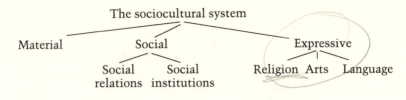

Figure 1.1. Components of the sociocultural system.

system includes both social relations and social institutions. Social relations concerns the ways people naturally interact with each other, taking into account conflict, animosities, jealousies, and other personal and individual features that are found in any group of humans. Social institutions are the standardized ways that people relate to each other, such as kinship groups, legal and educational institutions, or special organizations of musicians in guilds or performing groups. The third component of the sociocultural system is the **expressive,** primarily oriented to the cognitive and emotional needs of humans. The exact nature of these needs is not yet fully understood because it is difficult to distinguish universal human needs from those determined by individual societies. However, these needs are commonly considered to include at least the need to make sense of experience, to express one's self, and to obtain positive reactions from other people.

Culture, as part of the sociocultural system, is a difficult term to understand because it has several meanings. In the popular humanistic usage, culture is taken to mean a certain degree of erudition, or snobbishness, resulting from appreciation of the various fine arts, certain forms of etiquette, or even particular ways of speaking. In social science, culture has a much wider meaning. To some anthropologists, culture is another way of referring to the entire sociocultural system. To other anthropologists, culture consists basically of ideas or concepts individuals learn from society as part of the process of growing up. These socially learned concepts serve as the basis of human action, including the material (how to build a drum), the social (how to hire musicians), and the expressive (knowing when and how to sing the right song). The concepts serve as a model for action, but not as rules to be blindly followed. **Culture,** then, involves all of the techniques, values, and symbols that individuals learn from their society and use in adapting to the natural environment, to the social environment, and to their own inner drives.

The combination of these three components of the sociocultural system means that the artifacts created by humans, the patterned social relationships, and the approved types of expressive behavior all work together to generate what we know as the way of life of an ethnic group or socio-economic group. Society can only exist as people relate to each other with some commonly held understandings about communicating and behaving; culture can only exist in the minds of individuals and in the practices by which shared understandings are passed from one generation to the next.

Social scientists discuss society and culture so much that they tend to consider both a form of reality. Actually, social structure and culture are models formulated by the researcher from the regularities observed in behavior. A musical tradition or a musical culture is also a construct formulated in scholars' minds as they think abstractly. These things find their only true existence in the minds of people within the society. Music itself, however, consists of sound waves, thus it is physically real and not necessarily a mental construct. However, when one hears a very familiar tune in one's head, that music has then become a mental construct.

The idea of a sociocultural system is important in the study of music because it emphasizes that social dynamics are an integral part of the musical institutions and musical knowledge of peoples throughout the world. The most effective methods of researching the roots of musical behavior seek to relate the personal interactions of musicians and their audiences, the social institutions within which musicians work, and the ideas about music which are held in the society. The musical traditions of a society consist not only of the techniques of performing music, but also the ways of reacting to it, and the evaluation of good, mediocre, and poor performances. The musical system includes the motivation of both musicians and organizers of musical events. Music is not performed in a vacuum, nor can one assume that it is performed merely for amusement. Music has important links with economic arrangements, political action, religion, the other arts, and language. The holistic approach attempts to clarify all of these relationships.

Even though music is often considered only in terms of expressive culture, it has been shown that music is indeed related to the material and social aspects of culture as well. The term **musical segment** includes the technological, social, and ideational components involved in producing music.[1] Technology and the availability of materials often directly affect the manufacture of musical instruments. For example, the use of metals for musical instruments depends partly on the availability of metal ores and also the knowledge of metal working. The Piaroa Indians of South America, who lack the knowledge of metallurgy, use bark trumpets rather than metal

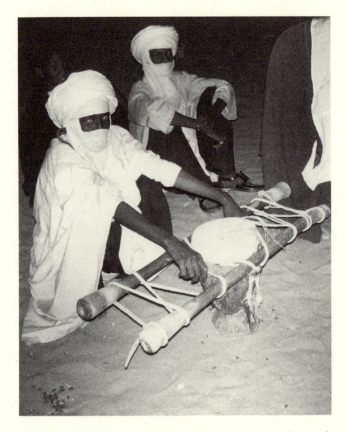

1.1. The Tuareg *tende* drum made from a mortar, with pestles used to secure the leather drumhead, rural Niger, 1977. (Photo by Caroline Card Wendt; used by permission.)

ones (*Columbia World Library,* record notes 1949). Musical activity is sometimes affected by the environment indirectly, as shown by societies that are nomadic because of scarce resources. Nomadic societies usually have few and rather small instruments. Some groups assemble instruments from materials they have on hand. The Tuareg of the Sahara Desert, for example, make their *tende* drum (Photo 1.1) by tying a piece of leather over the mortars used in food preparation (Card 1982:114). Music is closely related to social relations and social institutions because society develops norms that influence the ways people will behave musically. As an expressive feature of culture, music occurs to some extent in all societies, either as play, religion, or entertainment. Although Western society tends to view music as a form of decoration enhancing the activities of life, many societies view it as an essential feature.

Once the researcher has determined basic goals and theoretical perspectives, attention can be given to a specific research situation for planning the process of gathering data. Empirical observation under controlled conditions is the basic scientific means of testing hypotheses. The researcher formulates hypotheses concerning potential regularities and develops specific techniques to assure that data are relevant. In many sciences, controlled conditions require the use of experiments. When the subject of study is human beings, experiments are severely restricted because of limited ways people can be manipulated. Small experiments are occasionally possible; for example, while studying the songs of the Venda people in South Africa, John Blacking sometimes deliberately sang parts of a song wrong to discover the range of variation permitted in Venda society. He reasoned that if his variations were not corrected they were within the range of acceptability to the Venda people (1967:33).

Many social scientists compensate for restrictions on experiments by studying a variety of societies, since the natural developments through time have provided a sort of natural laboratory. Studying the music of any group of people today often involves going to their country and participating with them in the activities of their lives, including the musical aspects, as Blacking did. This practice is known as **participant observation,** and serves to take the place of experiments in the study of music of other societies. Participant observation is often called fieldwork, although the latter term can also refer to collecting field recordings without taking part in local activities.

Participant observation is particularly difficult because both the researcher and the objects of study are human beings. Empirical observation depends upon maintaining a high degree of objectivity, which means excluding personal feelings and prejudices from one's research. Naturally, in working with a specific group of people, the researcher develops strong feelings about them. Both positive feelings, such as gratitude and joy, and negative feelings, such as disgust or sorrow, may become so overwhelming that they threaten the objectivity of the research. These feelings often intensify as people perform music together. Rather than trying to avoid or deny natural human feelings, it is more feasible, as well as more suitable, to incorporate an appraisal of this human factor into an analysis of any situation.

The researcher should not only take care that personal feelings do not distort the research findings, but must also be aware that the

1.2. Njenge Nyamudo playing the mbira, Zimbabwe, 1972. (Photo by the author.)

social situation is somewhat different because of the presence of an outsider. During several months of research among the Shona in eastern Zimbabwe, I discovered that my study of the mbira (Ex. 1.2; Photo 1.2) was stimulating some members of the local community to become interested in playing it, including several sons of the player with whom I was working. This was not necessarily to be considered bad, but it did require some adjustment of understanding of what might have happened without the outsider's presence. The outsider can also cause different behavior at musical events when recording them, as shown by the following case in Northern India.

In Indrapur I recorded several women's pre-wedding song sessions characterized by considerable hilarity, not to say hysteria. It was obvious that the women were excited by having a strange male, especially one with something so magical as a tape recorder, sit with them and ask strange questions in a strange language. . . . Playing back the recordings certainly disturbed the normal flow of events and probably caused some self-consciousness. A friend later confirmed my suspicions, saying the women were distracted and agitated when I recorded them, and did not sing well. (Henry 1988:228)

Replication of research, which means the repetition of research with the same results, is often used to ensure empiricism and objectivity. However, when studying human behavior through participant observation, the researcher finds that constantly changing human situations make exact replication impossible. Nevertheless, a high degree of objectivity can be assured, provided one is careful in recording behavior and statements of informants. I was told many times of the traditional Shona belief that one's skills in playing the mbira developed through help from ancestors appearing in dreams. This verbal evidence was corroborated when people saw me playing and began to engage in heated discussion as to how a white man could be performing on the instrument. Undermining the Shona views of music was avoided when the local musicians assured the listeners that the skill involved in my playing was very limited, and that really great players had the help of the ancestors. In this case the fact that the information gained in a performance situation was compatible with what had been said earlier enhanced the validity and objectivity of the original statements.

Gathering reliable data depends upon noting the difference between the scientific perspective deliberately chosen by the outside observer and the characteristic commonsense perspective of the participant in the society under study. In anthropology these two perspectives have often been labeled the **etic** view and the **emic** view, respectively, using terms derived from linguistics.[2] Because the etic view represents the outsider, it has often been considered more objective. This view has often led researchers to focus on the material aspects of a society because of the emphasis given to objectivity in

science. The emic view has often been thought to be more subjective, and has consequently been given a smaller role in research,
although this practice has been challenged. The distinction between
the two perspectives is necessary and important, but it is equally
important to make sure that the two are not oversimplified. The etic
approach in a given research situation must include consideration
of the participants' actual behavior as well as the objectively verifi-
able material constraints influencing the participants. The emic approach, seen as the people's commonsense explanation of their behavior, also constitutes significant data. What the participants think
they are doing or intend to do may be as illuminating as what they
are doing. The importance of studying the ideals for behavior as well
as the behavior itself is a major reason for studying living groups
rather than recorded sound (Herndon and McLeod 1979:125).

Two different aspects of the commonsense perspective have frequently been overlooked because of failure to note the distinction
between practical consciousness and discursive consciousness (Giddens 1984:xxiii). **Practical consciousness** is the individual's knowledge of how to deal with particular situations, even though such
knowledge is seldom or ever put into words. Most of our practical
consciousness is derived from growing up in a particular society and
shaping our behavior to that of the people around us. It is basically
the commonsense perspective, and is seldom questioned. Practical
consciousness is apparent when a musician can perform on his instrument but is unable to explain it to anyone else. This aspect of
cultural knowledge has often been called implicit, covert, or tacit
culture. **Discursive consciousness** is that aspect of knowledge which
a person is able to verbalize or explain. It, too, is derived largely from
one's experiences in society, and is often called explicit, overt, or
manifest culture. Discursive consciousness includes the culturally
acceptable rationalizations about goals and motivations that are involved in human action, including music making. This form of discourse is characteristic of the aesthetic or philosophical perspective.
Both of these types of consciousness are operative and very important in understanding musical behavior.[3] They are both distinct
from the **unconscious,** which involves the universal human needs
mentioned earlier as the basis for expressive culture. These unconscious aspects of life seldom appear as discourse, but may be important motivations for musical behavior. In the Western world, musical discourse has taken the form of music theory and philosophy of
music. Discourse in many societies throughout the world is severely
limited, although many musicians will be producing and enjoying
extremely sophisticated music on the basis of practical conscious-

ness. However, since producing music has to be grounded in activity of the human mental system, some sort of mental structuring of the sounds or the movements necessary to produce them can be assumed to be present. One problem often facing researchers is that information given by informants is often confusing and even contradictory. This may sometimes be due to the informant's reluctance to reveal a society's unique knowledge; it may also be due to the fact that discourse in music is not commonly practiced in that society, so that no individual has ever thought through or verbalized the practical knowledge that is taken for granted. Because the value of discourse is sometimes not understood, the informant or musician might improvise a statement simply to please the researcher.

As Western music, with its complex system of discursive theory, has spread throughout the world, it has become increasingly prestigious to develop theories about musical features that were previously limited to the practical consciousness. Different musical systems seem to have features that lend themselves to discursive treatment and other features which do not. In Java, for example, musicians noted the complex Western theory of tuning, and tried to adapt it, encountering negative and frustrating results. Javanese music, however, has a formal system of complex cycles, (*gongan*, to be explained in Chapter 4) that lend themselves to discursive or theoretical treatment much more easily than do the formal aspects of Western music.

> The processes that have generated these many formal structures are so precise, so "scientific," and so consistent as to seem to have an autonomous existence outside the memories of men, while clearly this is not the case. Gamelan *gongan* structures have been created by men within an oral tradition that is specific and explicit about the correct manner of playing each instrument within each type of *gongan*, but which has not been explicit about the processes of creating new types of *gongan*. (Becker 1980: 143–144)

The important point here is that musical systems are made by humans, and they usually contain very complex phenomena produced without full awareness of the complexity. In this respect musical systems resemble languages.

Formulating a theoretical background and gathering reliable data are incomplete without analysis. Both the music itself and the social action related to it should be analyzed. The question has often been raised about whether an outsider with an analytical perspective can ever understand what the participant in another society is thinking and doing, particularly in such a subjective field as music. Certainly the outsider will never understand music or anything else in the same way or to the same extent as a participant. On the other hand, the participants, unless trained in research techniques, are unlikely to be aware of many factors related to the practical consciousness. The researcher complements the participant's knowledge with the power of analysis. While involved in the practical activities of life, the participant is often unaware of the wider implications or consequences of what is happening. The observer, concerned with discourse rather than practice, will develop a larger perspective through undertaking an analysis of the situation (Bourdieu 1977 : 106). Analysis often includes inferences derived from concrete situations of behavior and speech as the participant unknowingly reveals his practical consciousness. When learning to play the mbira in Zimbabwe, I was very much afraid of hitting the wrong note—a result of early piano lessons. One day the mbira expert who was helping me gave me a stern lecture. It was perfectly all right to hit the wrong note, any note would do, but *never slow down, and never stop!* This emphatic statement revealed the practical consciousness basic to the creation of Shona music as contrasted with that needed for Western music. Analysis by the observer must include not only the material conditions involved in musical activity, but also the nature of the practical consciousness of the participants in the society. The music sound itself is a creation of the practical consciousness, and recording and analyzing it provides an important key to the mental processes of the musician. The observer's perspective must also include an understanding of the discursive consciousness of the participants, achieved by listening carefully to what they say. Even though the observer will never fully understand many features of the life of the participant, analysis can provide a view of events that places the participants' lives and musical behavior in a clearer perspective.

Social analysis is enhanced by recognition of the different levels from which human activity may be viewed. On the most basic level, analysis can be limited to a certain piece of music or a specific performance. At a somewhat higher level, analysis can focus on the work of individual musicians. The next level consists of the music events themselves, where scholars often concentrate their activity because the event highlights the relationship between society and music. The community is a higher level at which musical behavior may be analyzed, such as, for example, the activity involved when a community decides to present its traditional music to tourists. A higher level of analysis is that of the ethnic group, often called a tribe or nation. This social unit often serves as the focus of research in social science. Presumably, the highest level of musical activity is the global level, which becomes most apparent in the modern rock music sweeping over the world.

Performance

As noted earlier, scientific objectivity rejects the tendency to evaluate. Where language is concerned, it is commonplace to distinguish between common ordinary speech on the one hand and formal language, oratory, or literature on the other. The first of these is considered a form of casual activity, whereas the others are considered to be more creative. When studying musical behavior, however, it is not common to distinguish between casual and creative renditions of music. The common distinction is between good and bad renditions. In approaching music from the scientific perspective, however, judgment of the effectiveness of any type of music will necessarily be related to its intended purposes. The scientific observer should give the same degree of serious consideration to casual renditions as to music presented as creative activity. By focusing on a distinction between casual and creative music activity rather than good or bad music, the analyst acquires a means of distinguishing different styles and genres of music without becoming evaluative.

The folklorist Richard Bauman has provided an objective framework for studying different types of language behavior by focusing on the concept of **performance** (1977 : 11). Performance in this sense occurs when the individual anticipates that a presentation, whether it be recounting a tale, singing, or playing, will be evaluated by an audience. Language in the performance context is considered creative behavior; outside the performance it is simply casual. The same distinction between casual rendition and creative performance operates in musical situations, and the difference between the two contexts is clearly indicated by several cues, which vary from one society to another. The term **marking** has been used to indicate the use of such cues in a musical situation to make this distinction (Stone 1982:98).[4] In the Western world the concert setting often serves as a marker, including special dress or costumes, the dimming lights, the applause and bow, and often the movements of the musician that have nothing to do with producing the sound. The lack of such markers is commonly regarded as absence of intention to be evaluated, so that a rehearsal or singing in the shower are not considered a performance.[5]

The concept of performance as a key to understanding creative activity is very relevant to music, and in any society the analyst must learn to observe the cues which mark the performance mode. Looking for markers in the cross-cultural situation will enable the researcher to gain a more accurate idea of what is occurring in the minds of the persons engaged in the activity. For example, the Kpelle of Liberia have a clear idea of the difference between a performance and behavior occurring outside the performance context. They habitually encircle the area of a performance to separate the performance area from ordinary space, so that evil spirits might be kept away from the performance. This practice also serves to alert everyone in the community that a performance is about to occur (Photo 1.3) (Stone 1982:101). Among the Inuit, also known as Eskimo, the first stanza of a drum dance song was devoted to a modest declaration of the singer's lack of ability, a clear indication that an evaluative response was expected (Cavanagh 1982:86).

Sometimes a community knows that the performance mode is intended because it customarily accompanies certain types of activity. Among Hungarian peasants the very act of singing dirges or mourning songs was considered a performance to be done by women. "People watch the performance very carefully and discuss it afterwards: 'She wailed beautifully,' 'She hasn't even mourned for him,' etc. They criticize the mourner if her sincerity is open to doubt, or if she has not come up to expectations" (Kodály 1960:76).

A final point concerning scientific method in research is that it is viewed in two different ways. One view maintains that scientists should restrict their efforts to those problems that are amenable to a suitably rigorous method. If a question poses severe methodological difficulties, it should be ignored in favor of questions where the methodological problems can be more satisfactorily solved. The other view maintains that some questions are very important, and they should be approached scientifically even though the problems of method are difficult. Rigorous use of what methods are available and relentless search for better methods constitute a form of challenge. The first of these approaches is more common in the natural sciences; the second is more common among social sciences, primarily because the study of human behavior is subject to so many variables that a flawless methodology is virtually impossible. Social scientists often proceed in spite of methodological difficulties because certain questions are so important that it is preferable to research with imperfect methods than not to research at all. Research into musical behavior as a social science is often not amenable to rigorous method; it is, however, an important topic in understand-

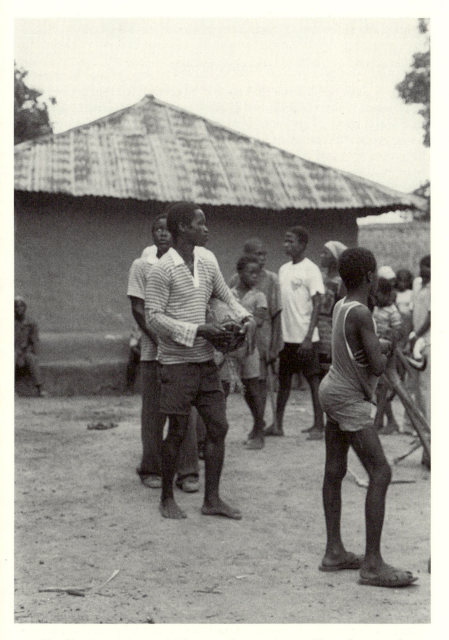

1.3. Kpelle entertainers circling as they enter a village for a performance, 1975. (Photo by Ruth M. Stone and Verlon L. Stone; used by
permission.)

ing what humans are doing as they create musical sounds to express themselves and enhance their lives in communities.

Research Ethics

Ethics is a scientific issue that should be considered especially carefully when doing research involving human beings. During the period when most of the non-Western world was ruled by European powers, the superiority of European culture was often assumed and its power was not to be challenged. Researchers in the past have been accused of supporting colonial power and exploiting people of the non-Western world. Today most researchers recognize the nature of exploitation. They are careful in handling information that may have political overtones, and they do not publish or even talk about matters considered secret by the people being studied. In the past, researchers and collectors have carried off musical instruments; even though the instruments were paid for, they may have been irreplaceable, thus depriving people of their music. Carelessness or exploitation in relation to recordings of ethnic music has frequently occurred, although today researchers as well as traditional musicians have become aware of the need to share any benefits accruing from the sale of recordings. Even in writing up research materials, full recognition is now given to the facts and insights provided by the local people. Undermining or changing other people's beliefs, as nearly occurred with my mbira playing, can often be harmful because it can weaken the world view on which people base their lives.

Theories of Society and Music

Studying music in the framework of social science raises the questions of how much the sociocultural system affects music and conversely, to what extent music can affect the sociocultural system. These questions have been approached in several different ways. During the nineteenth and early twentieth centuries, scholars were less concerned with explaining human behavior in specific sociocultural systems than they were with discovering why these systems differed from each other. Early explanations for the differences took the form of a postulated universal historical progression from savagery through various stages of barbarism to civilization. The less technologically advanced societies were placed somewhere on the continuum as a means of explaining why they were "backward," i.e., different from Western societies. In the early twentieth century it became apparent that these schemes of cultural progression were based primarily on conjecture, and scholars sought new ways of explaining why the many societies scattered throughout the globe were so diverse. The theories developed for this purpose affected scholars' ideas of music's relationship to society. The major approaches were neo-evolutionism, functionalism, and various interactionist and generative theories.

The Neo-evolutionary View

The neo-evolutionist approach explained differences between sociocultural systems on the basis of adaptation to the natural environment. Followers of this approach recognized the three parts of a sociocultural system mentioned earlier, but they emphasized a hierarchical arrangement (White 1949:364). The material or technological level was considered basic and determinative of the nature of a whole sociocultural system. The second level, the social, was seen to be subject to the types of subsistence activities required by environmental conditions. The third level was termed ideological rather than expressive, and it was viewed as the common beliefs necessary to maintain order and generally adaptive behavior in a society. These three levels of society have been compared to the layers of a cake.

The neo-evolutionary view has certain merits, but it has often resulted in unrealistic approaches to music or failure to consider it at all. Since music is not seen as directly related to the processes of producing goods, because it *is* frequently expressive, and because it cannot be visually measured, it has been assigned to the ideological subsystem. Since the technological level is considered to be determinative of the other two, music came to be widely considered a by-product or decoration of the major forces of social life—a frosting on the cake, so to speak. Because of this view, neo-evolutionary theory has contributed little to an understanding of music.

Research of musical behavior itself, however, shows that music is related to all three of the sociocultural components, as indicated earlier. Rather than resembling the frosting on a cake, musical life is more like a slice of the cake, the musical segment. Although it is often accurate to say that music serves an ideological purpose, it is misleading to say that it is to be understood solely as a part of the ideological component. Music, as one aspect of a sociocultural system, is the product of technological, social, and ideological forces, and is not solely the by-product of any one of them.

The relationship between society and music was explored from the neo-evolutionary perspective by Alan Lomax (1968). He used cross-cultural statistical techniques to compare singing styles from 233 different societies and relate them to subsistence systems. Recordings of ten songs from each group were rated by groups of college students according to thirty-seven variables, including the nature of singing groups, relation of instruments to group, melodic form, embellishments, volume, and raspiness. These features were correlated with information about the cultures that is contained in ethnographic accounts at the Human Relations Area Files at Yale University. Through this method Lomax found that:

song styles shift consistently with:
1. Productive range
2. Political level
3. Level of stratification of class
4. Severity of sexual mores
5. Balance of dominance between male and female
6. Level of social cohesiveness. (1968:6)

Many scholars of music realize that Lomax is doing something important, and that his work is both sophisticated and provocative. At the same time it is seen to be highly oversimplified.

One problem is whether his work is based on sufficiently large samples. For example, his portrayal of the music of village India as part of an "Old High Culture," indicates that it is characterized by an "'exclusive and elaborated dominance' where a solo performer, accompanied by an orchestra . . . sings a precisely enunciated, long, and complex text" (1968:97). Detailed research in village India, however, has revealed many types of musical styles not conforming to this characterization. A significant difference in styles is found, depending on whether the music is performed by specialists or by non-specialists. Many communal music groups actively perform devotional music, festival songs, and play songs in which the elaborated style is not found at all. Even when specialists perform, the characteristics described by Lomax do not dominate in their styles (Henry 1976). Lomax has assumed that song styles are homogeneous, which does not seem to be the case. How could such a diverse situation as village India be characterized by ten songs?

Another problem is the question of accurate rating of the styles. Many of the criteria are not well defined. Rating-scale items such as nasalization, raspiness, and enunciation could be factors involving a particular performer. Length of text and wordiness could vary from day to day with the same performer in traditions where verbal improvisation is important. American college students were trained to provide consistent ratings, but the consistency could have been provided by perceptions based on their own common cultural background.

Lomax's theoretical orientation is neo-evolutionary, since he seeks for causal connections between the economic and political systems of a society and the modes of expression. Only time and further study will confirm or deny the validity of Lomax's work. The question of the relations between the sociocultural system and music has continued to interest many scholars of worldwide music, and it will probably be seen that the question requires much more detailed investigation than Lomax was able to undertake.

Functionalism

Another reaction to nineteenth-century evolutionary theories was functionalism. It explained all sociocultural phenomena according to the contribution each feature of a society made to the group's continued well-being. An analogy was drawn between the social system and a living organism, in which all the parts make their contribution to the health of the entire system. A. R. Radcliffe-Brown was a major figure in formulating functionalism, and his description of dance among the Andaman Islanders of the Indian Ocean provides a good example of how function was used to explain the continued existence of music and dance in a society:

> Finally, in order to understand the function of the Andamanese dance it must be noted that every adult member of the community takes some part in it. All the able-bodied men join in the dance itself; all the women join in the chorus. If anyone through ill-health or old age is unable to take any active part, he or she is at least necessarily a spectator, for the dance takes place in the centre of the village in the open space toward which the huts usually face.
>
> The Andamanese dance (with its accompanying song) may therefore be described as an activity in which, by virtue of the effects of rhythm and melody, all the members of a community are able harmoniously to cooperate and act in unity; which requires on the part of the dancer a continual condition of tension free from strain; and which produces in those taking part in it a high degree of pleasure. . . .
>
> In this way the dance produces a condition in which the unity, harmony and concord of the community are at a maximum, and in which they are intensely felt by every member. It is to pro-

duce this condition, I would maintain, that is the primary social function of the dance. The well-being, or indeed the existence, of the society depends on the unity and harmony that obtain in it, and the dance, by making that unity intensely felt, is a means of maintaining it. For the dance affords an opportunity for the direct action of the community upon the individual, and we have seen that it exercises in the individual those sentiments by which the social harmony is maintained. (1922:248–249, 252)

As research continued among diverse societies around the world, it became apparent that functionalism as a theoretical approach had its limitations. In assuming a positive function for social practices, it did not allow for behavior that might have a negative effect on the life of a group, nor did it consider the possibility that some behavior might have neither positive nor negative effects. Another weakness of the approach was its assumption that a society had a stable way of life that indefinitely provided its members with satisfactory conditions for their lives. Functionalism was thus not equipped to consider the change inherent in human society.

Interactionist Views

Several approaches in the latter half of the century are variously called generative or symbolic interactionist (Barth 1966; Blumer 1969), and more recently practice theory (Bourdieu 1977). These perspectives focus on interaction among individuals and groups, and how this interaction generates the forms of social and expressive realities. As individuals seek to solve the problems and reach the goals in their own lives, they are constantly making decisions. They use the values and techniques which they learn from the people around them as a guide to behavior, but they do not slavishly follow it. People often flout the norms when it seems expedient to do so. The resulting pattern of decisions made by many individuals results in the modification of culture. These patterns provide the basis for scientific generalization. This approach to understanding society and culture serves much better than the neo-evolutionary or functional approaches as a basis for studying the relationships between society and music. Thus, both societies and music traditions are to be seen not as static entities but as common modes of action reproduced with varying degrees of continuity. This approach makes it possible to consider both the effect of society upon musical practices and the effects of music on the society.

One of the reasons for the importance of the levels of analysis

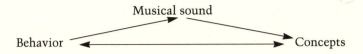

Figure 1.2. A model of musical process (modified from Merriam 1964: 32–33).

mentioned earlier is that they clarify certain differences in perspective. The neo-evolutionist view is based on very high, global levels of analysis. The generative perspective is on the personal and group levels of analysis. At high levels of analysis the role of music is rather difficult to discern. At the lower levels of analysis it is more easily seen, and sometimes music is quite pervasive.

Alan P. Merriam, a pioneer in the anthropological study of music, presented a model of musical behavior that complements the interactionist and generative approaches. He saw musical sound as a product or artifact of the behavior that produces it. This behavior is generated by concepts about music formed in the individual mind by interaction with other people in society. The sounds of music produced by musical behavior provide feedback to the performer and listener, either modifying or reinforcing the concepts (1964:32–33). Not all behavior related to music actually produces sound, such as the act of copying a musical manuscript or purchasing a recorded tape. Nevertheless, such behavior does influence the concepts about music. Moreover, nonmusical behavior is often important in generating musical events. Figure 1.2 modifies Merriam's model to indicate that both musical behavior and musical sound help determine the concepts.

Ethnomusicology and Music

The holistic study of music is a part of the scholarly discipline of ethnomusicology, although not all ethnomusicologists utilize that perspective. Formerly known as comparative musicology, ethnomusicology first appeared as the result of the interest of musicians in the music of non-Western peoples. Since ancient times, some people have found exotic music to be an interesting subject for observation, but such interest was usually limited to the sounds themselves. During the nineteenth century the origins of human cultural practices provided a central goal of research, for it was commonly believed that people with simple technologies must have other cultural features similar to those of our prehistoric ancestors. The general interest in origins spread to music, so that early studies of the music of tribal peoples focused on origins of music in relation to other schemes of origin. It has since been found that musical practices change considerably over time, and we have no way of knowing whether or not any of the music found and recorded in the past hundred years bears any resemblance at all to the music presumably created by prehistoric humans.

The prevailing mode of thought in the nineteenth century considered the music of small-scale non-literate societies to be "primitive." This idea was based on the erroneous notion that people who created it were somehow only beginning to understand the world around them, and they were making nothing but noise as they sang and danced. The term "primitive" has derogatory connotations and should be avoided, since we now know that all musical systems have some very complex and sophisticated qualities. The term "primitive" is often simply used to indicate something we cannot relate to, and it becomes an admission of defeat when one is undertaking a comparative study of music.

Nineteenth-century attitudes gradually dissipated as research in non-Western musical systems grew. Until the invention of recording devices in 1877, preserving musical sounds for study was both difficult and inaccurate. Even today, persons trained in notating European music find great difficulty in writing down non-Western musics, partly because their scales and rhythms are often not related to the European system of notation. Moreover, musicians in many societies are unaccustomed to breaking their music into small segments, nor do they customarily repeat performances several times the same way. After Edison's recording cylinders appeared, researchers were soon seeking to record as wide an assortment of non-Western music as possible. Fears were expressed that rapid westernization would soon cause the disappearance of indigenous forms of music. Ethnomusicological research at first consisted of putting such recordings in archives, and subsequently notating and analyzing the music. Many researchers, particularly Americans working with acculturated Indian groups, began to see the need for going out among the people in other societies and studying firsthand not only the music sound, but also how people conceptualized and valued the music they used. The participant observation methods of anthropology thus came to be associated with musicology. Today compact tape recorders and extensive scholarship have made possible the comparative study of a wide range of human societies and the musical cultures associated with them.[6]

Ethnomusicologists today have reached no clear consensus about their goals and methods. The idea that ethnomusicology is a form of discourse consisting of a scientific or scholarly approach to music is widely accepted. Some people calling themselves ethnomusicologists are essentially engaged in cross-cultural musical practice that might more aptly be called ethnomusicianship. When dealing with societies having extensive historical records and some form of music notation, the methods of ethnomusicology have tended to be more historical. Societies having no form of notation or any writing at all are usually researched through the methods of participant observation. In some ways, ethnomusicologists have tried to include in one discipline the diversity of materials that in other areas of study are considered separate. Whereas the study of language divides into sociolinguistics, structural linguistics, and comparative literature, ethnomusicology does not have separate terminology to distinguish between those who focus on social factors of music making, on musical structures, or on qualities of appreciation. The practice of ethnomusicology is proceeding well; it is the discourse which still causes problems.

The goals of holistic "sciencing" about music can be summarized as seeking explanations of human musical behavior. One might well ask, however, why such explanations are of any importance. The inclusive and integrative study of music provides us with new and different views of what music is all about. Other societies view music differently than we do; it is possible that we have something to learn from them. Studying music in relation to the processes of other sociocultural systems helps us see how our own musical practices are influenced by sociocultural factors that we have often failed to recognize. We should be led to consider such questions as to whether our society has a positive or negative influence on our musical life. To what extent is our musical life governed by commercial interests? Are our ideas about aesthetic values in music simply an historical accident, or do they actually describe an important feature of human musical activity? These and other questions provide some of the reasons for looking carefully at music in societies throughout the world.

CHAPTER TWO

The Sociocultural Matrix: Social Factors

IN THE NINETEENTH CENTURY, European societies were entranced with the idea of progress. The industrial revolution had begun to produce goods that raised standards of living to unprecedented heights. The progress that had taken place in European technology was assumed to characterize all of human life, including the expressive aspects of culture. Progress, in turn, was used to explain the differences in lifestyles of people throughout the world, including their musical practices. With a few exceptions, Europeans found non-European music bewildering and even distasteful, and they assumed that the cause was insufficient progress in musical knowledge.

As anthropologists went throughout the world in the early twentieth century, they discovered that people in non-Western societies, both literate and nonliterate, had quite sophisticated sociocultural systems even though their technology was often less complex than that of Europe. In every society, anthropologists found highly intelligent, articulate people who reflected seriously about the world in terms of the background provided by their societies. These discoveries led to the conclusion that the innate mental processes of all human beings are basically the same, and that other people's ways of doing things did not necessarily indicate a lack of progress. Thus, one of the major insights of anthropology developed: that one's society and culture are of major importance in determining what a person does. This was also found to be true of the behaviors characterizing whole groups of people, including their music. The fact that some societies in the world had relatively uncomplicated forms of music was no longer considered to lie in some fault or ignorance of the individuals concerned, but rather in the ways people in various societies learned to perform and appreciate music. Consequently, the explanation of widely diverse musical traditions has come to be attributed to differences in historical background and the dynamics of life in societies.

Using the term sociocultural matrix (d'Azevedo 1958:703) to refer to the social background of music emphasizes that the society and the culture have an impact on the nature of the music. Matrix has been defined as "something within which something else originates or develops" (*Webster's Ninth New Collegiate Dictionary*), a situation that applies to the relationship between a sociocultural system and its music. Many ethnomusicologists have pointed to the importance of the "social context" or "cultural context" of music. The term "context" does not preclude the tendency to think of music as somehow developing from within itself and simply being shaped by external circumstances, much as a tree develops from its genetic makeup but is influenced by the presence of surrounding buildings and other trees. References to the context of music frequently have the connotation of program notes—the explanations provided in the printed program at a concert or recital. Such explanations are intended to enhance the audience's appreciation of the music by presenting an idea of the romantic involvements or political difficulties of the composer. The context can be useful in determining the meaning of particular presentations of music, but thinking in terms of the matrix from which music develops is more useful in explaining why musical occasions and performances may take one form rather than another.

From the perspective of social science, music is seen exclusively as a feature of human behavior. Even the view that the calls of birds and whales are "songs" is an act of the human mind not likely shared by the animals involved. Since music is the result of human activity, and because humans behave in accordance with the cultural norms they have learned, it follows that music itself results from the sociocultural situation within which it is produced. A significant step in understanding the nature of musical behavior, then, is to clarify the different types of sociocultural situations in which people live and produce music.

Types of Societies

As noted in Chapter 1, classifying information is one of the intermediate goals of scientific study. Anthropologists have classified societies according to their gradual increase in size and complexity, although the differences between these societies are often not as distinct as the various categories make them appear. Since all societies in the world today have been incorporated into the world economic and political system to varying degrees, these classifications are often blurred. They are important, however, as they still describe the original types of social matrices that gave rise to the musical systems operating at the time Europeans began to study many of these societies.

As formulated by Morton H. Fried (1967), a basic distinction in classifying societies is the difference between stratified and non-stratified societies. Although stratified societies have existed for several millennia, they were preceded everywhere by nonstratified societies, many of which still existed as Europeans expanded their knowledge of the world from the fifteenth century onward. Nonstratified societies are basically those in which access to natural resources is not restricted by any individual or group. The forms of subsistence production characterizing such groups are either hunting and gathering (foraging) or horticulture (shifting agriculture). Because these production techniques seldom produce a surplus, no one can gain the power to dominate such societies by gaining control of excess production. Other nonstratified societies are found among pastoralists, who live off their herds of livestock. Although pastoral groups often produce a surplus, it does not create social divisions because constantly moving about for pastures assures social flexibility. Nonstratified societies are considered to be of two types, egalitarian and rank. Egalitarian societies seldom practice equality between men and women, but within their particular gender roles all individuals have equal opportunity to fulfill any social role for which their personal abilities qualify them. According to archaeologists, all humans at one time lived by hunting and gathering, and they all lived in egalitarian societies. Although some egalitarian societies are still found in the world today, they are becoming increasingly rare.

An example of an egalitarian society is provided by the Mbuti Pygmies in the Ituri Forest of northeastern Zaire in Central Africa (Turnbull 1961, 1965). They are primarily hunters and gatherers whose rain forest environment provides them everything they need for what they consider a comfortable existence. The women gather mushrooms, nuts, and berries, while the men hunt with bows and poison arrows. The favorite food of the Mbuti is honey, which they collect in season. They consider the forest to have a spirit, and their songs and dances are designed to keep the forest spirit happy. Song is thought to be the activity which most pleases the forest because it is considered cool, as is the shady forest. Song is pleasing because it requires breath, the "life force," as well as effort (Turnbull 1965:255).

Other egalitarian hunting and gathering societies with interesting musical practices are the Aborigines of Australia and the Inuit of

North America, more commonly known as Eskimo. The Aborigines are the original inhabitants of the continent of Australia who were largely displaced by English settlers arriving there in the nineteenth century. The Aborigines developed their civilization for more than forty thousand years with little or no contact with the outside world. Most of the Aboriginal groups living in the developed areas of Australia were wiped out or assimilated into Australian culture. The Aboriginal groups that have been able to continue their traditional ways of life down to the present time live mostly in the central desert or the tropical area of Arnhem Land. Each of the various bands or tribes had its own geographical area where it had the right to hunt and gather. A complex form of social organization based on clans symbolized by totems maintained the system. Their religious beliefs are based on a mythical time in the past, called the Dreamtime, that is considered to be the explanation and cause of everything that exists in the present. Their complex rituals reenact the events of the Dreamtime, through symbolic images, mimetic dances, and complex series of song cycles.

The inhabitants of the North American Arctic region have commonly been called Eskimo, but their own term, Inuit, has been adopted for referring to them because the term Eskimo has come to be considered pejorative. Traditionally the Inuit, from Greenland through Canada and Alaska to Siberia, lived entirely by hunting and fishing. Some of the more southerly groups hunted caribou in the summers, but the Inuit depended heavily upon marine mammals such as seals, walruses, and whales. They utilized the hides of these animals to make their major musical instrument, the frame drum. Their music was used for communicating with the supernatural and for relieving tension in the community (Ex. 2.1). Today they are becoming increasingly involved with the economies of Canada and the United States.

Rank societies are similar to egalitarian societies in that they do not have restrictions on access to natural resources. They are different, however, in that some social roles are restricted to certain groups or individuals. These restrictions are usually in the form of specific lineages or clans from which leaders are chosen. Rank societies are often considered to be transitional between nonstratified and stratified forms of society. Rank societies often have songs honoring the chief or other leader, but lack the elaborate elite music establishments characterizing truly stratified societies. The transitional nature of rank societies is seen on the small Polynesian island of Tikopia, located in the South Pacific between Fiji and the Solomon Islands. Its chiefs have an honored position in the society, and

often have more land than commoners, but they do not have the power to deprive the commoners of goods they need for their livelihood (Firth 1963:316).

Examples of rank societies include the Shona of Zimbabwe prior to the European invasion of their lands in the 1890s. Living by horticulture based on hoes and rotating fields, they were organized as rank societies under numerous autonomous chiefs. A chief was chosen from candidates whose eligibilities were based on membership in a leading lineage. Land was considered to belong to the entire community, and it was apportioned by the elders to members of the group for their use. Other resources, such as firewood or thatching grass, were available to everyone. Major music events were oriented toward rituals connected to the chief or to ancestral spirit mediums. The Venda in the northern part of South Africa also had a rank society, where there was no paramount chief, but local chiefs and headmen whose positions were determined by clan membership. The various local chiefs used musical organizations as a way of improving relations with each other (Blacking 1965:21).

Stratified societies are distinguished by the fact that certain groups or individuals control the natural resources, and restrict the access of other individuals in the society to those resources. Stratified societies have usually developed only where the means of producing subsistence goods have created a surplus. This process began several thousand years ago as agriculture intensified through the use of plows and fertilizer. More recently it has involved agriculture with power machinery.

When analyzing the forces influencing musical behavior, it is useful to distinguish between various types of stratified societies. One of these distinctions is between literate and nonliterate societies. Some societies, such as many groups in Africa and Polynesia, never had occasion to develop writing, but they maintained relatively sophisticated, stratified societies without it. The Aztec of pre-Columbian Mexico had developed a form of pictographic writing by the time of the Spanish conquest, but it was not used for writing music. The Aztec society was essentially a city-state that had conquered many surrounding city-states. They practiced a form of intensive agriculture and produced a surplus by growing crops in artificial gardens built up with silt from the lake bed. Although we have no way of knowing exactly how their music sounded, it is likely that some of the music of isolated Mexican Indian villages is similar to Aztec music. Of particular interest are the many descriptions of the organization and use of music left by the Spanish conquistadores in the sixteenth century. The highly stratified Aztec society had both

political leaders and priests. The latter operated the temples where human sacrifices were made, and organized the music that was used there. The city-states were primarily ceremonial centers, and music was a significant part of the ceremonies (Stevenson 1968).

The Tuareg of the Sahara Desert, before their domination by French colonial power, provide an example of stratified societies lacking a strong state system. Actually, the Tuareg consisted of several distinct but culturally related units. The stratification is seen in the division of these units into castes, meaning that members of various groups were restricted in their occupations, and had to marry within the same group. The dominant group was a warrior or noble caste, whose men were the fabled camel riders who wore blue veils. Religious specialists ranked close to the warriors, but were beneath them. Because religious specialists could originate in other groups, they did not constitute a caste. While the warrior caste provided protection from outsiders, the vassal tribes assured a food supply by providing care for the herds of goats. Beneath them was an artisan caste, whose members produced goods needed by the society. The lowest group consisted of a servile population—tenant farmers and slaves (Card 1982:19–28). Although members of other groups performed music, only the artisans were known as professional musicians because they performed for hire. Because of their low social position, artisans were able to perform music that was considered inappropriate for other classes (ibid.:145).

In stratified societies another major difference exists between those that are industrialized and those that are not. No stratified society was truly industrialized until the late eighteenth century, when the industrial revolution began, but for the last two hundred years or so the number and power of industrialized societies has been increasing, and the effect of this process has caused profound changes in musical behavior where it has occurred. The music of India developed in a stratified society that was at least to some degree literate but not industrialized. India as a Hindu country has been organized in terms of castes, in which the kinds of work people are expected to do are determined by their birth. Although India is now a republic, it was formerly a patchwork of stratified states led by princes or maharajahs. Their courts sponsored the classical cultivated music, which differed in many ways from the music of the common people. This southern Asian country was subjected to major invasions in the past, beginning with speakers of Indo-European languages between three and four thousand years ago, followed by the Moghul invasions of Islamic peoples in the sixteenth century. These incursions brought India a variety of musical influences, which were further changed by the domination of the British from the nineteenth century well into the twentieth one. The interplay of historical influences has led to differences between the musics of North and South India.

Industrialization became a major force in the world during the nineteenth century. One might assume that modern communications and technology would cause the musical practices of all industrial societies to be the same, but that has not happened. Japan provides an example of a highly industrialized society where modern rock music exists alongside staid court music hundreds of years old. Japan's traditional values emphasize cooperation and the importance of the group. Stratification in Japan is de-emphasized because of the way society is organized by focusing on the working group in which all levels are, theoretically at least, treated alike. Stratification is more apparent in the ranking of groups, such as schools and corporations, as much as from the ranking of individuals (Nakane 1970).

With modern transportation and communication the world has in many ways become one huge stratified society. This is the view of world system theory (Wolf 1982; Wallerstein 1983), which maintains that the power of international corporations overrides many features of the distinctive sociocultural systems that were formerly autonomous throughout the world. World stratification is seen in the distinction between the core, which consists of the industrialized countries, and the periphery, or the countries and areas of the world that now supply the basic raw materials and cheap labor. Some countries are semi-peripheral, either rising toward core status or becoming more peripheral. The core countries are able to direct the system to their own benefit, while the countries of the periphery are maintained as such by a local elite that depends on the core countries for maintaining their positions and their personal wealth. This view of the world situation is important in relation to music because of the power of the music industry and the general economic power of the core countries.

In summary, relating music to its sociocultural matrix involves five types of societies: nonstratified egalitarian, nonstratified rank, stratified nonliterate, stratified literate nonindustrialized, and stratified literate industrialized, as shown in Figure 2.1.

The influence of the type of society on musical practices is indirect, but some regularities are to be found. Among hunting and gathering peoples, as well as horticulturalists, music is often related to religious ritual, focusing on efforts to obtain food. Foraging and pastoral societies are nomadic, so their music does not involve the use

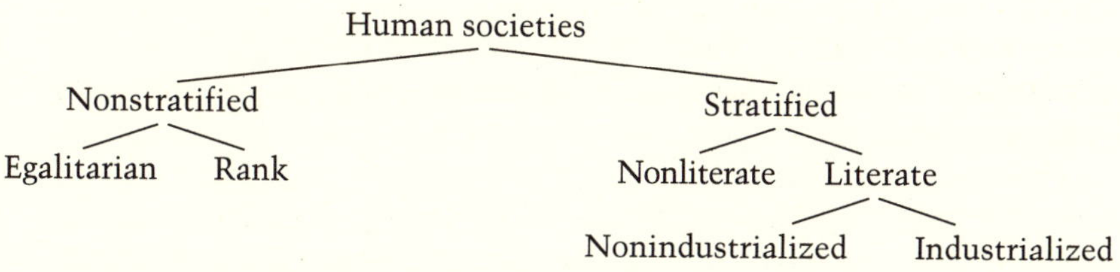

Figure 2.1. Types of human societies.

of heavy or cumbersome instruments. Musical activity among stratified societies is more often oriented to the expression of differences
in social standing. Because agricultural and industrial societies have
large populations, they are more likely to have diverse types of music following the forms of social stratification.

An important consequence of the stratification of societies is the
rather distinct differentiation of expressive cultures among the various groups. The sociologist Herbert J. Gans refers to expressive culture as "taste culture," emphasizing values and choice. He has suggested that differences in people's circumstances frequently divide a
society into different **taste publics** (1974:10–11). People who share
common resources, time, and education ordinarily have similar values that heavily influence the content and form of their taste culture. Those whose resources, time, and education are different will
develop different tastes. Gans uses the term high culture to refer to
the taste culture of the powerful, wealthy, and well-educated segments of society, and the term popular culture to refer to the taste
culture of the great mass of people in a stratified society. Since music is a part of taste culture, these distinctions are also relevant.
What has customarily been referred to as "art" or "serious" music
characterizes high culture; "folk" or "popular" music is found in
popular culture. All of these usages will be examined more carefully
in the following chapters. Nonstratified societies, which are usually
hunters and gatherers, pastoralists, or horticulturalists, have only
one taste public, whose music is referred to as "tribal," "traditional," or (improperly) "primitive." Using the simple phrase "music of small-scale societies" instead of these other terms provides a
way to avoid both inaccuracy and pejorative connotation.

Although the type of society affects the ways of making music in
broad and general terms, many other important factors operate at
the interpersonal and individual levels. The interpersonal level is
the musical event, where the musicians interact with other people
in their society.

Music Events and Music Complexes

One of the major effects of the sociocultural matrix on music is to determine the occasions on which music is performed—often called the **music event** or musical occasion. The event often serves as the basis for analyzing musical behavior, because it is in the event that social forces and musical sound actually come together. The motivation for musical events is a significant factor, for it means that people are choosing music over some other form of activity. Preparations for a musical performance, such as practicing the music, arranging the location, or organizing performers, are of major importance in understanding what is occurring at events. Although most music events involve performance, not all music events are determined by the presence of musical sound. A music lesson or a group of people conversing about music constitute a special kind of music event. Such lessons and conversations are often an important key to understanding many facets of the musical life of any society.

Although researchers sometimes focus on a study of one event (event analysis), it is much more common to deal as a unit with recurring cases of the same type of event. Humans seldom stage one event that is unique of its type. Usually the same types of events are regularly repeated, such as harvest festivals, marriages, or rock concerts. Thus it is possible to treat similar events together in what can be termed a **music complex**. A music complex is "a set of musical events having the same goal, conceptualized the same way, and supported by the same social group" (Kaemmer 1980).[1] The musical practices of any society, even a very small one, will probably consist of a series of music complexes. Both music events and music complexes are of several general types.

Individualistic music events and music complexes are those in which the impetus for a specific music event is the result of the personal motivations of the performer rather than a communally determined occasion. This is the type of music event where a person sings casually while washing clothes, or a beggar plays a guitar on the street. Among the Flathead and other Plains Indian groups in North America, young men traditionally engaged in a vision quest, in which they left the community and went out by themselves to obtain a vision that would guide them through their lives. Songs comprised an important part of the vision, and the song given to an individual during his vision was his personal song throughout his life (Merriam 1967:7ff).

An interesting example of an individualistic music event is given by Ian Cunnison as he describes the musician at a wedding among the Baggara people in the African nation of Sudan. Hammoda was marrying the sister of Hurgas, the chief (omda) of the Ganis tribe.

Hammoda was ready to marry. It was to be a quiet affair since he had been married before. There were few guests, and little celebration was expected apart from an evening of tea-drinking and feasting around the campfire. Hurgas was mellowed. A minstrel had heard of the wedding and rode up on a donkey with his one-string fiddle. The men sat around the fire and as the minstrel opened with his songs of love, the women came silently from the tents and sat at a respectful distance out of the firelight. Hurgas half closed his eyes and drank in the surroundings. He was a lover himself.

Folks call you the daughter of Ahmed
But to me you're the eye of a young gazelle
Ripple of sand under running water
Gold of a necklace from Omdurman
Lotus flower of the southern pool
Giraffe of the boundless grassy plains. . . .

But then the theme of the minstrel changed, his song became livelier and firmer, as he sang the praises of the men of Ganis dead and gone. Hurgas woke up, and as the wont is, took a piastre and dropped it into the hole in the minstrel's fiddle. Others followed suit as their own relatives were mentioned. The minstrel brought his song up to date and praised famous men of today:

His mother made the food for the elephant hunts
And Kibbeyry today leads the best of the horsemen
A granary of seed for next year's sowing. . . .

The women were stirred, and shrilled at the mention of the brave exploits of their kinsmen. And then the praise was of Hurgas himself. He had led the elephant on and the youths had speared it. His cattle were numbered like the blades of grass. The renown of his generosity was the fireside talk of distant tribes. His horse was black as the night. His women had the grace of horses. Hurgas could contain himself no longer. He seized his gun and shot into the air twice, three, four times. The sound brought people from neighbouring camps who came along and heard the praises of their Omda Hurgas. The half-moon had set by the time the

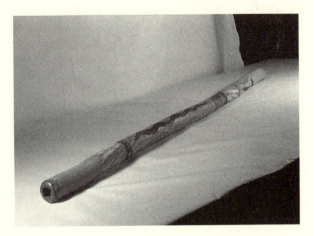

2.1. An Australian Aborigine didjeridu, 5'8" long. (Instrument in
William Hammond Mathers Museum, Bloomington, Indiana; photo
by the author.)

people dispersed, Hammoda went to his bride, and the minstrel
lay content with a fiddleful of coins. (1960: 322)

Communal music events and complexes are those in which a
community or group makes plans and actualizes the performance.
These performances may be common religious rituals, or they could
be the singing of work songs or entertainment songs. The persons
who perform may be those who are recognized as especially capable,
but no special arrangements are made for them. Events arranged by
a guild or association of performers would be communal in this
sense, even though they involve only part of a community. The Australian Aborigines (Ex. 2.2; Photo 2.1) provide an example of a communal music event:

During the day the members of the group have been scattered
on their economic and other activities, either in their own indigenous way or in relation to white men. Evening comes, and a
meal is eaten in family groups. Then as darkness descends and
camp fires sparkle, a didjeridu and the tapping of sticks are heard
from the dance-place or the Songman's camp. Gradually and casually men and women move over to the cleared ground. Perhaps
someone, hearing the preliminary sounds, has eagerly called out
"corroboree over there"—a Wongga, a Walaka, a Gunborg or other

dance title. Arriving there ourselves, we see the Songman sitting
or standing (according to the song and dance), with his rhythm
sticks in his hands, singing and beating time. Alongside of him is
a didjeridu player or "puller" as he is called, producing a deep
note of varied rhythm from a hollowed piece of wood about six
feet long and two or three inches internal diameter. He takes his
cue from the songman. The latter may be assisted by one or more
singers, but he is the leader—determining what is to be sung,
and if there be an unaccompanied recitative at the end of a verse,
he is the last to finish.

Further, we see some young men and some not so young, and a
few boys, dancing in ballet style. They enter the dance place from
the side of the ground opposite to the Songman, and dance towards him, raising dust with their accented stamping. There may
be a leading dancer, but he and his fellows are under the general
direction of the Songman, who is master of ceremonies. On one
edge of the ground, too, just after each song and dance commence,
some women and girls stand up and, without shifting their position, rhythmically move their feet, legs and arms in time with
the music. They are just as intent on their silent dancing as are
the more active men, and may be praised as good dancers. Nearby
in the various camps, old folk and parents with little ones on
their knees listen and watch, and beat the rhythm. (Elkin and
Jones 1958:92)

Contractual music events and complexes are those in which music is performed as the result of an arrangement (not necessarily a
written contract) between the musician and another party on a short-
term basis. The lack of an agent with a dominant profit motive distinguishes this from the commercial type of music event. Common
examples of contractual events are found where a shaman or spirit
healer, such as the Navajo curer, is summoned to a home to effect a
cure through a musical ritual. Contractual music events are also
found where musicians are engaged to perform on specific occasions, as among the Shona, where mbira players are contracted each
time they are needed to play at a spirit possession ceremony. Even
though the ritual itself is communal, the music is performed by a
specialist.

The artisans of the Tuareg provide an example of the contractual
type of music complex, since they were hired by the upper class to
perform at social events. Their remuneration commonly took the
form of gifts. Because they were expected to please their employers,
the artisans performed music to amuse and flatter, rather than ex-

press their own feelings. They were also able to adapt themselves to new and different styles of music (Card 1982:139).

Sponsored music complexes are found when performers are engaged on a long-term basis by agencies less concerned with profit than with entertainment, prestige, or influencing attitudes. This has often consisted of patronage, as when a nobleman provides the support for musicians to compose and perform music for the court. This type of sponsored music characterized much European musical activity during the seventeenth and eighteenth centuries. This was also the case in India, where classical Indian music was performed by musicians attached to the households of the wealthy and the aristocrats. The size and fame of the musical establishment added to the prestige of a ruler (Neuman 1990:86).

Sponsored music occurs not only in the palaces and drawing rooms of rulers, but also in certain religious contexts. Aztec temples were the center of important ceremonies, and each temple had groups of professional musicians who were affiliated with it. The religious cycle was 260 days, and every piece of music had a particular occasion on which it was performed. The musicians were formed into guilds, and were exempt from tribute to the government. They were also tenured and organized into grades. Although the names of the musicians were never recorded, it is reported that they enjoyed high status and prestige. Their duties included playing a musical fanfare to mark the passing hours, playing for dancers, and singing hymns and praises to accompany offerings. Also, one was chosen to accompany a deceased king to the other world (Stevenson 1968).

Modern governments in many areas also sponsor music. In Afghanistan, government sponsorship is the standard arrangement for musicians performing on radio or television. In this situation, counteracting the negative Moslem view of music was important.

With the establishment of a government radio station in Kabul in the 1940's, administered through the Ministry of Information and Culture, a new type of musician emerged. Like government bureaucrats, these musicians enjoyed official sanction and support; a majority of them began their musical careers at the radio. They were mainly young amateur musicians from socially established families (members of the extended royal family, or children of prime ministers, generals, or other officials), and their repertoire consisted of newly composed, popular songs. Their singing was accompanied by a large orchestra consisting of a conglomeration of Afghan and some Western instruments (piano, organ, trumpet). They developed a musical style that became distinctly associated with the radio and other government-sponsored institutions (theaters, concerts). These musicians represented a new, modern and urban class of artists known as *onarman* who were supposed to lend their own respectable standing to music and musicians as a whole. In fact, this respect was limited just to these modern artists, and extended to them only by the urban, middle class. The rest of the society tended to view them as traditional entertainers of low character and status. (Sakata 1983: 95–96)

Commercial music complexes are those characterized by the activities of an agent who serves as intermediary between the performers and the audience. Music is treated as a commodity, with emphasis on supply and demand and profitability. These complexes are prominent in the modern capitalist economy, and involve the record, radio, and music industries. However, anyone who organizes a music event primarily for the purpose of profit is engaging in a commercial music event.

Both sponsored and commercial music complexes tend to be controlled by those who have the financial resources to foster musical activities. The use of these resources is often determined not by the musicians or consumers themselves, but by the wishes of the patron or the agent. The group of people who exercise this type of control are often referred to as the **music establishment**. Their input is often crucial in determining the course of changes in music.

The entire musical culture of a society can best be understood by analysis of the various music complexes. No human societies are limited to only one type of music or music event. In some ways certain music events or music complexes are likely to be more closely related to other aspects of the culture than to other types of music complexes. The system of ritual in many societies will include music as a closely integrated aspect of the ritual. The ritual music will not necessarily be closely integrated with music used for work situations. Some musical cultures tend to consist of a collection of diverse musical occasions, while others exhibit closely integrated forms of behavior. Societies vary widely in the ways their musical activities are integrated with each other.

Although they constitute a very small society, the Mbuti Pygmies exemplify how the musical culture of a society is made up of several complexes. An individualistic complex consists of lullabies, individually motivated occasions when a mother tries to quiet a crying child. Because of the importance of egalitarian values to the Mbuti, their other music complexes are communal, but they are nevertheless distinct. One complex consists of the songs and dances of the Bantu villagers, sung when the Mbuti visit in the village, but not performed in the forest. Rhythmic games such as skipping or jumping hoops to the accompaniment of play songs form another complex. Another is the singing and dancing related to the hunt, where the dance movements suggest the movements of the game or of the hunter (Ex. 2.3). Another communal complex consists of the performance of songs when the group scatters to go in search of honey. During these songs the men imitate the honey gatherers and the women imitate the bees, attacking the men with embers as if they were stinging. The two most serious music complexes are the *elima* ceremony and the *molimo* festival, each with its specific songs. The *elima* ceremony occurs at the time of a girl's first menstrual period; the *molimo* festival takes place at times of crisis when the Mbuti sing to the forest, upon which their lives depend (Turnbull 1965).

Larger societies have the whole range of music complexes. In rural India, mendicant musicians constitute individualistic music complexes as they wander from place to place hoping to gather a few coins or bits of grain by playing or singing. Blind musicians board trains for this purpose, ride a while, then catch the train back to where they began. Other mendicants, called *jogi*, move from house to house singing and playing the *sarangi*, a kind of stringed instrument (Photo 2.2) (Henry 1988:159–160). A shamanic complex appears as a specialist called *ojha* conducts special nightly seances during which he sings a song to a goddess. He then goes into a trance, and by using the voice of the goddess he helps people solve their problems (ibid.:83). Contractual music complexes are seen in the practice of hiring bands to play at weddings (ibid.:193). In other cases certain musicians go to homes where sons have been born, and sing for pay (ibid.:64). The presentation of Indian classical music in the courts of the maharajahs and princes has already been mentioned as a form of sponsored music complex. The modern music and film industry represents the commercial type of complex.

The distinction between types of events and complexes serves not only as a useful tool for analysis of a given situation, it also helps clarify some of the basic relationships between forms of social life and the forms of musical activity. Certain regularities can be seen in the relationship between music complexes and the different types of societies. Nonstratified societies have only individualistic, contractual, and communal types of music complexes. In stratified societies all these types, plus sponsored and commercial music complexes, are found. The occurrence of the latter two types marks one

2.2. Mukh Ram, a *jogi*, playing the *sarangi*, Ghazipur District, Uttar Pradesh, India, 1972. (Photo by Edward O. Henry; used by permission.)

of the major differences between the musical practices of stratified and nonstratified societies.

Sometimes the presence of different styles of music in separate complexes is due to having borrowed both the music and its complex from different sources. This kind of situation is most obvious in Japan, where some music complexes are ancient borrowings from China, some are recent borrowings from Europe and America, and other complexes involve mixing the old and the new styles.

Social Roles in Musical Activities

People engaging in musical activities customarily behave in a manner socially acceptable for anyone in their position. These standardized ways of acting, called social roles, are important in understanding regularities in musical behavior, even though people do not follow the norms as automatically as social scientists once thought. The concept of social role is often connected with social status, since the role is the type of behavior expected of persons in a particular status.

A major goal of studying music from the social scientific perspective is to explain how society influences the music sound produced by any group of people. The social structure and the cultural understandings make much of their impact upon music through the musician. Those who create music constitute only one of several roles related to music making. While the others will be discussed in due course, focus is necessarily directed to the musician, whose action is indispensable to the existence of music.

Musician

The role of musician is of major importance, because performing musicians feel pressures from their society's views of themselves and their music. Those pressures can cause a marked effect on what the musicians do. The values of a society often determine what kind of people become musicians, what types of musicians are recognized, and what social position is given to musicians. The latter determines how musicians are given rewards, and how they are expected to act. Societies vary widely in their views of the role of musician.

In many societies, musical ability may be a relatively minor factor in determining who becomes a musician. Particularly in nonstratified societies, factors other than musicianship are important. The Suya Indians of the Amazon basin in Brazil sing mostly in ceremonies (Photo 2.3), where participation is guided by sex, age, and name sets. The latter are groups composed of people who share certain names. The Suya have two major types of songs, shout songs (*akia*) and unison songs (*ngere*). The shout songs are highly individual, and they are sung by men to honor their mothers and sisters (Ex. 2.4). The singing of unison songs is determined by name sets; they are sung by the men of each name set as they march through the village during a ceremony. Women do not sing at ceremonies; they constitute the audience. The women reciprocate the men's gift of song with their own gifts of food (A. Seeger 1979).

Throughout the world, one of the major factors determining status as a musician is sex or gender. Social scientists commonly make a distinction between the two, sex being biological and gender

2.3. Suya men singing in the Mouse Ceremony, 1975. (Photo by Anthony Seeger; used by permission.)

being socially determined. Thus the fact that most women have higher voices than men is due to sex; the exclusion of women from certain types of musical performances is related to gender. Gender is an important musical factor in many places, as highlighted by a situation such as the Suya, where only the men sing in most ceremonies. Among the Kaluli in Papua New Guinea the situation is the opposite of the Suya. In New Guinea it is the women who insert melody and text into their weeping to make it song. It is the men who are driven to weeping by the beauty of the singing of the women. Two of Feld's chapters (1982) are entitled "Weeping That Moves Women to Song" and "Song that Moves Men to Tears." The Warlpiri have separate songs and rituals for men and for women, with differences in the ways they perform. For rhythm, men clap boomerangs or clap their hands, while women cup their hands and

2.4. Indian women singing *sohar* songs, near Varanasi, 1978. (Photo by Edward O. Henry; used by permission.)

beat them on their thighs. In some types of songs a senior man leads with the first phrase of a section of song, followed by the other men singing the first line of a couplet. Women and children then join on the second line of the couplet (Wild 1975:86, 87).

Gender is a major feature of musical life in rural northern India, because men and women never sing together. Women not only sing more often, they also sing about topics that are primarily female interests, such as giving birth to a son, relations with in-laws, and the mother goddess (Photo 2.4). Men and women also have different styles, with men's singing characterized by strong regular rhythms, and women's with more melody and irregular rhythms (Henry 1988: 144). The singing ability of a woman is recognized and brings prestige to her and her family (ibid.:108).

Although the musical roles within a society tend to differ according to gender, it is not always the men who play the most significant instruments. Among the Tuareg, only the women play the *anzad*, a one-stringed bowed lute (Ex. 2.5; see Photo 5.4). The *anzad* was primarily played by women of the warrior caste, because only they had time to perfect the difficult technique.

> The *anzad* . . . is believed capable of inspiring men to heroic deeds and it is thought to give courage to warriors in time of battle. Its music evokes images of love and beauty, and it symbolizes the noblest ideals and sentiments in Tuareg culture. (Card 1982:74)

The instrument was formerly played to protect the warriors with what was considered a magical power. Playing this instrument gave status to women because they could refrain from playing it for a warrior if they felt he had not been sufficiently courageous or heroic. The prospect of this form of public censure was enough to drive men to do their utmost in battle (ibid.:76). The instrument was also used for entertainment, primarily at courtship gatherings, so it became identified with love and passion. Moreover, some *anzad* songs are associated with pre-Islamic features of Tuareg culture. These factors have caused conservative Moslems to try to suppress use of the instrument. Although the religious leaders are sincere in their belief that the welfare of the community is at stake, some Tuareg women see the opposition to the *anzad* as opposition to a meaningful status for women (ibid.:78).

The reasons for gender distinctions in musical life are not clear, and certainly vary from one place to another. They appear to be related to general differences in gender role within each society. Matrilineal societies determine lineage membership through females, and they emphasize relations between mothers and daughters; patrilineal societies, with lineage membership determined through males, emphasize relations between fathers and sons. In such situations it is customary for the social lives of men and women to be distinct, so it would be natural for musical life to follow the same pattern. In societies without lineages (bilateral), where the nuclear family and the husband-wife relationship are of major importance, distinctions between the social domains of the sexes are not necessarily as distinct. With the exception of modern industrial societies, women have customarily found their major place in the domestic sphere because of the requirements of childbearing and nursing. This situation has left the men to care for the public domain involving both political and economic relations between groups, as well as public rituals. Its use in rituals has been another reason that men's music has often been distinctive, and often appeared to be more significant than women's.

Gender differences in musical style may have causes other than the meaning and use of the music. Among the Tuareg, for example, men sing a particular type of song with a tense and piercing quality, whereas women sing the same type in a much more relaxed way. The difference is simply due to the fact that men and women sing these songs at the same pitch (Card 1982:99).

Age is another factor that sometimes determines who performs as a musician. In Macedonia it has been common practice to give up music when mourning for close kin. Although the period of mourning does not last indefinitely, the older a person gets, the greater the likelihood of losing parents and brothers and sisters, so that older people become less active musically (N. Sachs 1975:163–164). Among the Yirkalla in Arnhem Land, Australia, young girls sing extensively when they are baby-sitting their younger siblings, but as they grow older they are limited to performing a type of ritual wailing (R. Waterman 1971:173).

Important in determining the role of the musician, social and political factors are often mixed with other factors, such as gender. Because musicians in India were considered low caste, it was thought inappropriate for high-caste people to perform music, at least in public. Among the Venda in South Africa young men of chiefly families are expected not to perform music because of their important political roles, but the women in such families are required to practice and learn extensive series of songs for important rituals (Blacking 1973:46–47). In West Africa the praise singer (*griot*) is a member of an endogamous group that resembles a caste, even though the entire society is not organized that way. In some places the caste includes both musicians and blacksmiths.

Sometimes economic factors restrict who can become musicians. Classical music performance in the West, for example, is often the prerogative of upper-class individuals whose families have the resources to provide the young with expensive training. Because of the expensive equipment used in rock bands, "in other countries with a larger spread of income it is no coincidence that rock groups are often formed by the children of upper-middle-class families" (Wallis and Malm 1984:275). In less materialistic societies, social position seems to be more important than economics in determining who becomes a musician.

Distinguishing one type of musician from another is important in many societies, and wide variation exists in the ways this is done. Many societies commonly distinguish between the amateur and the professional. The term "professional" is used extensively in the literature of the cross-cultural study of music, but it has often been given different meanings by various scholars. In Western society formal training is considered the criterion of the professional in the "art" music establishment. In nonliterate societies reading music is completely irrelevant, yet many highly skilled musicians support themselves completely with their music. This factor sets them off from others who pursue musical performance as a supplement to their income, or even for no recompense at all. It is often useful to reserve the term **professional** for musicians obtaining the necessities of life through their musical activities, and describe part-time practitioners as semi-professionals or **specialists**.

Afghanistan, a Moslem country, provides an interesting example of the complexity that can mark the distinctions among musicians. The Afghans have two criteria for distinguishing between amateur and professional musicians. One is whether the arrangements for musical performances are made in a social or a business context, respectively. The other criterion is whether or not the individual was born into a family of professional musicians. Those born into that group constitute a type of caste, in which members customarily marry other members of the same group. Some people in this group become barbers either full- or part-time. Musicians belonging to the group are considered professional even if they work part-time as barbers, but they occupy a very low social status (Sakata 1983:76). These hereditary musicians are pejoratively called *dalak;* the non-hereditary musicians are called *shauqi*. The kind of instrument played serves to indicate the status of a musician. Only the hereditary musicians play the two instruments *sorna* and *dohl*. The *sorna* is considered polluted because it is a double reed instrument, and the musician puts the entire reed into his mouth, thus contaminating it with spittle (Photo 2.5) (1983:79). Other instruments, such as a plucked lute, jaws harp[2] (see Photo 4.13), and flute, are seldom played professionally by the hereditary musicians. While Sakata was working with musicians in Afghanistan, the nonhereditary musicians were very careful not to be perceived as working with her, because that would give them the appearance of professional status, and low social standing.

In Western civilization a distinction is traditionally made between composer and performer, because it is the composer who chooses and arranges the specific sounds that the performer is to actualize. In other societies, where improvisation is the rule, the performer has extensive leeway in creating a great variety of tonal and rhythmic patterns, while the composer may only determine the

2.5. A *sorna* player from Herat, Afghanistan, 1967. Circular breathing causes the cheeks to be puffed out. (Photo by Sumio Thomas Sakata; used by permission.)

general outline. In such societies a distinction is not always made between composer and performer, or else the role of composer is considered less important than it is in the West.

Western observers have often unquestioningly assumed either that the composers of tribal or folk music were unknown, or that instead of being composed, the music developed as a result of a group process. In egalitarian and nonliterate societies little attention is given to publicizing the names of outstanding musicians. They are not, however, characteristically forgotten in their own groups. Even when musicians are unknown, music probably did not result from group creation alone, since certain individuals have usually provided the initial outline. Modification of a basic outline is easy in a society lacking specific music notation, since changes or improvements are easily incorporated into customary ways of performing.

It has often been observed that in many places the musician occupies an inferior position in society (Kimberlin 1980:232–236). Where a society is organized in castes, as in India, musicians usually come from the lower echelons. The low status of the hereditary musicians in Afghanistan is possibly derived from the caste system in India (Sakata 1983:79). Even in nonstratified societies, musicians occupy low statuses. Robin Horton noted that the performers of the Ekine masquerade dances among the Kalabari peoples of Nigeria are carefree and not necessarily bound to observe the moral standards for sexual behavior as followed by the rest of society (1973:612–613). Merriam has discussed the status of musicians fully in his *Anthropology of Music*, where he noted that in Zaire among the Basongye,[3] musicians are expected to be drunkards, monetarily irresponsible, and sexually deviant. In describing the social position of Songye musicians as ambivalent, he points out that although they can be ordered about as servants, their services are indispensable to the society. He concludes that the Songye musician is of such great importance to the society that deviant conduct is tolerated (1964:134).

The position of musicians may reflect the values given to various types of music. In classical Indian music the prestige of musicians varies according to which instrument they play. Players of solo instruments such as vina or sitar have much higher status than performers on accompanying instruments like the tabla. Singers have even higher status. One goal of many musicians is to bring about higher status for their particular instrument (Neuman 1990:92–94).

The low position of musicians in many places seems to be related to a music community's basic values concerning human relations. Where a society has egalitarian ideals, the extraordinary and enviable skill of the musician would tend to foster arrogance were it not for the humbling effect of a social role viewed with disdain by the society as a whole. When a society is basically stratified, the position of musicians as servants under the patronage system would by itself serve to put them in a subordinate position.

Low social status is not always the lot of musicians. Among the Inuit, drummers have a high social status (Johnston 1976:18). In many places the blind are frequently given a valued role in society by becoming musicians. In Japan the rights of blind people as performers of certain instruments were protected by the government in the mid-nineteenth century (Kishibe 1984:11). In capitalist societies where music becomes commercially important, the musician is likely to be considered a valuable commodity. Whether the position of the musician is especially low or especially high, it seldom seems to be ordinary; it is consistently polarized one way or another, resembling the position of artists (Anderson 1979:90).

Musicians are often organized into guilds, which serve to improve their socio-economic situation. Guilds are common in many parts of the world, notably Japan and India, where they often sponsor musical performances and serve as a means of controlling the financial arrangements for musicians. In Japan, where they are called *ryu*, the guilds have existed for fifteen centuries (Harich-Schneider 1973:29). They are basically family groups, but they do not hesitate to incorporate other members who are interested and display ability. The term is often translated as "school," because different guilds are characterized by distinctive ways of performing. Guilds in Japan are formed for each kind of instrument, as well as for different styles of theater, flower arranging, tea ceremony, and other arts. Guilds in India, called *gharana*, are apparently not so old as those in Japan. They seem to have been established as a means whereby musicians sought to legitimize their status as professional performers rather than simply low-status servants (Neuman 1990).

Different roles of musicians are even found within a particular performance ensemble. Among the Aymara Indians of the Andean Plateau several different roles exist within the communal music groups organized to perform at religious festivals. Each group will have a *guia*, or major leader, who is chosen informally because of his musical knowledge. He must know performance techniques on the different instruments and also the pieces in the group's repertoire so that he will always be able to cue performers. Another role is that of *maestro*, the men who play the various instruments. They too must be expert musicians, since they carry the major responsibility for playing the music and for creating new songs. A third role in this situation is rather distinctive, being filled by ad hoc members of the ensemble, who are not as skilled as the *maestros*. Even though they do not appear for rehearsals or sessions for composing new songs, they are still accepted in the group (Photo 2.6) (Turino 1989).

In any performance involving ensembles, a variety of roles among musicians is required to ensure coordination. Very few societies have leaders, like conductors, who do not play. Often the leading performer will give visual cues with head or hand. Sometimes the cues are aural, a part of the musical performance. Among the Kpelle (see Photo 1.3), numerous roles are distinguished within the performing group. The vocal soloist has a supporting soloist as a counterpart. The master drummer also has a counterpart, the supporting drummer (Photo 2.7). All of these together are counterbalanced with the chorus, which also has a distinction between the main chorus and a few who perform a counterpart. The role of audience is not emphasized by the Kpelle, because those who are not participating in the music are considered to be outside the bounds of the performance. Other roles exist in certain types of performances. The "question-asking-person" provides cues that enable a storyteller-singer to proceed through the performance. Also a part of the group, although not part of the performance roles, are the agent and the *posia* (police) and their counterparts *soya* (soldiers), who keep order. Spirits that provide supernatural aid, as well as spirits of deceased

2.6. Aymara musicians playing panpipes, Conima, Peru. (Photo by
Thomas Turino; used by permission.)

2.7. Musical roles of drummers among the Kpelle, contrasting the master drum, played with hands, and the supporting drum, played with sticks, 1975. (Photo by Ruth M. Stone and Verlon L. Stone; used by permission.)

ancestors or noted players, are also considered a part of the performance group (Stone 1982:81–83).

Other Social Roles

Although the role of musician is of overwhelming importance, the presence of other persons in all music-related activities must not be overlooked. While people sometimes play or sing alone, such as the African cattle herder amusing himself with a hastily fashioned flute, most performances involve an audience. When everyone is participating in communal music events the distinction between performers and audience is not clear. In some cases, as with the Kpelle mentioned previously, no one could rightly be considered audience. In broader terms, the audience is one special kind of role often termed **consumer**. The consumers are basically the ones for whom the music is being performed. Although consumers are usually the listeners, the role can include the persons utilizing a musical performance in other ways, such as the family of a sick person who has hired a shaman to sing for a cure. In addition, the consumer may also include the purchasers of records, cassettes, or compact discs.

Another important role in analyzing musical behavior is that of **agent**. The agent instigates and often organizes musical performances, even though possibly not participating in the actual event. In capitalist societies the agent's purpose is to make a profit from the music performance, rather than to relate to it as an expressive activity. When music is treated as a commodity, as it often is nowadays, the agent could be termed the seller. When governments sponsor music, the role of agent would be filled by a bureaucrat who organizes groups to convey desired social messages through musical performances. The role of agent is not limited to complex societies. In nonstratified societies the agent, as a person sent by a family to procure a singer for a curing ceremony, would often be termed a go-between. The role of agent is seen among the Kpelle of Liberia:

Kpelle performing groups sometimes include a *pele-kalon* (chief of performance). Although he is not usually visibly active in the performance situation itself, he serves as a counterpart to the entire ensemble in its internal relations and in respect to the people outside its boundaries. He settles disputes among group members, serves as a liaison to the town chief, and negotiates performance conditions and arrangements for the group. (Stone 1982:81)

A role similar to agent is found among the Warlpiri Aborigines of Australia. Their society is divided into two patrilineal moieties (halves), so that when the members of one moiety (the owners/performers) wish to conduct one of their rituals, which focus on song and dance, the members of the other moiety (the managers) make the preparations of the ritual area and supervise the proceedings. Although the managers sometimes take part in the singing, they do not always do so, nor is that their major role (Wild 1975:39, 117–118).

In some situations the role of **critic** is important, involving a person who engages in discourse about an artistic or aesthetic activity. The critic enables the researcher to gain a clearer idea of the musical concepts of the community; but even more important, such discourse becomes a part of the process of developing concepts about music within the society.

Specifically musical roles are not the only ones that are important. In many societies, particularly those based primarily on personal interaction, kinship relationships are important in musical events. The people of Tikopia, for example, use different kinds of laments for various categories of kin (Firth 1990:5off).

Conclusion

The impact of a society on its members' musical activity, although indirect, is often very strong. Egalitarian societies are usually limited to individualistic, contractual, and communal music complexes. Rank societies, such as those occurring in pastoral or horticultural groups, can have distinctions in terms of musical obligations or musical styles, but they are still not characterized by sponsored musical complexes or patronage.

Stratified societies are characterized by major differences in musical behavior and musical performance because of the prevalence of patronage. The sponsored music complexes that exist in stratified societies encourage more complex music for several reasons. One reason is the requirement that the music basically be intended for listening. In India, for example, music involving group participation is sung by masses of people in the villages and countryside. Because it is sung on communal music occasions, the music must be kept simple so that large groups will be able to learn it and participate. On the other hand, classical Indian music, having developed within the patronage system, is intended to be performed by professionals while the audience sits and listens. To maintain the interest of listeners, the music necessarily contains considerable complexity (Henry 1976:51, 53).

Another reason for the importance of patronage is that it facilitates specialization and professionalism among musicians and theoreticians who can devote extensive time to music. They can thus elaborate musical styles and develop extensive patterns of performances, as well as discourse about music. Whenever music serves as an indicator of prestige, extensive musical developments are likely to appear as a result of competition between patrons. Both patronage and commercialization are likely to influence the nature of musical sound, since those who support the performances can decide which performers they will support and which they will not.

CHAPTER THREE

The Sociocultural Matrix: Conceptual Factors

THE SOCIOCULTURAL MATRIX includes not only the social relationships between people and the standardized social institutions, but
also the cultural concepts or understandings shared by people of a
community. Many of these shared concepts relate to music, and they
largely determine what people do musically. These concepts concern the values and motivations leading to musical performances,
as well as the knowledge and skill necessary to produce and understand music.

The cultural concepts involve both the content of the discursive
consciousness of a people and their implicit values and knowledge
that operate only at the practical level. This dual nature of the basic
concepts makes them especially difficult for the observer to understand. When the concepts are at the practical level people are virtually incapable of talking about them. A researcher questioning an
individual about personal views of music will receive a reply in
terms of conventional discourse of the society. Lacking standard discourse, a reply will be improvised in accordance with what the informant thinks the researcher wants. It may never occur to informants that an outsider might not view things the same way they do.

This subconscious nature of much musical knowledge makes it
necessary to observe many facets of people's behavior other than
music. Observing how people behave at a musical event is as important as analysis of how they sing and play their instruments. Often,
casual references to music provide an indication of its value, such as
in the case of the Shona, whom I heard frequently remark that some
music was so good it made them leave their cooking pots to boil
over. Frequently, it is helpful to consider the role of music in myths
and stories. The role of Blackfoot music is shown in their myths of
origin, which include the supernaturals singing to humans (Nettl
1989:95).

Concepts of What Music Is

Many of the concepts about music serve to relate music to other spheres of activity. As pointed out in Chapter 1, in order to compare the music of different societies it is necessary to be certain that the comparison includes similar things. Obviously, different words are used to refer to musical behavior, but societies also differ in the type of activity of which they consider music to be a subcategory. In Western society, professional musicians consider music to be one of the fine arts, meaning that it is one of several ways of creating beauty. They tend to judge all music as either good or bad in those terms. Many other people in modern society consider music to be a subdivision of the larger field of entertainment. In some places music is considered a subcategory of ritual. Among the Australian Aborigines, songs are categorized by the type of ritual with which they are used. They do not have children's songs or special songs for nonritual purposes, although some of their ritual songs can be sung casually. It is the same case with the Navajo, whose songs are basically a form of ritual as well. Music, particularly singing, is considered in some places to be a form of speech. For example, the Suya of Brazil consider songs to be a category of verbal communication. The Suya language makes a clear distinction between speech, instruction, and invocation (A. Seeger 1987:26). However, what the Suya call invocation might appear to the outsider to be another type of song, since invocations are performed in a type of chanting voice that includes different pitches. The Tuareg in the Sahara Desert consider music to be an extension of the verbal arts (Card 1982:47). Music elsewhere is categorized as a special type of natural sound. In Japan and New Guinea, musical sounds are conventionally conceptualized in the same terms as animal sounds, with the latter often being considered to be a form of animal speech. The Netsilik group of Inuit also consider music as simply one type of the sounds of nature, with animals, as well as people, composing and singing songs (Cavanagh 1982:144).

It is common practice in many societies to think of their songs as belonging to several categories, which often determine the appropriate music for a given occasion. The people of Tikopia divide their songs into two basic categories: recreational songs (mako) and laments (fuatanga) (Firth 1990:6). When a community is in mourning, the recreational or dance songs are not performed (ibid.:28). The Australian Aborigines of Arnhem Land classify their songs as secret, sacred, and secular. The secret songs are used in rituals from which women and children are excluded. They are sometimes sung in other rituals where the whole community is present, but they have secret words that are only explained to men. The sacred songs are sung in the more common rituals, such as those for mourning, and no restrictions are placed on singing those songs in informal situations. The secular songs are performed in a wide range of situations not necessarily connected with ritual; they are characterized by the use of the didjeridu (Elkin and Jones 1958:5) (see Photo 2.1). Similar distinctions characterize the music of the Warlpiri (Wild 1975:10–12).

The method of distinguishing between individual pieces of music is one more way that concepts about music may vary widely from one place to another. In Western society it is customary to consider the melody and rhythm as the determining features of a song, and although one can put different words to a tune, it not considered a new song, but the same song with new words. Some societies consider the text to determine the identity of a song, even if the tune is the same for several songs. Among the Kaluli in New Guinea "the creative moment of text coming to mind and flowing into the pool of swirling melody is the act of musical composition" (Feld 1982:214). Among the Aymara, relatively small changes in various phrases are considered to constitute a new song (Turino 1989). The music of China and Japan uses the same sounds interchangeably in various theatrical works. The sounds are not considered a song or a piece of music in themselves, but rather a particular sound effect to be used as needed.

The Blackfoot of Montana distinguish songs not only in terms of their sound and usage but also by the people and events associated with them. The melody of a song is an important distinguishing feature, but what sounds like the same song to the outsider would traditionally be considered a different song to the Blackfoot because of its close connection with the vision of a particular individual. Two identical songs become different because of their association with a different event: "You can make the same song twice, as you can make two identical drums or headdresses" (Nettl 1989:57).

How individual songs are distinguished is of more than purely academic interest, since it is closely related to matters of copyright and royalty payments. This problem is clearly seen in relation to calypso music of the Caribbean area.

Up to 1970 musicologists have estimated that about fifty melody types had been developed by the calypsonians. These fifty basic structures were used over and over again, and were traded freely between different composers. The uniqueness of a new calypso was to be found in the *combination* of choice of topic, text and melody, with the emphasis on the first two. This is quite a normal situation in folk music cultures. The identity of the actual composer becomes irrelevant in the traditional system. This "positive" public domain attitude can of course be totally exploited by the legally wise when exposed to a system where the first registered copyright claimant is accepted as the legal owner. (Wallis and Malm 1984:199)

An important feature of the conceptual aspect of music is the way music is seen as fitting into a society's world view or general scheme of reality. The nature of that relationship influences the way people think music is created. In many societies the origins of music, and even of specific songs, are seen to be supernatural. Among the Suya, allegedly supernatural origins determined the acceptability of song texts. The teachers of new songs were "men without spirits," meaning that they were ill because their souls had left their bodies. The souls had gone to reside with the animals, which were considered the source of new songs (A. Seeger 1987). The Kaluli considered songs to come from the dead through the mouth of a medium as the latter sang at a seance. Ideas like those of the Suya and Kaluli indicate recognition of the powerful impact music exerts on human beings, since people seldom attribute supernatural origin to insignificant things (Feld 1982).

The link between world view and music often influences the significance given to music. The people of Java have linked the brass instruments of their ensembles with the powers of the universe through the association between volcanic fires and the fires needed to smelt ore for making the musical instruments (Photo 3.1). The power of volcanic activity in that part of the world is seen to resemble the power of the traditional political leaders as they control the manufacture of the major musical instruments (Becker 1988).

Music is often considered to have supernatural power, presumably because it is ephemeral, it cannot be seen, and it deeply moves people's emotions. For the Blackfoot, songs provide a way for the supernaturals to communicate with humans, thus validating ritual and religious beliefs (Nettl 1989:128). Myths of origin of various rituals often include songs as an important feature (ibid.:95). Because of this connection, music is considered to have extensive power so that it actually *does* such things as curing illness (ibid.:146).

Eta Harich-Schneider tells of a Japanese myth describing the power of the music of a famous musician, Hakuga. When a burglar robbed his house, Hakuga found that his flute had been left behind. He be-

3.1. A Javanese metallophone, several of which are used in the gamelan ensemble. (Instrument in William Hammond Mathers Museum, Bloomington, Indiana; photo by the author.)

gan playing it, and according to the story, the music was so beautiful that the burglar, upon hearing it, stopped fleeing, returned with the stolen goods, and asked forgiveness (1973:191–192). Even though this story may not have a factual basis, its existence indicates the kind of power attributed to music. A similar indication of power is the old Shinto idea in Japan that musical art is a gift of the gods (Kishibe 1984:15).

The general world view often provides explanations for different degrees of musical ability among people. Although many societies do not have the role of professional musician, people everywhere can perceive the difference between a mediocre and an exciting performance. Egalitarian societies are inclined to explain unusual ability in terms of supernatural powers, thus avoiding individual tendencies to become too proud and overbearing. Societies in which clans and lineages are important often consider musical ability to run in families.

Another important concept about music is a society's view of the accessibility of its own music to outsiders (Nettl 1985:114–117). Such views vary considerably, from the Western assumption that anyone can learn Western music to the view of some societies that outsiders could not possibly learn their music. The accessibility of Shona music to outsiders was basically the question that disturbed the Shona as they witnessed an outsider playing their mbira. The postulated accessibility of one's music to outsiders is an important factor in considering questions of music change.

A third important concept about music concerns the rights of individuals to perform particular works of music. This principle is seen in copyright laws, but it operates in many small-scale societies as well. Among the Warlpiri of Australia, new songs or song cycles were considered to originate with spirit-agents of the Dreamtime. Many times the spirits would give songs to one individual when the song was intended to belong to a ritual of a different group. In such a case the receiver of the song would teach it to members of the proper group, and once he gave it away he would no longer use it (Wild 1975:54–55).

Ownership of songs was formerly very important among the Blackfoot, partly because of the association of specific songs with the vision quest. Some songs were associated with tribal ritual or social dances, and they could be sung by anyone. Songs related to medicine bundle ceremonies and other rituals could be shared, given away, or sold. Other songs were not transferable, particularly those which were given a person for use at times of crisis (Nettl 1989:141). Today the idea of individually owned songs still exists among the Blackfoot; although songs are sometimes used as gifts, they are no longer sold (ibid.:143). The concept of ownership being related to one's experience validates the statement that "each song is its owner's even when it sounds like someone else's" (ibid.:168).

The general value given to music often conflicts with other values in a society. For example, among the Aymara Indians of the Andean Plateau, social values seem to conflict with musical values, affecting the way their music sounds (see Photo 2.6). The musical values include "sounding as one," where no individual and no instrument stands out. They also like a dense sound, where instruments are played so they blend and also produce numerous overtones. As noted earlier, the group leader and the main performers have the responsibility of assuring the quality of performance of each ensemble, which they do by practicing and preparing new songs. The conflicting social value of communal participation, however, permits the ad hoc members to join the group at performances. Because they have not practiced with the group, their presence often muddies the clarity of the group's performance. However, the ideal of community inclusiveness forces the primary performers to accept outsiders and

work together as best they can, although the end product is inferior
(Turino 1989). In other words, *being* unified is more important than
sounding unified.

In many societies, music is perceived and discussed in terms of
senses other than hearing, such as taste or sight. In English this appears in such terms as sour note, wide range, or hot rhythm. Merriam (1964:87) has labeled this phenomenon "intersense transfer,"
and it is a feature of the variable concepts about music. Intersense
transfer is shown by the names given to various pitches. Where English uses the terms "low" and "high" (spatial qualities) to refer to
pitch, many African societies use the terms equivalent to "large" or
"small." In other areas, sexual characteristics are applied to pitches
by referring to them as "male" (low) or "female" (high). Intersense
transfer is shown in the Kaluli practice of using a term equivalent
to "hardening" for referring to the act of bringing a song to a climax
so it will make people cry (Feld 1982:211–212). Perceiving musical
sounds in terms of nonmusical meaning is related to the ideas of
analogy and metaphor, important concepts of Chapter 5.

The concepts about music include the ideal ways of presenting
music, often called **performance practice**. One aspect of performance
practice is the optimum size of musical ensembles. In classical music of India the ideal performing group consists of four people,
whereas the ideal symphony orchestra playing twentieth-century
Western classical music has at least a hundred players. Performance
practice also includes nonmusical movements involved in performance. Japanese drumming includes prescribed flourishes of the
arms as part of proper performance. Western classical performers often engage in exaggerated swaying movements of the head and body
to show emotion as they play. Rock musicians are more inclined to
move their whole body to add to the effect of the music.

Social Legitimization of Music

The term **legitimacy** has long been used in political science to indicate the forms of political power acceptable to the people of a society.[1] When applied to expressive culture, legitimacy is essentially
the acknowledgment by people in a society that certain forms of
creative activity are recognized and positively valued, and that
people who perform or produce in those areas should receive some
type of recognition for their work. Although any innovative individual behavior is creative, legitimacy develops patterns of routinely
acceptable creative activity within a social group. The concept of
legitimacy does not necessarily mean that certain kinds of activity

are forbidden, but simply that some forms of expression are valued more highly than others. In relation to music, legitimacy means that some musical activities will be considered very important, and others will hardly be recognized at all.

Legitimacy is basically the result of processes involving the gradual acceptance of particular types of music by various groups in a society. When the leaders in a society adopt a music complex or a musical style to enhance their prestige or strengthen their position, legitimacy usually follows their influence. When the powerless people in a society express themselves through a particular type of music, that music becomes legitimate for them. The commercial promulgation of recorded music gives that kind of music an air of legitimacy. In some countries peripheral to the world economy the very act of being recorded gives additional legitimacy to the work of a local musician. Legitimacy also results when certain types of music maintain their value and acceptance over a long period of time.

Legitimacy, as determined by a society, is different from performance as an individual's intention to be evaluated. It is related, however, since legitimacy is indicated when a society develops markers that enable performers to communicate their expectations of evaluative reactions. The musician who engages in a legitimate type of music is not always being subjected to evaluation, as seen in the obvious difference between rehearsal and performance in many societies. However, when that performer intends to be evaluated, the socially determined markers are used. If the mode of performance is not legitimate in the society, the performer may have to invent a personal way of indicating a willingness or eagerness to be evaluated.

Some ways of indicating legitimacy occur in both stratified and nonstratified societies. In addition to markers, the existence of discourse is one criterion of determining legitimacy; the very fact that a society has forms of language for discussing a particular creative activity indicates the legitimacy of that activity (Bourdieu 1977:170–171). For some groups, discourse regarding music is very highly developed, but for other groups it is not. Another indication of the legitimacy of particular musical genres is their existence as a part of ritual, which relates them to the society's world view. Legitimacy is often shown by the acclaim or respect given to performers.

A significant indication of musical legitimacy is the type of rewards a society provides to the musician. In stratified societies, musicians obtain extensive rewards because the ruling classes sponsor musicians, enabling them to devote all their time to creating and performing music, and to theorizing about it. The very act of sponsoring musicians at the temple or the court serves to legitimize their activities. Legitimized musical practices are often organized in guilds or schools that regulate training of the young, provide security, set standards, and facilitate dissemination of the group's creative work. Legitimacy also means that the society provides ways of disseminating its music by such means as the press, the broadcast media, or the educational system. It has been suggested that one reason guilds (*gharana*) developed in India was to provide musicians with a degree of legitimacy.

The development of the modern music industry has resulted in financial success as both a cause and result of legitimacy. The sale of many recordings leads to recognition and legitimacy in the popular culture. It is assumed that only the best performers sell many records, but sales are also influenced by skill in arranging promotion. Legitimization through economic success operates not only for individual performers, but also for broad types of music. Folk music was originally the music of rural people, but in the United States it has now spread from the countryside to urban areas and has become established as a type of popular music.

Whereas a nonstratified society characteristically has the same pattern of legitimacy for everyone, the differences between social strata in a stratified society will be reflected in different patterns of legitimacy for different taste publics. Each of these groups has different tastes in music, thus distinguishing several different areas of legitimization. Stratified societies vary in the ways they note the legitimacy of the music of different social groups. People in Afghanistan make a distinction between composed song and folk song (Sakata 1983:188). In Hungary art music was distinguished from folk music as a difference between published and unpublished music (Kodály 1960). While folk music and popular music are considered legitimate by their own taste publics, those types of music are often not considered fully legitimate by the elite.

Recognizing that various taste publics in a stratified society legitimize different kinds of music helps avoid inaccurate and derogatory terminology. In stratified societies the term "high culture" commonly indicates that the product or performance is of higher quality. However, in sociological circles, the basic meaning is that "high culture" represents the tastes and sponsorship of the upper classes. When discourse provides legitimacy, special terms such as "fine art" mark many forms of creative behavior that are legitimized by the elite in Western society. "Art music" and "serious music" usually mean in English the types of music legitimized by the elite music establishment: those who provide support for opera, ballet, and symphony orchestras in great cities. Legitimacy is also indicated by the commissioning of special compositions of a certain style or having been the pupil of a famous musician. Elsewhere, legitimacy as high culture is often shown by performances of music in temples, the courts of the aristocrats, or music halls endowed by the wealthy.

Popular culture at one time was indistinguishable from folk culture, but more recently it has become associated with the taste that is developed from the promulgation of certain genres by the music industry. In many situations the consumers of popular music are aware of the characteristics of the legitimized music of high culture, but prefer their own patterns of legitimacy in their musical activities. Legitimacy within popular culture is often determined by financial success.

In both high culture and popular culture the ideal is to have legitimacy determined by the quality of the product, even though the two taste cultures may vary in their definition of quality. The ideal may not always happen if people with the power to make decisions regarding musical performances use nonmusical means to further their own objectives.

Because different subgroups in a complex stratified society have their own patterns of legitimacy, the patterns set by the elite are neither universally accepted nor unchanging. For many years jazz was legitimate among African-Americans, but not in the groups where legitimacy was determined by the elite. Jazz musicians were not nationally recognized as artists. Today this situation has changed so that jazz is now legitimate "art," with jazz musicians appearing in the White House, and conservatories of music hiring professors of jazz.[2] Although rock music is not yet recognized as legitimate in conservatories of music, the young widely regard it as such. Today, leaders in government are sometimes granting performance opportunities to rock musicians. In the early 1990s rap's legitimacy as an art form was limited to a relatively small social group.

Because the terms art music, classical music, and serious music have connotations of snobbery and elitism, they should be avoided or redefined when objectivity is desired. Many aficionados of folk music, jazz, and rock do not like being told that their expressive creations are neither serious nor artistic.

The forms of music common in non-Western societies have achieved no form of legitimacy in Western society because few people have heard those types of music, and even fewer understand them. The efforts of some ethnomusicologists are directed toward making their own society more aware of musics in other societies, a goal that could lead to some degree of legitimacy for such music. Care must be taken, however, that such activities do not result simply in greater economic exploitation of the music of relatively isolated groups throughout the world.

Legitimacy provides very specific advantages for those who participate in legitimate forms of musical activity. In small-scale societies the practice of legitimate forms of creative activity often frees an individual from onerous productive tasks. Thus, musicians spending time in religious ritual are considered to be performing a useful service for their people. They are therefore not subject to criticism for not helping physically in production tasks. Skill in a legitimate musical idiom also provides coveted recognition, whereas skill in nonlegitimate music tends to go unnoticed.

The changing patterns of legitimacy in the Soviet Union following the October revolution of 1917 show how legitimacy operates. Before the revolution, professional musicians worked at the court and in conservatories and received their support from those institutions. The czar had power to control performances of music. As unrest was growing in Russia in 1905, the composer Rimsky-Korsakov, who supported a reform movement, was dismissed from his teaching post at the conservatory, and a performance of one of his operas was cancelled (Schwarz 1983:4). After the revolution, the court orchestras became city orchestras, and the conservatories came under increasing pressure from the Communist Party to change their curriculum and admittance policies in order to serve the working-class people. The newly established pattern of legitimacy radically altered the norms under which musicians customarily worked. "Musical opportunism flourished among hack musicians, but even serious composers were not averse to switching to 'revolutionary thematics' as a means for survival" (Schwarz 1983:33). Later, the Union of Soviet Composers became the organization that provided musicians with financial support, housing benefits, and vacation opportunities. This change meant that the kinds of music that had been encouraged under the czars, such as modern and avant-garde trends, were no longer permitted, and mediocre music was encouraged as long as it extolled the revolution.

Music is one of the many activities that humans are constantly noting and evaluating. Legitimacy is one of the major criteria used in evaluating musical performances. Other major criteria will be discussed in later chapters. The important point here is that legitimacy represents a criterion based on social relationships, while aesthetic criteria have to do with intrinsic qualities of the music itself.

Music as an Aspect of Expressive Culture

Expressive culture consists of more than expression; it also includes forms of play, means of communicating information, and aesthetic appreciation. Music is only one of several ways that humans enjoy these things. Also included are sports and games, folklore, religion, language, literature, art, dance, and theater. Music often occurs in combination with other aspects of expressive culture, some of which exert an influence on music.

Although all societies have some form of music, its importance in relation to other forms of expressive culture varies widely among different societies. Jacques Maquet has used the term **aesthetic locus** (1979:30) to refer to the type of aesthetic activity most prized in a particular social group. This variation in the types of principal aesthetic forms can account for the fact that some societies have numerous occasions for musical expression, whereas others have very few. Thus, among the Navajo, music would not be considered a part of the aesthetic locus; instead, it is a form of religious power. Music is often combined with other forms of expressive culture, particularly with religion in ritual, with language in song, and with dance and drama in theater.

Ritual

Music and ritual are often so intertwined that it is difficult to determine with any certainty which one is affecting the other. One area in which religion is often considered to dominate music is in establishing timetables for rituals that also serve as important music events. Three major types of ritual often involve the use of music: rites of passage, calendrical rituals, and crisis rituals.

Rites of passage are used in many societies to symbolize the progression of individuals through life, particularly in relation to changing social statuses. Rites of passage are naturally divided into three stages—often called separation, transition, and incorporation.[3] Music is often a very important part of such ceremonies, because it frequently marks the division between the stages of the ritual. In rural India a tonsure ceremony accompanied by special songs is performed for a baby boy. His head is shaved and the hair is offered to a mother goddess. This marks the transition of the child from a polluted to a nonpolluted condition (Henry 1988:64). Many societies include initiation at puberty as a rite of passage from childhood to adulthood. Funeral rites are intended to assure the passage of the deceased to another world.

Weddings are rites of passage everywhere, marking the change from single to married status. Music was an important part of traditional weddings among the rural Macedonians in the southern part of Yugoslavia. Rather than merely singing or playing to celebrate festivities, they used specific songs to indicate important sections of the ritual. Before the wedding, bagpipe players went from house to house performing a song of invitation to inform the whole community of the approaching festivities (N. Sachs 1975 : 181). The preparations for the wedding included baking a special bread, so they sang a song for kneading dough, symbolizing that the bride was going to rise to a new status. A later song for baking bread referred to the groom as a young fool, whose heat of sexual desire would soon be cooled. Other songs moved the focus from the newlyweds to the relationship between the families. The song that accompanied the weaving of the bride's wedding crown indicated the kind of reception the bride was to be given in her new family. The songs sung as the groom was washed and shaved by his kinsmen instead of a professional barber symbolized his solidarity with them. Other songs were sung as the groom left his house to fetch his bride, and as he arrived at the bride's house. Songs also accompanied the feasting and the giving of gifts, followed by those concerning the bride's farewell to her family. The following morning the groom went "from house to house carrying warmed sweetened plum or grape brandy which he shares with his kin in celebration of the consummation of his marriage" (N. Sachs 1975 : 301ff). The significant feature here is that the meanings given to the various parts of the ritual are reflected in the songs.

Calendrical rituals occur at regular times throughout the year to mark the changing seasons. They are often connected with the agricultural cycle, taking the form of fertility ceremonies or harvest festivals. Many festive periods in the large-scale religions of the world, Passover or Christmas for example, occur at particular seasons of the year, although agricultural activities are no longer offered as the reasons for them. Celebration of special anniversaries is also a form of calendrical ritual. The Blackfoot hold their North American Indian Days powwow on the four days following July 4 (Nettl 1989 : 40) (Photo 3.2).

A calendrical ritual still performed by rural Macedonians is the Koleda, celebrated in the winter, since it was probably associated with the winter solstice in pre-Christian times. The ritual is limited to men, who meet around a large bonfire outside the village on six consecutive nights preceding the Orthodox Christmas. After an exchange of food, the men perform Koleda chants, a specific type of

3.2. Blackfoot dancers at North American Indian Days, Browning, Montana, July 1984. (Photo by Wanda Nettl; used by permission.)

performance that many do not consider to be songs because they have no melody. Women, girls, and small children are excluded from these rites because the texts of the songs are often obscene (N. Sachs 1975:169–70).

In rural India calendrical rituals are directed to a female goddess believed to cause smallpox. These rituals take place every year during the monsoons, and include offerings and sacrifices. The songs are sung during the rituals to please the goddess. Processions around the village are thought to distract the goddess and protect the village from attacks of smallpox (Henry 1988:81–82).

Crisis rites form a third major type of ritual forms in many societies. Occasions for crisis rites include epidemics, droughts, floods, earthquakes, volcanic eruptions, solar eclipses, and animal disease. Because rites connected with these events may not occur regularly, they are less likely to include complex musical activity. Especially important are the crisis rites for curing illness. Such rituals form the basis of much shamanic activity, which is often performed with singing.

The Tuareg have a pre-Islamic crisis rite for curing. After having a white cloth with a short cord and tassel placed on the head, the sick person is seated in the center of a courtyard on a pile of cushions. *Tende* drumming and songs are performed while the patient sways gently, swinging the tassel. This continues as long as an hour, until the patient falls exhausted or goes into a trance. The nature of the ceremony affects the music because it is slower than the usual *tende* music and is always in duple time to synchronize with the swaying. Men make unusual raspy vocal effects to accompany the singing of the women (Card 1982:146–149).

Religion assumes major importance in many small-scale societies because it serves as the only means of coping with the powers of the universe. Such ideas can affect the course of musical behavior as societies restrict the teaching and learning of music to those whom they consider capable of handling it properly.

Language

Language and music often affect each other. Ritual is closely inter-related with both because of the importance of language in religious texts. Many humans sing with words they do not understand, often because an archaic form of language is considered more ritually powerful than ordinary speech, as in the Latin Mass. Sometimes rituals and music are borrowed together. Even though the meaning of the text is unknown, it is used anyway because it is a part of the ritual. The Warlpiri have learned songs from their northern neighbors, and now perform those songs using their neighbors' language (Wild 1975:119). Singing with meaningless words is often practiced outside the ritual context. The prestige of foreign art forms is often a reason for such practices, including the use of Latin and French throughout Europe for many centuries.

Singing is also performed with sounds that carry no meaning, called **vocables** or nonsense syllables. The Suya refer to such syl-lables with a term equivalent to "song words." Among the Navajo such sounds provide clues to the type of music being performed, even though they carry no semantic meaning (McAllester 1984:26). The Blackfoot consider the music of whites to be very strange be-cause it uses so many words. They view vocables as an intrinsic part of a song, and they always sing vocables the same way and sing them together. To some extent the Blackfoot vocables resemble those used by many other Native American groups, when using stan-dard sounds and varying them with the pitch of the singing (Nettl 1989:71) (Ex. 4.1).

In some societies music is subordinate to language, while in other societies the reverse is true. Up until the last century, Japan had very little instrumental music; music was dominated by the texts (Ki-shibe 1984:17). In parts of Micronesia and Polynesia, the music it-self is overshadowed by the meter of the language. On the other hand, the people of Tikopia modify their diction when it is sung,

INTONATION		MEANINGS
High level	(—)	Mother
High rising	(⌣)	Hemp
Dipping/falling rising	(⌄)	Horse
High falling	(⌐)	To scold

Figure 3.1. Importance of tone in Mandarin Chinese language.

changing vowels and repeating the first syllable of words (Firth 1990:40).

Music dominates the text in the music of India and of much European music, where many notes may be sung to one syllable of text, an effect known as melisma. In women's songs of rural India extra vowels or syllables are added to make the text fit the music. Vowels are also lengthened or shortened as the music requires (Henry 1988: 108). The Navajo language uses tonal level and length of vowels to make distinctions between words. In singing, however, both of these features are subordinated to the music (Reichard 1950:279).

Where language is not definitely subordinate, the nature of musical sounds is often profoundly influenced by specific qualities of a language. **Tonal languages**, in which the tones of a word affect the meaning, cause a severe restriction on melodic inventiveness. For example, Mandarin Chinese has four different tones. As shown in Figure 3.1, the word "ma" has four meanings, depending upon which tone is used (Li and Thompson 1987:299).

The Chinese example involves semantic tone, but in other languages tonal differences are grammatical. In the Shona language, one group of sounds can mean "he went" (wáéndà, high-high-low), "when he has gone" (wáèndá, high-low-high), or "the one who has gone" (wàéndà, low-high-low), depending upon the tones. When such restrictions occur on the rise and fall of language, members of those societies will naturally deal with tune and rhythm in different ways from people in the Western world. This factor is probably a major reason why music from Africa, where most languages are tonal, has developed rhythmic, rather than melodic or harmonic, complexity. It could also account for the Chinese emphasis on tonal color and pattern rather than melody. The relationship of language tone to music is not inflexible, and values in this respect have been known to change.

Many European languages are more concerned with stress, as in the difference between the words "con'tent" and "content'." Languages which emphasize stress tend to restrict the rhythmic variety in songs, but have few restrictions on the rise and fall of pitches. The Czech language customarily places the stress on the first syllable of a word, but erroneous stress does not change the meaning as it does in English. Nevertheless, in Czech folk music the musical stress usually coincides with the language stress (Nettl 1964:289).

The close links between the sounds of language and the sounds of music are utilized in many societies as an aesthetic quality. These links are one of the reasons why it is so difficult to make suitable translations of songs and operas.

Theater

Other forms of expressive culture closely related to music include dance and drama. Theater is the essence of combining music with other forms of expression, since it often incorporates literature (both oral and written), mime, dance, and visual forms. Drama occurs not only in formal theater, but in the presentation of a skillful story teller, often accompanied by songs. Drama often takes the form of puppetry as well as live mime. Shadow puppets are very popular on the Indonesian island of Java, where intricately carved figures are cast upon a sheet as a puppeteer manipulates them against a strong light. The puppeteer not only operates the puppets, but also declaims poetry, sings, and directs the instrumental ensemble. The puppets present ancient Hindu and pre-Hindu stories from Indonesian religious history. Similar stories are also presented by live dancer-actors, who wear elaborate costumes and combine dance with forms of poetry and song (Kartomi 1980).

Dance is not always allied with music. In traditional Polynesian society, dancing was often performed with poetry. Both there and in many parts of Asia, the movements of dance express the thought of the words rather than the rhythm of the music. Although folk dance is often the reaction of people to rhythm, in some forms of dance the visual impact assumes major importance.

Concepts about music and its relation to the other parts of culture constitute the ideology concerning music, but the importance of such concepts should not overshadow the fact that actually producing music is also based on concepts. The concepts used for making music are called musicianship, and refer to the shared knowledge required for producing musical sounds themselves. These concepts form the basis not only for the skills of performance, including pitch, rhythm, and patterns of performance, but also for the skills of hearing and appreciating music. The listeners provide the performers with an audience, and they must learn to recognize the musical elements of their own tradition. The audience also knows the difference between a good performance and a poor one. Musicianship is an aspect of practical consciousness; when the production of music is subjected to discourse it becomes music theory. The absence of music theory in a society by no means indicates a lack of musicianship. The ways that elements of musicianship vary from one society to another provide the material for Chapter 4.

The concepts required to actually produce the music itself include the knowledge needed for construction of musical instruments. Many instruments that appear to be simple actually require extensive knowledge for manufacture. The Shona mbira is a good example (Photo 3.3). One must know which kind of wood is best and how to carve it into the tray shape. The keys are more complex. They must have the right thickness and gradual thinning to produce a pleasant tone quality. Thickness also determines how long a key must be to produce the correct pitch; inconsistent thickness makes it impossible to space the keys with gradual lengths so the player's fingers can reach all of them easily.

Socialization in Music

The sociocultural matrix influences not only the musicians, but all the members of the society. A group's ongoing musical practices are the result of the experiences of the performers, audience, agents, and critics as they grow from babyhood to adulthood. A universal feature of human life is the replication in every generation of the techniques, values, and symbols that characterize a particular mode of human life. The instilling of these qualities in the young is called **socialization** or enculturation.[4] The major point is that for musical performances to take place, people everywhere must undergo a process of learning the acceptable forms of musical activity in their society.

Each of the roles involved in music requires considerable learning. A major part of musical training is attaining the skills of playing an instrument and learning the songs of one's social group. Learning to produce music involves the unconscious structuring of what one hears, similar to the process of learning language. Constantly hearing musical performances provides feedback into the mental structures of the hearer and aids in the development of habits about what sounds right and what does not, as indicated in Figure 1.2.

3.3. Mombo Nemasasi constructing a mbira, 1971. (Photo by the author.)

Much of this process takes place in the practical consciousness, but in many societies discursive sources of information about music are also important.

Societies vary in the emphasis given to rehearsal. The amount of time spent in rehearsal is indicative of the value given to musical performance. The people of Tikopia rehearse for their dances and songs (Firth 1990:91). Horton (1973) notes that the Kalabari people of southern Nigeria rehearse for Ekine masked dances but not for ordinary rituals.

Learning the musical system of one's society involves more than skills of performance; it includes familiarity with the theories and values concerning music as understood in the society. This knowledge is often implicitly learned from the context of use, but also explicitly taught through discourse about musical events. Even for nonperformers, musical learning involves many features, including the meanings attached to music, the values given to various kinds of music, and knowledge of the appropriate type of music for specific occasions. Values given to music are closely related to the meaning of music (Chapter 5).

One of the most widely used ways of learning music is by imitation, working out the sounds by trial and error. Children all over the world naturally imitate adult activities, and this practice is an important means of learning music. Children often seek to reproduce on an instrument the sounds that they have been accustomed to hearing. This type of learning is very common in nonliterate societies. Margaret Mead, the anthropologist, has described this process among the Manus people of Papua New Guinea:

> Whenever there is a dance there is an orchestra of slit drums of all sizes played by the most proficient drummers in the village. The very small boys of four and five settle themselves beside small hollow log ends or pieces of bamboo and drum away indefatigably in time with the orchestra. This period of open and unashamed imitation is followed by a period of embarrassment, so that it is impossible to persuade a boy of ten or twelve to touch a drum in public, but in the boy's house when only a few older boys are present, he will practice, making good use of the flexibility of wrist and sense of rhythm learned earlier. Girls practice less, for only one drum beat, the simple death beat, falls to their hands in later life. (1968 [1930]:44)

Some societies, like the Shona, have theories of supernatural origin to explain the ability to perform. From the analytical perspective, such theories may be viewed as a way of interpreting the unconscious process of sorting out in one's mind sounds that one has often heard. Shona children are permitted to attend musical performances as long as there is space for them and they do not make a disturbance. When drums are not being used by the adults, the chil-

3.4. Shona boys with drums, 1972. (Photo by the author.)

dren are free to play on them (Photo 3.4). Sometimes a child will have a toy instrument on which to work out rhythms.

Learning by rote often involves instruction in which the learner imitates a teacher or demonstrator. In India a class consists of a teacher who plays a portion of music, followed by the students who repeat from memory what they have heard. Elsewhere teachers often hold the hands of players as they move on drums or xylophones. In Ghana "less talented persons are made to lie on the ground barebacked and face-downwards, while the master sits astride them and beats the rhythms into their body and soul" (Cudjoe 1953:284).

Learning by imitation marks a major difference between Oriental and Occidental approaches to the arts. Imitation was the preferred teaching method of Confucius, being used in China for hundreds of years and becoming the standard method in Japan.

> The Western teacher believes in an educational principle leading from an inner understanding to the exterior activity . . . The Oriental believes in the reverse method: from faithful and literal imitation of the teacher in all exterior manifestations the final understanding of the principles will gradually emerge. (Harich-Schneider 1973:547–548)

The learning process is different in traditions emphasizing improvisational techniques. In Java the learning process takes place in several stages. First, in a process lasting several years, the child gradually picks up the sounds of the music during performances in his community. The older child or youth eventually begins to learn one instrument. This process does not involve learning specific pieces of music, but rather mastering a large number of formulas that will serve as the basis for improvising on his instrument. Only after mastering the formulas and the ways of incorporating them into an ongoing ensemble performance is one considered a real musician (Becker 1980:20).

Mnemonic devices are often used as an aid to the memory, particularly verbal syllables that stand for different features of rhythm. In areas such as India and Africa, where drumming is complex, each type of drum stroke is given a particular syllable, so that their recitation as vocables serves as a guide to the strokes to be played. Indicative of the vocables that are used in many societies to express drum rhythms are those of the Eve (or Ewe) people of Ghana in their *atsimevu* rhythms. The Eve use such vocables not only in rehearsal, but also in discussions with each other about various ways of playing. In Eve the syllables represent different strokes that are used on the drum. Although the actual syllables used vary from place to place, and even among individuals, the most common uses have been noted by David Locke, as in Figure 3.2. The syllables are learned as rhythmic speech, with each syllable clearly stating how the drum is to be struck and the rhythm itself indicating when. Figure 3.3 indicates this combination (Locke 1978:598).

In the Western world, notation is an important tool of teaching and learning music, although the proper way of performing specific types of music is usually passed on from teacher to pupil. Music notation has frequently followed the development of verbal literacy in a society. Some societies in Asia have a form of notation, but it serves as a reminder of the general direction of a musical performance rather than providing an explicit statement as to which notes should and should not be performed. In most societies a performer must have a conception of the sound of a piece of music before being able to play it. Western music notation is unique in enabling someone to play a piece of music without having heard it before, although stylistic nuances must still be learned aurally.

The way an individual learns is not the only question involved in music learning; the organization of music in society is also significant. Where learning is expected to occur naturally as the result of

ga: the hand is bounced in the center of the drum head
de: a stick is bounced in the center of the drum head
gi or ge: the fingers are bounced at the edge of the drum head
dzi: the fingers are pressed rather than bounced at the edge of the
  drum head
tsi: a stick is pressed rather than bounced in the center of the
  drum head
tõ: a stick is bounced against a damped drum head
kpa: a stick is bounced against the side of the drum

These basic syllables are supplemented by a few others to indicate
common strokes:

kere: a combination of de followed by gi
gere: a combination of gi followed by de
dza: ga and kpa together
n: used as a suffix to denote a longer duration or damping the
  drum head after a strong de

Figure 3.2. Eve rhythmic syllables (adapted from Locke 1978: 506–
507).

de ge   ge de   gan   de ge   ge de   gan

Figure 3.3. Eve mnemonic syllables. The pitch of these tones is
indefinite.

trial and error, imitation, or supernatural intervention, it is not common to find formal instruction. Where learning is seen to require
formal instruction, institutions are often established for that purpose.
  One type of formal instruction is an apprenticeship, where an individual undertakes the instruction of young people in exchange for
their help in the domestic situation or in musical performances.
Such arrangements are often based on kinship. Sometimes groups of
teachers and apprentices are organized into guilds where music instruction is a major responsibility. They preserve performance standards and also seek to avoid developing a surplus of musicians. If the
art form represented by a guild is somewhat esoteric, specialists recognize the importance of providing themselves with an audience
who can understand and appreciate the performances. They there-

fore train not only performers, but also an audience that will have some understanding of what the performers are doing. For this reason, some of the Noh theater guilds in Japan are willing to instruct foreigners as potential followers. In some societies, rituals of initiation are used to teach music to the initiates. Such teaching is usually limited to learning songs, but the time devoted to them helps inculcate musical values in the children. In modern industrial societies instruction in music sometimes constitutes a part of the general education curriculum, and in other cases special music schools are developed.

Conclusion

Enculturation is the major channel through which the features of a sociocultural system make an impact on music. Recognizing its importance in determining musical tastes should increase acceptance of musical values different from one's own. Particularly in stratified societies, the differences between the musical tastes of high culture and popular culture should not be seen as some sort of musical arrogance or deficiency among people with whom one does not share musical tastes. The next chapter deals with the ways that different societies have structured music so that no matter how bizarre it might sound to outsiders, it is found agreeable and exciting to people who have experienced it during the process of growing up.

CHAPTER FOUR

Musicianship

UPON HEARING MUSIC to which they are not accustomed, people will often miss many of its significant features. Curt Sachs tells the story of a friend who took an excellent Albanian folk musician to hear Beethoven's Ninth Symphony. When asked to give his impression of the music, the Albanian replied that it was "Fine—but very, very plain" (1962:218). Early European travelers to other parts of the world often reflected ethnocentric views as they reported on the distastefulness of the music of exotic places or even its complete disorder. Moreover, these unusual ways of making music were often considered wrong and in need of European improvement and development. The study of non-Western forms of music through the years has revealed that people perform with unusual pitch combinations or incomprehensible rhythms because their society has come to consider those forms correct and desirable. Learning something of how other musical styles are created will not only relieve many Westerners of a false sense of superiority in musical matters, but will also expand the range of musical sounds that one can enjoy.

Comparative studies of human behavior are possible because all human beings share many needs and many common experiences as they participate in life and relate to the world around them. Just as humans share biological relationships that provide a basis for kinship systems, so they share experience with universal acoustical phenomena used in creating music. Musical sound consists of sound waves produced by a vibrating object, such as the membrane of a drum head, the string of a guitar, or the human vocal cords. Once sound waves are produced, they move through the air and strike the eardrum, which sends impulses to the brain. The brain sorts the impulses and either organizes them as music or interprets them as noise if they cannot be organized. Sound waves do not rise and fall like the waves of the ocean, but they consist of successive compressions and decompressions of air. They can be visualized as resembling the legs of millipedes as they walk, or something like the thick and thin lines of the bar codes that activate computers at grocery checkout counters. The characteristics of the sound waves determine the nature of the sounds. The sound waves themselves are a property of physics; the ways of perceiving and manipulating them are a part of human culture and constitute the elements of musicianship.

Pitch and Scales

The pitch of a musical sound is determined by the number of decompressions of air that occur each second, commonly known as vibrations per second (v.p.s.) or hertz (Hz). Many vibrations per second produce a high note, and fewer vibrations a low note. Some of the lowest notes we can hear, such as the deep bass notes of a pipe organ, are approximately 16 vibrations per second. The highest vibrations per second that we are able to hear are several thousand; for example, the highest note on the piano is 4,186 v.p.s. In Western music a standard pitch has been determined by assigning specific letter names to certain numbers of vibrations. For example, the A above middle C on the piano is 440 v.p.s. in the United States. Using a standard pitch enables a large number of instruments to be played together without sounding out of tune. In many musical traditions people are not concerned with a standard pitch, and they tune instruments to sound well with other instruments for a specific occasion or even to suit the most convenient level for a singer. Such tunings are determined by the tones in relation to each other rather than a fixed number of vibrations per second. At any level, the relationship of the sounds to each other is the same. This fixed relationship of pitches is expressed in the Western diatonic major scale with the names do, re, mi, fa, so, la, and ti, which indicate specific ratios between tones and can be sung or played in any key. For many people these syllables are associated with the song "Do-Re-Mi" by Rodgers and Hammerstein from *The Sound of Music*. The descending diatonic scale is found in the first line of the Christmas hymn "Joy to the World" (noted by Pantaleoni 1985:45). The lack of standard pitch is commonly experienced when a group begins a song at one level, finds it too high, and starts again at a lower pitch.

The term **interval** refers to the difference in v.p.s. between tones of two different pitches. The octave is one kind of interval to be found in music. It represents two tones, with the higher having twice the number of vibrations per second as the lower, thus representing a ratio of two to one. Thus, if the A above middle C is 440 v.p.s., the A above that is 880 v.p.s. and the A below middle C is 220 v.p.s. The octave is usually experienced when men and women sing the same melody together, and the women naturally sing an octave higher than the men.

Although all human groups recognize the interval of the octave, societies differ in the way the octave is treated. Some societies deliberately tune their musical instruments so that octaves are not quite a true doubling of the v.p.s. In Bali, the *penjoreg* tuning, in which two instruments an octave apart are tuned with a somewhat less than exact octave, gives the music a shimmering effect which is highly desired (Hood 1971:233). Among the Shona, some mbira players tune their instruments to include a larger octave, while others use a smaller octave (Berliner 1978:69). Some societies consider octave notes to be equivalent to each other, so that a singer may skip to a different octave if the required notes become too high or too low. Writing of a dance of the Venda people in South Africa, Blacking notes:

> During the course of freer musical expression, a variety of melodies come out "on top" because in the excitement of the dance the pitch of the girls' voices rises, and when they cannot reach a tone they transpose it down a fifth or an octave. Thus, falling intervals may sometimes express the feeling, "I can't reach the next tone!" (1973:71)

Tikopia singers (McLean 1990:108) and Hungarian peasants (Devereux 1971:199) have been noted to skip to an upper octave when the notes are too low.

The differences between other intervals are also expressed as ratios. The characteristics of vibrating strings or blown pipes naturally produce a certain series of intervals. Vibrating strings, as on a guitar or violin, are important because they sometimes vibrate as a whole, and sometimes in parts. When a string is made to vibrate for only half its length, it makes a sound an octave higher than the full string because the number of v.p.s. is doubled. A string vibrating two thirds of its length gives an interval based on a ratio of two to three. It is called a fifth in the terminology of Western music because it represents the fifth tone of the scale. The fifth is so prominent that it is sung in some societies by men and women who think they are singing in unison (see Henry 1988 : 109). The ancient Chinese discovered that if a bamboo flute is blown easily it produces a medium pitched sound, but if it is blown hard it produces a sound considerably higher than an octave. The interval is actually an octave plus a fifth, and the phenomenon is called the overblown fifth. Other intervals are expressed by smaller ratios.

The **pitch inventory** refers to all of the pitches within an octave which are used in a specific music tradition or in a particular piece of music. All societies, including those without a system of discourse about music, use a limited number of tones in their songs; these tones constitute their pitch inventory even if they do not perceive them as such or do not have a term for it. Scale is a term used to refer to the notes of the pitch inventory that are used in particular pieces of music. Thus, Western music has a pitch inventory of twelve notes within an octave, called the chromatic scale. It also has the diatonic scale, which has seven different notes in the octave, with the lowest note repeated an octave higher. Societies have many different ways of creating their pitch inventories, so that what may sound out of tune in one society is simply the way another society prefers to tune its instruments.

When the various natural ratios of the intervals of a scale are put together, they don't quite add up to the octave, so the natural scale has never been quite satisfactory. The ancient Greeks developed a scale by mathematically creating ratios that would correlate with the octave. Since then, Western civilization has developed the chromatic scale of twelve notes within the octave. Because each interval is equal, it is called the tempered scale. This scale includes all the keys on the piano within one octave, and it enables musicians to begin any piece on any note of the scale and have it still sound the same. This modification took place because moving from one tonal center (key) to another within a piece of music became very popular in the late seventeenth century, about the time of J. S. Bach. Some scales, such as those of Java, appear to use intervals that do not match the natural scale at all.

Scales are often described by the number of notes occurring within an octave. Although the Western chromatic scale includes twelve tones, the commonly used major and minor scales, with seven notes between octaves, are called heptatonic. Some societies use hexatonic scales, with six notes. The term pentatonic is used to refer to scales with five tones, such as those of the Chinese. One form of pentatonic scale has no semitones (half steps), and consists of the notes do, re, mi, so, and la, or

performed on any pitch level. The sound of this scale is produced by
playing only the black notes of a piano. This scale, called the an-
hemitonic pentatonic because it lacks a semitone, is very common
in many societies, and in some European folk music. Some societies
utilize an even wider number of tones within the octave than the
European chromatic scale. Most instruments of India are designed
to sound many tones within the octave as the player slightly shifts
the standard pitches. In such cases these notes are inserted between
the notes of the main melodic outline to serve as decoration or
embellishment.

Sometimes scales are determined by nonmusical factors. The Chinese have a basic pentatonic scale partly because of a philosophical
commitment to the number five. They do, however, use other notes
as passing tones and in embellishments. An ancient lute in Southwest Asia had strings divided on a mathematical rather than a musical principle. Each of two strings was divided into forty parts, with
only the use of the first five parts indicated by frets on the fingerboard (C. Sachs 1940:257).

In many societies the tuning of instruments is not fixed, as it is in
the Western world. Mbira players in Zimbabwe enjoy changing the
tuning of their instruments from time to time because they can thus
enjoy a variety of sounds but still perform the pieces they have already learned. Various gamelan groups in Java have different tunings,
which are not a matter of distress and criticism but "a source of
pleasure and interest to the listener." Discourse about the tunings
is also a source of pleasure (Becker 1980:xvi).

The scales used in various music systems throughout the world
are analyzed according to the size of intervals separating the various
tones. To facilitate comparing the size of intervals in the music of
different societies, Alexander Ellis devised a system of **cents**. Although the ratio between intervals is the same no matter whether
the pitch is high or low, the number of vibrations per second varies
considerably between high notes and low notes (Figure 4.1). Ellis'
cents system, based on the twelve-tone equal-tempered scale, as-
signs the quantity of 100 cents to each semitone or half step so the
octave is 1,200 cents.

Since intervals in other music systems are often different from

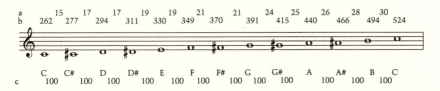

Figure 4.1. Measurement of intervals. a: The intervals of a half step are unequal when given as differences in vibrations per second. b: The vibrations per second for each note on the staff. c: The intervals of a half step are equal in the cents system.

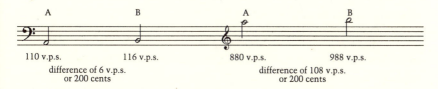

Figure 4.2. Although great differences in v.p.s. exist, we *hear* no difference.

intervals in European music, it is important to be able to describe them with a system of measurement that is the same at all octaves. With the cents system, an interval of 500 cents would be a fourth—the larger fourth that characterizes some music systems would be something over 500 cents, and the perfect fourth that is not equal tempered is 498 cents. An interval of 175 cents, as in the Tepehua thought songs of Mexico discussed in the following chapter, is somewhat less than a whole tone. With Ellis' system the difference between A and B in any range would always be 200 cents. This system is much easier to handle than the variable number of vibrations per second (Figure 4.2).

Timbre and Tone Quality

The nature of a musical tone is determined not only by the basic number of vibrations per second, but also by other vibrations occurring at the same time. Most musical sounds blend several frequencies, producing what is called a fundamental tone with overtones. The **fundamental tone** is what we hear as the basic pitch, and the varying **overtones** produce additional sounds that enable us to distinguish between different instruments even when they are sound-

4.1. Matias Chipadze playing the musical bow, Zimbabwe, 1972. (Photo by the author.)

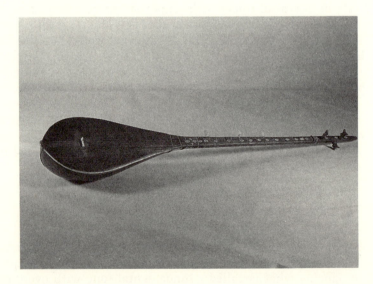

4.2. Lute, 38½″ long, from Afghanistan, played by plucking. (Instrument in William Hammond Mathers Museum, Bloomington, Indiana; photo by the author.)

ing the same pitch. This difference is called **timbre** or tone color. The resonator of a musical instrument often brings out different overtones, much as the shape of the mouth changes the notes which one hears when playing a jaws harp (see Photo 4.13).

Because the different musical instruments are a major source of variety in timbre, musicians show great concern with the various types of instruments and how they produce sounds. Instruments are thus classified in a variety of ways in different societies. The conventional classification system in Western civilization divides instruments into strings, woodwinds, brass, and percussion. The Chinese, on the other hand, have eight categories of instruments based on the materials used to make them. These categories are metal, stone (gongs), earth (clay), leather, silk (strings), wood, gourd, and bamboo (Harich-Schneider 1973:134). The early ethnomusicologists Erich von Hornbostel and Curt Sachs (1961) arranged musical instruments into four major groups based on the method of producing the vibrations. Their classification is now widely used for cross-cultural description and comparison of instruments, as well as for museum displays.

The first category of the Hornbostel-Sachs classification system is **chordophones**. These instruments produce sounds by plucked, bowed, or hammered strings. Different categories of chordophones are distinguished by the shape of the resonator and its relation to the strings. If an instrument has one string that is held taut by a bow, it is called a **musical bow** (Photo 4.1). Either a gourd or the oral cavity of the player can serve as a resonator. The pitch of the string can be changed by pressing on it as it is played, or by connecting the middle part of it to the bow. **Lutes** are a classification in which the instrument has strings extending from the resonator over a fingerboard, like the violin or guitar (Photo 4.2). **Lyres** have strings which are parallel to the resonator but are fastened to a framework rather than a fingerboard. **Harps** have strings also attached to a framework, but they are placed perpendicular to the resonator rather than parallel to it (Photo 4.3). **Zithers** are chordophones in which the strings cover the resonator (Photo 4.4). This is the classification that includes the European harpsichord and piano, as well as the dulcimer, the Japanese koto (Photo 4.5), and related instruments.

Another major group of instruments are **aerophones**, whose sound is produced by activating an enclosed portion of air. Usually the player blows into the instrument, but the air can be provided mechanically, as in a pipe organ. The distinctive timbres are created as some instruments produce sounds when the player blows into an empty object like a flute, an ocarina, or panpipes (Photo 4.6). Some

4.3. A Burmese harp, 33″ long. (Instrument in William Hammond Mathers Museum, Bloomington, Indiana; photo by the author.)

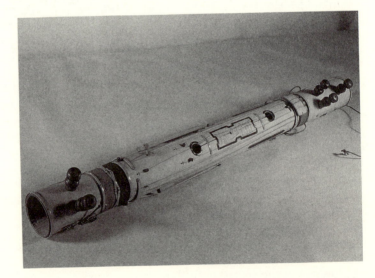

4.4. A tube zither, 34″ long, from Madagascar. (Instrument in William Hammond Mathers Museum, Bloomington, Indiana; photo by the author.)

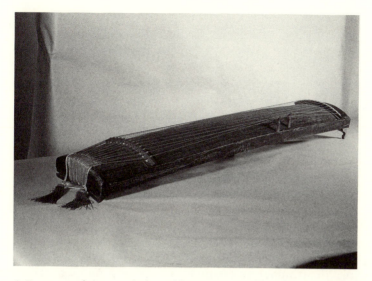

4.5. A Japanese koto, 53½″ long. (Instrument in William Hammond Mathers Museum, Bloomington, Indiana; photo by the author.)

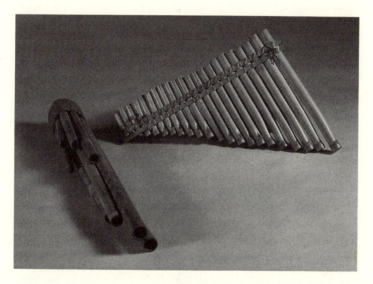

4.6. Panpipes. Solomon Island pipes are arranged as a bundle; the longest pipe is 15″. Pipes from Brazil are arranged in a line, with the longest one, 7½″, at one end. (Instruments in William Hammond Mathers Museum, Bloomington, Indiana; photo by the author.)

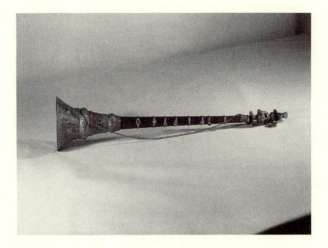

4.7. A shawm, a double-reed instrument, from Nepal. This one is 23" long. (Instrument in William Hammond Mathers Museum, Bloomington, Indiana; photo by the author.)

aerophones have reeds which flutter when blown so they produce a distinctive sound. One reed, as in the clarinet, produces a less nasal tone than the double reeds of the oboe and shawm (Photo 4.7). The sound-producing vibration is sometimes made by the player's lips, as with the trumpet. The bullroarer, which is used in many places to depict spirits, is a piece of wood carved so that it produces a whistling sound as it is swung around the player's head at the end of a string.

In some parts of the world aerophones are played with a technique called circular breathing (see Photo 2.5). The mouth of the performer serves as a type of air chamber, as the player inhales through the nose while the air from the mouth continues to play the instrument. This is why pictures of players in Southwest Asia often show them with cheeks puffed out. Today many jazz musicians use circular breathing. Students of this technique practice by breathing as they blow into a glass of water with a straw and maintain a steady flow of bubbles.

The third group is **membranophones**, with which the sound is produced by a membrane, usually leather. This classification consists primarily of drums, although not all instruments commonly called drums are included. Drums are beaten by hand as well as by sticks, and some, called friction drums, are played by rubbing a string attached to the membrane (Photo 4.8). Some drums are closed

4.8. A friction drum, 17″ high, from Angola. Protruding through the drumhead is the thong used for playing the instrument. (Instrument in William Hammond Mathers Museum, Bloomington, Indiana; photo by the author.)

4.9. A closed drum, 27½″ high, from Ecuador, and an open drum, 17½″ high, from Ghana. (Instruments in William Hammond Mathers Museum, Bloomington, Indiana; photo by the author.)

at the bottom, like a kettledrum, and others are open at the end opposite the drumhead (Photo 4.9). Hourglass drums are smaller in the center than on each end, and the membranes on each end are attached by strings. The player can then change the pitch of the drum by constricting the strings so that the membrane is stretched. The frame drum is simply a skin stretched over a round frame without any resonating chamber.

The last category, **idiophones**, includes instruments that vibrate without any special tension (C. Sachs 1940:69), basically those not belonging in any of the other groups. Idiophones produce sound through the vibration of the body of the instrument itself, such as a rattle. Xylophones (Photo 4.10) belong to this category, as do the plucked iron prongs (mbira, see Photo 1.2) that are widespread in Africa. Slit-drums are a form of idiophone because they have no membrane, but are carved so that the wood itself vibrates, often producing at least two different pitches (Photo 4.11). Steel drums, bells, and gongs (Photo 4.12) are all idiophones. The difference between bells and gongs lies in how the instruments are struck: bells resound by being struck on the edge, while gongs sound best when struck in the center. Jaws harps are also considered idiophones (Photo 4.13).

Since the development of electronic technology an additional classification of **electrophones** has been suggested. This group includes all instruments where the sound is produced by electronic impulses amplified through a loudspeaker.

Timbre is not only a matter of the difference between instruments; it also can be varied with modifications in the way instruments are played. The mute on a violin changes the way the strings vibrate; the mute on a trumpet changes the shape of the resonator. Timbre is a particularly important feature of music in East Asia. The Japanese not only have a great variety of drums and flutes, they have many ways of controlling the timbre. On the *shamisen* plucked lute of Japan:

> The lower bridge varies in size and weight according to the genre of the music, giving a variety of timbre of a delicate, but distinguishable difference. The strings are struck and plucked by a plectrum shaped in the form of a leaf from the Ginko [sic] tree. The shape, size and weight of the plectrum also vary according to the genre of music, giving quite a remarkable variety of timbre. These variations of timbre are a very important element of Shamisen music. (Kishibe 1984:75)

Although timbre refers specifically to the nature of overtones, many societies change the sound effects of their instruments by

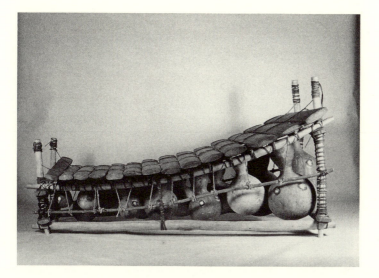

4.10. Xylophone, 41" long, 21" high, from Ghana. (Instrument in William Hammond Mathers Museum, Bloomington, Indiana; photo by the author.)

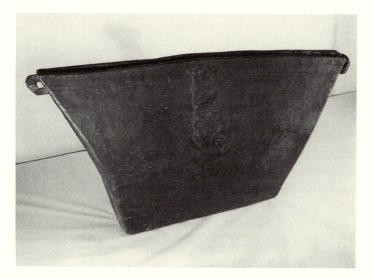

4.11. A slit-drum, 22" high, 43" long, from Angola. (Instrument in William Hammond Mathers Museum, Bloomington, Indiana; photo by the author.)

4.12. Gongs, *6″* to *12″* in diameter, of the type used in the gamelan, from Sunda, Java. (Instruments in William Hammond Mathers Museum, Bloomington, Indiana; photo by the author.)

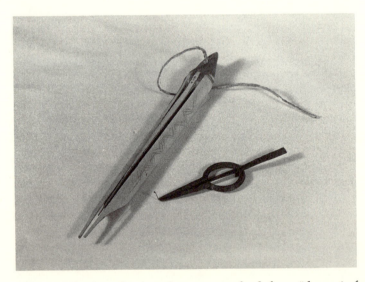

4.13. Two jaws harps. The wooden one on the left, *12″* long, is from Kiwai Island, Papua New Guinea; the metal one, *5″* long, is from Pakistan. (Instruments in William Hammond Mathers Museum, Bloomington, Indiana; photo by the author.)

various modifications. The Tuareg produce a buzzing sound by attaching a metal jangle to their *tahardent,* a three-stringed plucked lute (Card 1982:163). In Japan, drummers change the sound quality of drums as they attach small strips of paper to the back of the heads of the drums used in Noh plays (Photo 4.14) (Kishibe 1984:53). The sound of the koto is changed by scraping the string instead of plucking it (ibid.:57).

Timbre is produced not only by various instruments, but also by the various techniques of singing. The open singing style of Italian opera is vastly different from the crooning of the 1940s or the loud aggressive singing of modern rock musicians. Singing in Asia is often nasal and sounds pinched, but much emphasis is given to the ability of the singer to produce different types of tone quality. Singing styles are carefully cultivated. In North India each guild (*gharana*) of singers cultivates different vocal sounds (Wade 1979:176). The Blackfoot cultivate a distinctive singing style that is one of the central features of Blackfoot music, and it serves to distinguish their music from that of whites (Ex. 4.1; see Photo 3.2) (Nettl 1989:67). Tibetan monks have developed a technique of singing two notes at once, producing a fundamental note and shaping their throat cavities so that certain overtones are emphasized. Vocal style is a matter of what a social group considers desirable rather than a question of some people being able to sing well and others not. Like other features of music, the definition of a good singer varies from one society to another and from one taste public to another. It often includes more criteria than simply the production of certain tone qualities. These criteria include the number of songs known, stamina, and the ability to improvise creative texts.

Rhythm

Whereas pitch and timbre are physical characteristics of a musical tone, other aspects of musicianship are related to the arrangement of musical sounds in relation to time. Rhythm and form are the most important of these elements. Rhythm means more than a basic beat. Not only does the presence or absence of sound create patterns, but so does the loudness, or the intensity, of sound waves. Loudness gives emphasis to certain tones to make them stand out in relation to other tones. Sometimes emphasis on certain tones results from the nature of the tones surrounding them.

Rhythm is often conceptualized differently in various societies. In Tikopia, a pause to take a breath is considered outside of the rhyth-

4.14. Tsuzumi drum, about 10½″ tall, used in Noh plays, Japan. (Instrument in William Hammond Mathers Museum, Bloomington, Indiana; photo by the author.)

mic pattern, so that it randomly adds what outsiders would consider an extra beat (McLean 1990:108).

Sometimes no pattern of accent, stress, or rests is present, so the movement of music is termed **free rhythm**. This type of rhythm appears in certain types of chant or improvised solo singing such as lullabies. Most of the world's music is characterized by **metric rhythm**, that is, rhythm measured in some way. Rhythm is patterned in many different ways by people in various societies. Metric rhythms are basically duple, triple, or asymmetrical. Duple rhythms are those in which two beats appear to belong together; triple rhythms have three beats perceived as a grouping. In Tikopia some songs can be sung in either duple or triple rhythms, which determines a distinction in song type (McLean 1990:113–114). The music of China, Japan, and Bali traditionally had only duple rhythms. The traditional music of Korea, on the other hand, utilized only triple rhythms (Kishibe 1984:22). No matter how many beats are conceptualized together, the beats can also be divided into divisions of two (binary) or three (ternary). Consequently, metrical patterns of this type are sometimes called divisive rhythms.

Asymmetrical or irregular rhythms consist of patterns combining groups of two and groups of three equal pulses, such as 2 + 3 + 2 or 2 + 2 + 2 + 3. These rhythmic patterns have often been called additive because they appear to be formed by adding small pulses together into different sized beats.[1] Although not found in East Asia or most of Europe, asymmetrical rhythms are common in many parts of the world. A common rhythm of this type

occurs in groups as far apart as the hill tribes of Asia and the Indians of North America.[2] Asymmetrical rhythms are common in the Balkans where they are called *aksak*, a Turkish word with the literal meaning of "limping." In rural Macedonia a popular dance, "Za Ramo Oro," was danced to any tune with the pattern 3 + 2 + 2 (N. Sachs 1975:212). The lack of rhythmic patterns like these would provide a reason for the Albanian musician to consider Beethoven's music so very plain.

Asymmetrical rhythms make it possible to create rather distinctive patterns of rhythm instead of the regularly recurring beats and measures of European music. Just as the different sized intervals make the various pitches in a scale distinctive, so the asymmetrical rhythmic patterns create distinctive moments for inserting counter-rhythms. Asymmetrical patterns provide the basis for rhythmic complexity in Africa, where they are used extensively. African musical complexity is based on using both regular and additive rhythms simultaneously, a practice called **polyrhythm**. African music often consists of different instrumental and vocal parts, with each having its own rhythmic pattern. Many African pieces are based on units of twelve rapid pulses, with the units divided into rhythmic patterns in different ways. Such patterns as 3 + 3 + 3 + 3, 4 + 4 + 4, 2 + 2 + 2 + 3 + 3, 2 + 3 + 2 + 2 + 3, and numerous other combinations, are often played together. Cross-rhythms occur when these rhythmic patterns are played so that the tones of the patterns sound at different times.

The rhythmic basis of the classical music of India is the **tala**, a rhythmic pattern which underlies an entire piece of music. It is often irregular, consisting of a mixture of two-pulse and three-pulse units. The drummers play intricate variations upon these patterns, which are difficult for the non-Indian to hear. Indian audiences know the tala and maintain it in their minds during a performance, often with the aid of finger and hand movements. Thus, they can appreciate the variations which the performer is making, as well as the ways the singer or player of the melodic instrument is relating to the rhythm. The drummer creates variations on the basic tala and demonstrates skill in returning to the most important beat at the right time (Wade 1979:115–127).

An interesting combination of nonmetrical, yet measured, rhythm is found in the Japanese elastic or breath rhythm (Malm 1977:197). This rhythm is a rather rapid accelerando of drum beats, beginning slowly and progressing to a rapid beat reminiscent of expelling the breath. It is found primarily in Buddhist chant, in ancient Japanese court music, and in the music of the Noh theater.

Melody

Rhythm and pitch together often result in **melody**, although not all use of pitch results in melody as understood in Western music. Melodies combine pitches with patterns of rhythm to produce a distinctive line of sounds. Melodies do not necessarily include all notes of a scale, and some notes of the scale are given more emphasis than others. Much Oriental music uses standard melodic patterns that are repeated as needed to provide sound effects for productions with drama and text (Kishibe 1984:25). What might be termed melodic fragments characterize the *ngororombe* bamboo pipe music of northeastern Zimbabwe. Players perform in a small ensemble, each man having two, sometimes three, bamboo pipes. He plays them in one of four or five fixed patterns that often include sung notes. Since the pitches and patterns of the pipes differ, they produce a full and rich sound together, but it is not characterized by a strong melodic element (Kaemmer 1975:97–98).

Hocket is a technique that provides a melodic line through coordinating the performance of many people. Each individual produces one to three notes that are timed with other performers so that the ensemble provides melodies of a full range. This is the technique used in the English handbell tradition. The performers in the ensemble have a bell in each hand, and a particular bell is played when its pitch is needed in the melody. In the *tshikona* national dance of the Venda, each player has only one pipe. The musicians use the hocket technique to make melodies as well as the characteristic harmonies (Ex. 4.2). The egalitarian Mbuti Pygmies use hocket in their singing, thus avoiding the extra attention that would otherwise be drawn to a soloist.

Tonal orientation refers to the relative importance of the various tones in the pitch inventory. The same amount of emphasis is seldom given to all the possible tones in a performance, so that different pitches serve different functions (Wade 1979:65). Many musical traditions have standardized forms of tonal orientation, called **modes**. Modes are distinguished by the ways certain notes are highlighted in relation to the tones surrounding them. The closest that Western music comes to modes is the difference between the major and the minor keys. The tonal orientation of the various modes is indicated through greater repetition of the basic tones, the usage of the tones above and below them, and the endings of musical sections. The latter provide a feeling of completion or relaxation. The ancient Greeks developed a variety of modes, each of which is more or less equivalent to a heptatonic scale based on each of the white notes of the piano. The Inuit have many songs using a pentatonic scale, but different tones of the scale become the tonal center according to the emphasis given them. Thus, even with a five-toned scale, the Inuit have four different modes used in different songs (Cavanagh 1982:106).

The classical music of India is characterized by configurations of notes called **raga**. A raga is similar to a mode, but it includes other features in addition to the emphasis given to the various notes. Each raga gains its distinctiveness by the particular pitches involved, the rise and fall of the melody, the intonations used, and by the nature of the embellishments (Wade 1979:68–74). At a concert of Indian music each piece is characterized by one raga, and the opening of the piece is used to establish the raga in the listeners' minds. The performer then proceeds to create variations within the constraints of the raga, just as the drummer improvises within the rhythms of the tala.

Form

Form, like rhythm, marks the passage of music through time, but form involves larger units that create a type of pattern as a performance proceeds. A major distinction in form exists between linear and cyclic forms. **Linear** form occurs in fixed pieces of music having a definite beginning and ending. Frequently, two or three characteristic parts are repeated in a certain order. Linear forms characterize most types of European music, in which pieces often progress from a beginning to a climax and then an ending. A very common linear form in European music is called the ABA form, since it consists of an opening theme (A), followed by something rather different (B), then a return to the beginning material (A). This form characterizes European folk songs, hymn tunes, and, in a more complex way, sonata form. The Japanese have another type of linear form, which they call *jo-ha-kyu*. "Jo means introduction, Ha exposition, and Kyu conclusion. The tempo of each is slow, moderate and fast, respectively. The form is not based on the idea of symmetry A-B-A, but the idea of A-B-C" (Kishibe 1984:29). A kind of linear form, called incomplete repetition, is found in the songs of the Blackfoot. The leader begins a song with the principal motif, which is then followed by a repetition by another singer. After that, parts of the motif are repeated at a lower pitch level (Nettl 1989:100). As the Blackfoot themselves expressed it: "Our songs have a beginning, middle, and end. After beginning, somebody raises the leader, and then all sing" (ibid.:172). There is no specific length for the last portion of the song.

The second major type of musical form is often termed **cyclic**, in that it consists of repeated cycles. Cyclic form is the basis of musics characterized by improvisation, in which a basic musical idea is continuously repeated, but varied with each repetition. This type of structure makes possible the creation of music of considerable complexity, even in a society without music notation. Much music of India is of this type, as the soloist develops melodies based on the raga while the drummer creates variations on repetitions of the tala rhythmic pattern.

On the Indonesian islands of Java and Bali the recurrence of cycles is an important characteristic of the gamelan ensembles (Photo 4.15). Gamelan is an Indonesian word that means literally "orchestra" or

4.15. Gamelan from Surakarta, Central Java, 1986. (Photo by Arthur P. Durkee; used by permission.)

"music ensemble." The word orchestra is not used to refer to the gamelan since the instruments and the sound are both very different from the Western orchestra. Many of the instruments of the gamelan are made of bronze, so the whole ensemble has a metallic sound. One cycle of gamelan music is a type of long musical phrase. It is called the *gongan*, denoting that the cycle is determined by the gong. The English word "gong" is borrowed from the Indonesian word that denotes the largest gong in the gamelan orchestra. The smaller secondary gongs are called *kethuk, kempul,* and *kenong*. The *gongan* cycle is marked by the large gong, then subdivided by the sounds of the other gongs. In one form the *kenong* divides the cycle in half, and each half is divided into halves by the *kempul*. Each of the quarters is divided by the *kethuk*. The listener is able to follow the cycles because of the distinct sound of each of the gongs, as in Figure 4.3.

African music has a cyclic form termed **call and response**, in which one person leads out with a phrase, and the rest of the people join in with a reply. The call and response form can be repeated indefinitely, and often the leader creates considerable variation. This form characterizes not only African music, but also spiritual songs of African-Americans and much of the recreational music of the Ca-

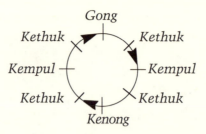

Figure 4.3. Cycle of gong sounds (adapted from Malm 1977: 44).

ribbean area. Jazz, which is in part a derivative of African music, is also characterized by cyclic form, as the performers improvise on the basis of a standard harmonic structure.

One type of form appears to be cyclic in detail, but linear in its overall pattern. **Strophic form** has characteristics of linear form, since each verse has a definite beginning and end; it also resembles cyclic form in that the verses are repeated. In these forms the tune is repeated with different sets of words, like the verses in English folk songs, which may or may not be followed by a refrain. The strophic form does not appear everywhere in the world.

Some musical forms customarily end with a **coda**, which indicates the imminent conclusion of a piece or performance. Among the Flathead, a coda indicates that a song is borrowed rather than being one of the old Flathead songs. The word they use for a coda is translated "tail" (Merriam 1967:41).

Multipart Music

Very few societies have extensive amounts of music sung by only one individual or by groups performing everything in unison. Whenever more than one part is occurring we have the phenomenon of **multipart music** (Kauffman 1970:5-6). The presence of multiple parts in Western music is called polyphony, but the term is closely connected with specific European features, so that the term multipart is preferable for purposes of cross-cultural study and comparison. The nature of the multiple parts differs considerably from one society to another.

A common type of multipart music occurs when the various musical parts produce different pitches at the same time. A simple form of this practice is the **drone**, common over a wide area stretching from India to Ireland. The drone is one or two notes that are repeated

continuously throughout a piece of music, providing a contrast to
the other notes that are played or sung. The drone of bagpipes provides a distinctive sound to the music of Scotland, Ireland, and parts
of eastern Europe. In Moslem West Asia and the Balkans, reed instruments are made as a pair so one player can sustain a drone and
also provide a melody (Photo 4.16). Flute players among the northern Tuareg often maintain a vocal drone as they play (Card 1982:63).
In India the classical music performer creates elaborate variations in
relation to the note of the drone during development of the raga. The
skill shown in returning to it is a source of great pleasure for the
Indian audience.

Multipart music is closely associated with the practice of **harmony**, but the two features are not quite the same. Harmony refers
not only to notes that are sounding together (chords), but also to
notes that are perceived together even though they may sound successively. Harmony is basically the progression from one type of prescribed sound combination to another. European polyphony is the
simultaneous use of several melodic lines that fit into a common
harmonic structure. Chords in Western music require a third and a
fifth note above the root note, with emphasis on the third. Chords
among the Shona emphasize the fifth, with the third often being
omitted. The result is heard as parallel fifths and fourths that move

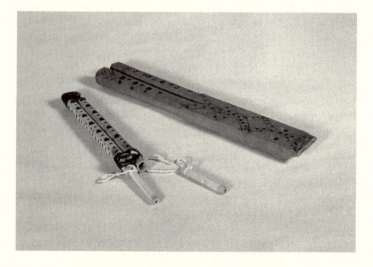

4.16. Dual aerophones, from Turkey (*left*, 9″ long) and Macedonia
(*right*, 14¼″ long). Instruments in William Hammond Mathers Museum, Bloomington, Indiana; photo by the author.

in patterns involving leaps of thirds and fourths (Ex. 1.2). In Bulgaria
and in parts of West Africa, multipart music occurs as performers
sound together the interval of a second.[3]

Sometimes melodies overlap, creating another type of multipart
music. In call and response songs the response often begins before
the call or solo part is finished, thus producing two parts at once.
Popular rounds like "Three Blind Mice" are an example of the same
melody overlapping. This practice is called **canon**, which is a feature
of many types of music. In classical music of India the *sarangi* accompanying instrument often echoes the melodic line of the vocal-
ist (Neuman 1990:121). The Kaluli use multipart music sounding
like canon or musical imitation. A major feature of Kaluli treatment
of sound is basically overlapping parts. Steven Feld calls attention
to a Kaluli term, *dulugu ganalan,* meaning "lift-up-over sounding"
(1988:76). This feature relates to the way singers build up sound by
superimposing musical ideas on each other (Ex. 4.3). Such use of
sound is symbolically related to the overlapping sounds of the forest
and of people working together.

Sometimes the effect of multiple parts is gained by deliberately
performing related parts with one slightly behind the other. When
singing *gisaro* songs, the Kaluli practice a type of canon on the basic
descending melodic outline. When a singer begins a line, the chorus
repeats the same thing a split second after the singer (Feld 1982:
176–77). The Japanese deliberately perform with the rhythm of the
instruments slightly behind the singers. This is an important aesthetic feature; a performance in which the voice and instruments
sound together would be considered childish (Kishibe 1984:26).

Some societies achieve polyrhythmic effects by having instrumental parts that vary rhythmically from the singing parts. Early observers of Native American music came to the conclusion that the
people did not bother to coordinate melody and rhythm. Recently,
analysis of the rhythm of a Dakota song shows that the rhythm is
based on a rapid pulse, expressed as a vibrato in the singing. The
drumming is carefully coordinated with this rapid pulse, providing
a system of metric restriction that sounds remarkably free (Pantaleoni 1987). In Blackfoot music a similar process seems to operate,
since it is considered necessary for the musicians to keep separate
rhythms for melody and drumming (Nettl 1989:119). This kind of
performance sounds like a lack of coordination to outsiders, but the
performers and their audience appreciate the effect.

Elsewhere, rhythmic coordination seems to be the only feature
holding the parts together. Suya shout songs (*akia*) (Ex. 2.4) are a
type of multipart performance in which a large group of men will

all be singing their individual songs simultaneously as they shake their rattles together. The songs are all different because each man wants his sisters to be able to distinguish his song from the others. Anthony Seeger notes that performance of this type of song actually requires effort on the part of the musician. In order to have his song heard it must be sung with a high strained voice and be noticeably different in melody, rhythm, and text (A. Seeger 1979:383).

The polyrhythms and cross-rhythms of Africa are essentially another type of multipart music. Regarding musical values among the Kpelle of West Africa, Ruth M. Stone writes:

Ideally music, especially that for dance, is performed as fast as is possible without loss of synchronization and precision. The emphasis is not on the quantitative time between drum beats, but rather, on the qualitative synchronization working toward ever greater precision. It is more desirable to combine many different parts than to play at a significantly faster tempo. (1982:76)

Many societies put a high value on the multipart features of their music. Having several things happening at once is one basis of interest in music, since it is possible for the listener to shift attention from one aspect of the music to another. This statement is as true with the polyphonic music of the West as it is with the music of many societies around the world.

When multiple parts occur, the emphasis given to various parts varies from society to society. Among the Aymara of Peru the part in the center is the main part, and higher and lower parts are considered decorative. In West Africa the steadily repeated pattern that provides rhythmic orientation is in high-pitched sounds, and it is the lower-pitched drums that do most variation (Pantaleoni 1985:283). In Western music it is the opposite, with the lower voices providing the basic harmonic orientation, while greater variability comes from the upper voices.

The elements of music presented in this chapter are the basic building blocks used by people everywhere in working out music that is pleasing to them. Familiarity with these terms is essential in dealing with questions concerning the meaning, the use and function, and the processes of change in music.

CHAPTER FIVE

Meaning in Music

THE QUESTION OF MEANING in music is closely related to the concepts about music as described in Chapter 3. However, people not only give meaning to music, they also use music to convey meanings. Where Chapter 3 dealt primarily with the ways different societies think about music, this chapter is more concerned with how the experience of music is translated by the individual into thoughts and feelings. Meanings are essentially individual, but they become of interest to social science when they are shared among members of a social group. The meaning of music is broader than concepts about music because many of the meanings are not musical at all. Such meanings help explain why people engage in musical events and how musical behavior might produce certain musical styles.

Music has popularly been called a universal language because it is obviously an effective means of communication. Music *is* indeed universal; no human group without some type of music has ever been discovered. But as with spoken language, it is not always possible for everyone to understand what is being communicated. Anyone who has listened to highly exotic music and found it meaningless, or even unpleasant, will agree that no one form of music will convey the same meaning, or even *any* meaning, to all people. The idea of music as a universal language sounds reasonable as long as one is considering only the areas comprising Western civilization. However, once one ventures into regions of Asia, Africa, and the Americas where indigenous music is customarily used, it is easily seen that music is not a universal language as that term is commonly understood.

The meaning of music is more closely related to an individual's perception than it is to the nature of the music itself. We humans are very selective in our perceptions, since our sense organs pick up more stimuli than our cognitive capacities can handle efficiently. Many sights and sounds escape our notice entirely unless we focus our attention upon them. This focus of attention is one of the primary features of meaning. In a broad sense the meaning of anything is seen in the way humans react to it: if we don't react to a stimulus, then it is truly meaningless. Other features of meaning appear as affective reactions. In both cases the reactions or meanings range from the casual notice of a request or cue on one hand to fits of tears or laughter on the other. Meaning has customarily been expressed intellectually in terms of symbols. For an expressive aspect of culture it is important to supplement symbolism by considering the aesthetic dimension that relates affect and emotion to a society's values.

In general, meaning is found when humans relate something in their current experience with previous experiences stored in their memories. Thus, most meanings are personal and based on a form of **association.** One reason we fail to appreciate some types of exotic music is that we lack any previous experience with it. In some ways musical meaning is unique to every person, particularly as individuals experience certain music at especially sad or joyful moments in life. A great deal of musical meaning is formed as one grows up gradually absorbing the skills of perceiving specific musical features as well as the meanings one's society attaches to them. Thus, many elements of meaning are shared by persons in the same society, acting on their shared symbols and values. Broadly shared musical meanings serve as the motivation for organizing musical events, and for performing music.

The meanings of music are basically of three types. Music often acquires meaning in terms of what it *says,* called **symbolic** or referential meaning. A second type of meaning, termed **aesthetic,** nonreferential, or absolute, concerns what music *is*—what the sounds convey without reference to anything else. In many societies the principal meaning of music is pragmatic, that is, it is used to obtain utilitarian benefits. **Pragmatic** meaning concerns what music *does.* In the latter case, music is more closely related to adaptive culture than to expressive culture. Pragmatic uses and meanings of music will thus be the subject of the following chapter, while symbolic and aesthetic meanings will be considered in this one.

Music as Symbol

Human life is based on symbols. They serve as the basis for language, which enables us to pass cultural knowledge from one generation to the next. Symbols also permeate religion, which concerns major questions about the meaning of life. They are also crucial in the arts, which occupy a central place in our enjoyment of life and in maintaining emotional stability. Only humans are capable of the complex symbolizing that occurs in language, religion, and the arts.

Symbol is a difficult word to define adequately, since it is used in many different ways. A widely used definition of symbol was suggested by Charles S. Peirce (1960). He viewed symbols as only one of three kinds of signs. The **index** was a sign in which a physical connection existed between the sign and its meaning (the referent). For example, thunder serving as an index indicates a storm. A second type of sign was the **icon,** which was characterized by some type of resemblance between the icon and its referent. In this case the roll of a drum imitating a storm would be an icon. When music serves as an icon, the relationship is often termed **iconicity.** Peirce limited the term "symbol" to a third type of sign, in which the relationship between the sign and the referent is completely arbitrary. The flags indicating a storm at a marina would be symbols in this sense. The meanings of most words in language are also this type of symbol. Peirce's view is somewhat restrictive, however, since popular ideas of symbol and the definitions used in psychology consider the symbol to be anything that stands for something else. Peirce's scheme is useful in distinguishing index from icon; a symbol in his sense of the word is less confusingly referred to as "arbitrary symbol."[1]

Because music can convey meanings about many other things, it frequently serves as a symbol. A particularly useful definition of **symbol** for considering the symbolic aspects of music is "objects, acts, concepts or linguistic formations that stand *ambiguously* for a multiplicity of disparate meanings, evoke sentiments and emotions, and impel men to action" (Cohen 1974: Preface). Music is included in this definition because musical instruments and sound waves are objects, and the production of music is an act. Since music is an important symbol, behavior that creates music is rightfully considered a form of symbolic behavior. Part of the ambiguity in musical meaning comes from the fact that the same performance or piece of music may carry different meanings at the same time. Many types of symbols that carry several meanings at the same time have been termed **multivocalic** (Turner 1967).

The ambiguity of symbols is important because it enables people to manipulate symbolic meanings for their own purposes. This manipulation often takes the form of repudiating the messages that are expressed through socially recognized art forms. The potential for this practice, called **repudiability** (Devereux 1971:204), enables performers to express themselves, yet, if necessary, repudiate or deny any meanings that might cause inconvenience, embarrassment, or even serious political complications. Music often adds the element of repudiability to song texts by enabling the performers to deny personal involvement with the words of the text, alleging simply an interest in enjoying the tune. For example, many Shona political songs in Zimbabwe could be easily explained in terms of traditional beliefs about lions or birds. The song *"Totamba nakashiri kamambo"* literally means "we are playing with the chief's little bird." It doesn't make a great deal of sense until one realizes that during the Shona uprising against the European colonialists in 1896, the "chief's little bird" referred to the spirit mediums who went from one chieftainship to another to coordinate the struggle (Ranger 1967). In the context of the independence struggle of the 1970s the song had very deep meaning, yet one could easily avoid giving an accurate explanation to the casual inquirer.

Although music as a symbol is expected to convey meaning, as a form of self-expression it may sometimes fail to do so. The terms "expression" and "communication" are not interchangeable, as many people often assume. **Expression** simply means that thoughts or feelings have been put into some kind of medium; whether or not the message is picked up by someone else does not affect the act of expression. **Communication** conveys the idea that two parties are involved, a sender and a receiver, and that some sort of message passes between them. Whenever artists, musicians, or dancers are concerned only with giving form to their feelings, they are basically expressing themselves. If the form of expression is meaningless to anyone else, the result is limited to expression. On the other hand, if the forms of expression do carry meaning to someone else, the result is both expression and communication. Sometimes the message picked up by the receiver is not the same as that intended by the sender, resulting in distorted communication. Because symbols in the arts are highly ambiguous, the sender may have a range of messages, any of which may result in communication when picked up by the receiver. Messages may involve both ideas and feelings. Messages or information that are primarily ideas or concepts are dealt with in terms of **cognition;** communication of feelings is a matter of **affect.**[2]

Meaning in music operates at the levels of both discursive and practical consciousness, as well as the unconscious. The meaning of a piece of music is in the discursive consciousness when one can describe it to someone else. Meaning resulting from practical consciousness, on the other hand, is characterized by a lack of awareness. The failure of a society to verbalize certain aspects of meaning in discourse does not always indicate the absence of those features of meaning. Often the only way such meaning can be determined is by the outside observer, who is able to infer meanings from analysis of behavior in the group. The outside observer lacks the assumptions that often blind the participant. The situation somewhat resembles the role of grammar in language. Young children of four and five years can handle a language very well, and follow the rules of grammar. Their inability to verbalize those rules does not mean that the rules do not exist.

Another important feature of symbolism in music is the fact that meanings may be combined so that the meaning of several symbols together is different from the total of each one. Sometimes this type of symbolism operates at different levels. The simplest level is the **motif,** a basic pattern of melody and rhythm that occurs repeatedly throughout a larger piece of music. Meanings given to motifs are clearly seen in Prokofiev's *Peter and the Wolf,* where different themes are assigned to the various characters by a narrator. The themes of the characters are then combined musically when a procession of all of the animals is taking place. Thus different motifs are combined to create increasingly complex symbolism.

In some music traditions different songs are joined together to form song cycles. This form of symbolism is seen in the music used by the Australian Aborigines in rituals related to their myths of the Dreamtime. They use song cycles to recount ancient mythical journeys, with each song representing a stop on the journey. Each song has its own meaning, but each also contributes to the overall meaning of the entire event. These songs are coordinated with sections of ritual as the journeys are reenacted, as shown in a description of one particular cycle:

> The song cycle starts at Ngawantzi near Linnekar Creek, a tributary of the Ord River, plain country where Abe has been. From there it goes to a place called Palangayi and then to Inverway (European cattle station). From Inverway it goes to Nongra Lake, where the spirit-agent looked at bloodwood trees and sang about them. From Nongra Lake Abe and the spirit-agent travelled to Walumaninpa, about thirty miles west of Hooker Creek, and there the spirit-agent looked into the distance at some clouds and sang about them. From there they travelled to Hooker Creek, where the spirit-agent looked at a thick line of trees along the creek south of the settlement, and sang about them as far as Tipitipul. They then travelled to the nineteen-mile bore and to wakaRakaRa, a Whirlwind Dreaming site near the bore which belongs to the Burindji and Mudbura tribes. There the spirit-

agent looked at a dead spirit-agent there himself when he was chasing a goanna—it just consisted of bones. It was because Abe had seen this that the spirit-agent taught him the songs about it. (Wild 1975:56)

How music operates as a type of symbol becomes clearer by distinguishing the ways that music may convey meaning. When meaning is purposefully formulated in the music by the persons creating it, the result is **denotative meaning.** Because it is purposeful, this kind of meaning is usually overt, meaning that it is in the discursive consciousness of the participants. Music also conveys **connotative meaning,** which is inferred by the listener from experience with the music. This type of meaning is often the product of practical consciousness, although not necessarily. The difference between denotative and connotative meaning is not always distinct, but awareness of the two types provides a framework for considering the numerous ways that music conveys meanings.

Denotative Meaning

Music sometimes conveys denotative meaning as an icon when the sounds of the music bear a resemblance to some other reality. This type of iconicity is seen as imitation as well as analogy. When imitation of other sounds is incorporated into the music by the creator or performer, it is a type of aural representation, similar to the visual representation of pictures. The degree of resemblance between the music and its referent varies considerably, so that the nature of a resemblance must often be learned. Although the resemblance between the sounds of a large drum and thunder, or between flute sounds and bird songs is easily recognized by many people, the meaning could be completely missed if the sounds are somewhat distorted for stylistic reasons. Thus, in Japanese kabuki a steady one-tone drum beat denoting water (*mizuoto*) is basically arbitrary. However, a more complex drumbeat representing waves (*namioto*) is iconic, with surges of intensity in the drumbeats resembling the surging of waves (Purcell n.d.). A well-known piece for the Japanese *shakuhachi* (flute, Photo 5.1) imitates the mating cry of the hart (Harich-Schneider 1973:99). The Chinese represent the sound of the mythical phoenix bird by a high-pitched double-reed aerophone, the *sona* (Photo 5.2). Many small-scale societies frequently use imitations of animals. South American Indian shamans often use the cries of animals as they perform their curing chants. Africans use the cries of cats, roosters, etc. for a comic effect. In Western classical

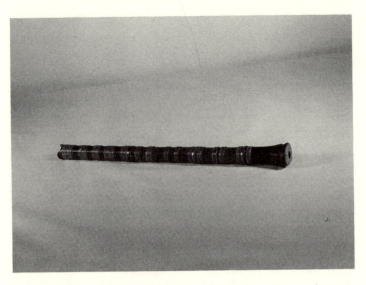

5.1. A *shakuhachi,* notched flute, 21″ long, from Japan. (Instrument in William Hammond Mathers Museum, Bloomington, Indiana; photo by the author.)

5.2. A *sona,* a double-reed instrument, from China. This one is 14″ long. (Instrument in William Hammond Mathers Museum, Bloomington, Indiana; photo by the author.)

music, storms are depicted in sound, as in Beethoven's *Pastoral Symphony, No.6,* Rossini's *William Tell Overture* and Vivaldi's *The Four Seasons.*

In music, arbitrary symbolism is a more common denotative meaning than icon, and in this sense the meanings resemble the meanings in language. The hearer learns to recognize arbitrary denotative meanings in music in a variety of ways. The clearest and probably the most important is through the words or lyrics of a song. In human societies vocal music is more common than solely instrumental music; in fact, some societies have very few instruments. Because much music is embodied in song, the symbolism and meaning of the musical sounds themselves are often closely related to and even dependent upon texts. In many cases words and music have a complementary relationship—the text embodies the message of a song, and the music intensifies the appropriate feelings. The study of song texts is primarily a literary study. Because this book basically deals with music, this section will focus on how music has meaning apart from the words.

Music without texts seldom carries specific denotative meanings, although it can be made to do so. Like words in language, motifs in music are often given arbitrary denotative meanings which are then combined with each other. Richard Wagner and other opera composers provide many motifs whose meanings are learned through association as the motifs accompany the appearance of particular characters or certain elements of the action. In a performance recorded among the Piaroa Indians of Venezuela, each of several supernatural beings has its own motif, which is heard during ritual as each spirit enters the sacred house (*Columbia World Library* 1949). In some parts of Africa certain drum rhythms are assigned conventional meanings so that when people hear particular rhythms they know what kind of event is occurring (Blacking 1973:33, 38—41).

The structures of music rarely convey complex syntactic meanings in the manner of language. However, Charles L. Boiles (1967) has described a case in which the meaning of music is syntactic in the sense that several musical symbols are combined to provide larger musical meaning. This case comes from the Tepehua people of the eastern coast of Mexico. What Boiles calls "thought-songs" are performed on a violin and guitar during a number of local ceremonies generally concerned with the well-being of the members of the community. Different songs accompany various phases of the ritual, and the local people understand from the music itself what is happening in the ritual. Boiles' analysis divides each song into two parts (continua) with each part having four rhythmic sections (motives). The rhythmic pattern of the continuum expresses the general context or topic of the song; thus ♫♩♩♩ indicates sacrifice and ♫♩♩♩ means asking pardon. The pattern ♫♫ occurring in this and in other motives refers to an intercessor. Additional details are provided by the intervals. The seven-tone scale is divided into equidistant intervals of approximately 175 cents each, and the size of interval and whether it rises or falls give additional meaning. Thus, for example, repetition of the same pitch indicates reference to a place. Other intervals show various actions or feelings, as seen in Figure 5.1. The last quarter note of a motive shows whether the action is in the past, present, or future, according to whether it follows a higher pitch, the same pitch, or a lower pitch. Boiles' analysis includes many additional complexities, but these examples provide a basic idea of the principle involved. Although this semantic structure is limited, it does indicate that music *can* be given a semantic meaning, as these rhythmic patterns and intervals are combined in many different ways.

Arbitrary meanings, such as those of the Tepehua songs, often operate simply by being widely known in a society. Where instrumental music is common, a society provides ways to inform its members what meanings are to be conveyed by certain kinds of music. In many societies the meanings of specific instrumental music pieces are known to the whole community, and passed on to children through explanation or experience in the context of performance. Western society often relies on program notes at concerts to explain what the music is about. The titles given to an instrumental piece serve the same purpose, such as *The Sorcerer's Apprentice* or *Don Juan*.

In many parts of the world, particularly Africa, drumming conveys arbitrary meanings. It is considered more than simply an accompaniment to song and dance; it is a full-fledged musical idiom on its own. It provides not only complex patterns of rhythm, but in many cases a wide variety of timbre and pitch. In areas with tonal languages the pitch possibilities of drums are used to reproduce language tones. Thus drumming, as a form of icon, can actually convey linguistic messages. This practice is the basis of the "talking drums" formerly used to communicate over long distances in Zaire. It also provides a means of proclaiming social commentary during musical performances in West Africa.

In many situations meaning is assigned not only to rhythms and melodies, but also to systems of modes. This type of tonal orientation is an important feature of the ragas of India, and is the basis of traditionally considering certain pieces as suitable for specific times

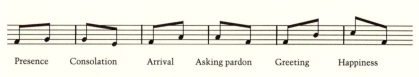

Presence   Consolation   Arrival   Asking pardon   Greeting   Happiness

Figure 5.1. Tepehua musical meanings.

of the day. The music of Java also has specific modes for various
times of day (Becker 1980:78). For many years the Aborigines of
Australia were considered to have the simplest, most "primitive"
music in the world because of the small range of many of their
songs. Richard A. Waterman (1971:172) finally pointed out that the
Yirkalla Aborigines used different modes to identify the songs of
each lineage. Thus, the people of each lineage restricted their ritual
songs to certain combinations of notes in order to provide a sound
distinctively different from other lineages. Thus it was shown that
instead of having a "primitive" or backward tonal system, the Aborigines had a narrow tonal range in many of their songs due to a
complex type of musical symbolic system.

People often apply meanings to musical instruments. The Warlpiri use a large and a small bullroarer in a fertility ritual called the
Two Mothers ritual. The bullroarers as objects are given meanings
identifying the smaller one with the elder sister, who is more dangerous and important, and the larger one with the younger sister.
Where the sounds are concerned, the larger low-pitched bullroarer
represents the Two Mothers, and the smaller high-pitched instrument represents evil spirits (Wild 1975:115–116). A type of iconic
meaning is often attached to flutes and other long, thin instruments
because of their resemblance to the male genitalia. However, this
form of symbolism is overlooked by some ethnic groups.

Certain types of musical structure convey meaning as cues that
direct the course of the performance or aid the listener in knowing
what is happening in the music. The importance of cues is seen
among the Flathead Indians, where Merriam notes:

In the War Dance sequences, the songs are started rather
abruptly and the unwary may be caught off guard until it is no-
ticed that the leading singer usually puts the fingers of his left
hand on the edge of the drum, as if muffling it, and then taps
lightly to give the tempo. The dancers are warned of the approaching end of a War Dance song when the musicians halve the beat
and increase its intensity; after a brief pause, the drumming is
recommenced and the coda sung. Singers who have had consider-

able experience with X know that he wishes to put this cue into motion when he makes a small circle in the air with his drum stick. (1967:42)

Among the Kpelle in West Africa a singer can indicate in several ways when a chorus is supposed to enter. One cue is the use of a descending melodic line; another cue is to decrease the amount of text within the melodic line. A third way is simply to use the vowels "ee" or "oo." Sometimes these cues are used alone, but to avoid ambiguity two or three of them are often used together (Stone 1982:108ff). Cues of this nature are particularly important in group performances of improvisational types of music.

Connotative Meaning

Connotative meaning is perceived by the listener, either consciously or subconsciously, even though the musician did not intentionally put it there. Connotative meaning operates in two ways: situational experience and analogy. **Situational meaning** occurs when music originally heard as part of a significant experience causes one to recall later the feelings accompanying the original experience. A common form of such meaning occurs when lovers give special significance to a particular song as they first experience it together. Situational meanings are a result of mental association, but they are not specifically incorporated into musical performance the way denotative meanings are. One reason careful analysis of musical events contributes so much to research is because the performance context provides important clues to the meaning of the music. Such clues are not unlike the program notes concerning a composer's state of mind at the time a piece was composed, but they are the result of informal social action rather than specific input.

Categorization of song types is often affected by situational meaning. Among the Shona of Zimbabwe, songs that were known to older people as hunting songs would be identified by younger people as spirit possession songs. The meaning of the song for each group depended on whether they first heard it as part of a hunting ritual, which ceased being performed many years ago, or as part of an ancestral spirit ceremony, a type of ritual that still occurs.

Situational meaning is not limited to the actual event where a performance occurs. The whole political, religious, or economic context of a society can influence the meaning of a musical performance. In Afghanistan the view that music is related to warmth or heat contributes to the idea that it is somehow dangerous or im-

moral (Slobin 1976:25). In Macedonia some of the folk songs refer
to the bravery of guerrillas who fought against the Turks until the
latter were driven from the Balkans in the early twentieth century.
To the older people who had experienced life under the Turks these
songs conveyed sadness, referring to the loss of life, the abduction of
women, the economic oppression, and the dishonor. To the younger
people who had never experienced such conditions, the songs were
considered to depict the bravery, honor, and freedom-loving qualities of the heroes, and were thus considered happy songs (N. Sachs
1975:335–336).

The *tende* mortar drum of the Tuareg (see Photo 1.1) carries several types of symbolism attributable to the general social situation.
The term *tende* refers not only to the drum itself, but also to the
musical events at which it is played. This type of music has been
used by the Tuareg only since the early twentieth century, so that it
represents not only the nobility among the Tuareg, but also the
people of lower status. It represents the values and perspectives of
traditional Tuareg life in the "bush" as opposed to modernization and
urbanization. When interacting with other Tuareg, the nobles prefer
the *anzad* because it symbolizes their unique status. In inter-ethnic
situations, they use the *tende* to affirm their Tuareg identity, and it
has become "the true folk music of the Tuareg" (Card 1982:154).

Analogy is a type of connotative meaning that appears when an
individual detects a relationship between similar types of phenomena. Analogy is a common human way of thinking, a largely subconscious form of icon that is less specific than imitation. As related to
music, analogy consists of consciously perceived or unconsciously
sensed similarities between music and other aspects of life. It is seen
in the concept of intersense transfer mentioned earlier. Analogy
means that music carries meaning because its structures bear resemblance to the social conditions of a specific society or to various
aspects of human life in general. For example, a similarity is often
noted between harmony in music and harmony in society. This was
so important to the Chinese that they established a department
of music in the government over two thousand years ago (Picken
1957:96). They viewed noise in relation to music the same as chaos
in relation to an ordered society.

The human tendency to appreciate analogous forms has been suggested as a major reason for similarities or **coherence** between musical forms and the forms of socially determined concepts about life
and the organization of society.[3] Since the perception of these forms
is often below the level of consciousness, it is a characteristic feature of practical consciousness. The most widely known example of

coherence is found in India, where the Hindu concept of reincarna-
tion causes life to be considered an endless series of cycles. The form
of classical Indian music, also based on cycles, reinforces this basic
feature of Indian life. Cycles also provide coherence in Java, where
their significance is more than a feature of musical structure. Cycles
traditionally represented the acceptance of calmness and serenity in
life as exemplified by the nobility. Elongated cycles in court music
thus reflected the supreme importance of stability, both in society
and in musical structures (Becker 1980:27–28.) Unlike India and
Java, Western society emphasizes the linear aspects of life, such as
birth, maturation, and death. Western music is linear rather than
cyclic, since it gradually builds up to a climax and then quickly ta-
pers off. Coherence has been suggested in the way the hierarchical
societies of Western civilization are reflected in the hierarchy of a
modern symphony orchestra and its audience (Pantaleoni 1985:399–
400). It is very difficult to demonstrate conclusively that these elements of coherence actually do contribute to the cognitive and affective processes involved in musical meaning. A growing number of
cases indicates that the idea of coherence does bear some validity.

Coherence appears as dualism among the Suya. Like many Amazonian societies, they divide many aspects of their lives into two
parts. Two divisions of the community as a whole, called moieties,
appear at their ceremonies, and each of the shout songs they sing
has two halves. At one of their major ceremonies the first half of
each song is sung by boys at the east side of the men's house, representing one moiety. Then they march in two rows and sing at the
west side of the men's house, which represents the other moiety
(A. Seeger 1987:18–19). Dualism is even carried to the Suya concepts of song as they distinguish the shout songs representing a high
voice or "small throat" from the unison songs considered low voice
or "big throat" (ibid.:100).

A case of coherence between musical behavior and the major
forms of social life is shown in Conima, an Aymara community of
the Peruvian highlands. The major musical groups are ensembles of
panpipe players who play at community fiestas (see Photo 2.6). Each
ensemble is divided into three groups of pipes, broadly arranged into
high, medium, and low voices. In contrast to European music, where
the soprano and bass voices are most important, the Peruvian groups
consider the middle voice the most important and the others as accompaniment. This pattern of giving major importance to the center, with development on the periphery, also occurs in Andean weaving, where the pattern is developed from the center outward. Both
forms parallel the local concepts of social organization. Living on

the sides of the Andes mountains means adapting to a climate that varies with the altitude. By having a primary community in the center with peripheral communities at higher and lower elevations, the people can enhance their economic life by trade and cooperation. The situation of life on a mountainside is considered similar to the parts of a body, with the torso maintaining life with the assistance of the head and the limbs. Similar forms in music serve to reaffirm this basic mode of adaptation and orientation to life (Turino 1989).

Coherence has been suggested as an important feature of music among the Mbuti Pygmies. The highly egalitarian characteristics of their society are also found in their musical activity. What appears to the Western ear as singing, such as lullabies and play songs, are considered by the Mbuti to be sound rather than song. Because of the egalitarian values of the Mbuti, the only types of singing that they consider to be truly legitimate music are those songs requiring group participation. The practice of singing in hocket and without recognized soloists expresses their commitment to group values (Turnbull 1965:255–56). Edward O. Henry (1976:63) has noted that many societies in North America are very egalitarian, but they do not have "groupy" types of music. This does not necessarily invalidate the suggestion that coherence is important to the Mbuti; it may simply indicate that in North America other factors are more important in giving meaning to music.

Some of the analogical meaning of music may be entirely unconscious because it relates to basic human experience rather than experience in a specific society. Time is one such area of meaning, since music basically exists in time. Blacking has described music as creating "a world of virtual time" (1973:27, 51), saying in effect that the passage of time in music is a miniature model of the passage of time in human life. Sometimes in real life it takes months, or even years, to work out our plans; in music it can be done in a few moments. Moreover, in real life we find it difficult if not impossible to control events ourselves, but in music we can.

However, the analogical meaning of time is not the same in all societies. For example, the Kpelle of Liberia view time in music as "going down the road" (Stone 1982:71), so that it is more than the simple passage of time. It involves the quality of experience similar to the act of walking down a road meeting and interacting with neighbors and kin. Thus in Kpelle music the quality of the moment's experience is emphasized more than the passage of time.

Some societies have carried analogy to an extreme by organizing their views of reality in terms of sets of opposites, often called **binary oppositions,** another form of dualism. When music is included in these sets of oppositions it affords a glimpse of the way in which music is integrated with other sets of meaning within a society. Sakata has presented a set of binary oppositions from the Persian-speaking areas of Afghanistan:

> Throughout the discussion of musical and musician terms, several features have consistently recurred. These features fall naturally into a system of binary oppositions which give insight into the relationship of the various conditions which influence the final conceptualizations of music and musician:

Music	Literature
Foreign	Native
Professional	Amateur
Instrumental	Vocal
Urban	Rural
Male	Female
Formal	Informal
Specific	General
Segregation	Nonsegregation
Censure	Praise
Variety of Styles	Lack of Variety of Styles
Terminology Abundance	Lack of Terminology

(1983:105)

Two types of meaning often occur together in what is called a **metaphor.** A metaphor is essentially a type of meaning conveyed when the referent or meaning of one symbol becomes another symbol, thus providing an extension of meaning. The term metaphor originally referred to the use of words when the meaning of a given word was extended to something else that it resembled. For example, the sounds represented by the letters t-u-r-k-e-y serve as an abstract symbol for a kind of edible bird popular in America at Thanksgiving. Because the bird is widely considered to be rather stupid, the term has assumed an iconic meaning when referring to a human being, indicating someone who is not viewed as very bright. The sounds are an abstract symbol for the bird; the bird, in turn, is seen as an icon for stupidity, so that when applied to a person the two symbols together become a metaphor. Strictly speaking, metaphor includes the idea of beyond (meta-) the bearer (-phore) of meaning. When the term "metaphor" is used to refer to music rather than language, the absence of the link between a word and its original meaning is often overlooked, so that some references to music as a metaphor would be more accurately described as analogy. One rea-

5.3. A Kaluli man dancing in the *gisaro* ceremony, central Papua New Guinea. (Photo by Shari Robertson; used by permission.)

son the phoenix bird imitation occurs frequently in Chinese music is that it represents more than simply a bird, as indicated by its sound. To the Chinese, this mythical bird represents the greatest of birds, since it dominates the southern part of the heavens and symbolizes the sun and warmth (Morgan 1942:8). The relation of the sound to a bird is imitation; the parallel characteristic of a phoenix bird representing the ruler of the south is a meaning commonly known in Chinese society. The two meanings together create a metaphor—the sound of the bird symbolizing the warmth of the sun.

Music as a type of metaphor linked to a people's world view is further exemplified by the Kaluli of New Guinea. The Kaluli believe that when they die their spirits go to live in birds, so that birds are considered "spirit reflections" of the dead. For this reason people do not hunt birds near their longhouses. When birds sing, it is considered the voices of the dead speaking to the people. Several species of doves have calls with a descending pitch pattern, and this pattern serves as a basis for much Kaluli song. Central to this metaphor is a myth concerning a boy who became a *muni* bird. The boy was refused food when he requested some from his older sister. Because food sharing and reciprocity are highly valued by the Kaluli, the boy felt abandoned and he turned into a bird. The song of the *muni* bird has become the basis of the most important and moving song form among the Kaluli, the *gisaro* (Photo 5.3). A descending note pattern

is used in weeping, frequently with words added at the third note. As the text becomes more elaborate the weeping becomes song. This kind of song becomes very moving as a metaphor because it re- sembles the sound of the *muni* bird, which recalls a story of failure of sharing and reciprocity. By inserting the names of known people and places, the singer can make a reference to specific dead loved ones, as if the birds/loved ones were speaking (Feld 1982; Schieffelin 1976).

Music as Aesthetic

In earlier chapters of this book, references to aesthetic factors in music have assumed a common understanding on the part of the reader as to what aesthetic is. It is now time to deal with the term more explicitly. Whereas the symbolic meanings of music involve its reference to other aspects of experience, those meanings termed aesthetic, absolute, or nonreferential are found in the music itself without reference to other features of experience. Although music is not always considered an aesthetic experience, the nature of its meaning cannot be fully understood without taking potential aes- thetic qualities into account. The study of aesthetic phenomena, called aesthetics, is properly a branch of philosophy, whose major purpose is to provide a basis for evaluation. Although the Western aesthetic has long been concerned with concepts of beauty, it has more recently developed into a treatment of the overall value given to the "fine arts." Thus, the term "aesthetic" today often refers to the general value given to the music legitimated by the elite, includ- ing symbolic or pragmatic values not necessarily associated with aspects of beauty. In this book, aesthetic is used in terms of its ear- lier and narrower meaning related to beauty.

When one wants to discover how people in other societies value their music, one cannot assume that its value is limited to the sym- bolic and pragmatic, since aesthetic features are often considered very important. For example, the aesthetic of a musician in India is described as "his set of values about music itself" (Neuman 1990:80). The holistic approach to music includes interest in the extent to which aesthetic qualities are relevant to the meaning of music in societies outside of Western civilization. Such aesthetic apprecia- tion may be, and often is, an expression of practical consciousness that needs to be empirically determined. In such research, aesthetic must be defined in a specific way that may differ from the definition of Western philosophy. Because aesthetics originally consisted of discourse concerning the nature of beauty, many cross-cultural researchers have tried to discover in non-Western societies a cluster of concepts that more or less cover the meanings of the word "beauty." Such efforts have been inconclusive since many societies lack a word with a similar range of meanings. In a paper on aesthetics in anthropology, Warren L. d'Azevedo defined the aesthetic as "the qualitative feature of the event involving the enhancement of experience and the present enjoyment of the intrinsic qualities of things" (1958: 706). This view of aesthetic provides a framework that includes the Western concept of beautiful, but also allows for the fact that other societies might appreciate other kinds of intrinsic qualities. D'Azevedo's definition explicitly excludes those symbolic or pragmatic meanings in music that are related to nonmusical experience.

Intrinsic qualities in music include features such as tone quality, rhythmic patterns, or melodies that are appreciated for their own sake. The intrinsic qualities are similar to what is commonly termed "style," defined as the observable nature of the medium. A style, however, is often simply a way of identifying music, and it may have symbolic or pragmatic meanings attached to it. The major aesthetic issue is whether a style is valued for the intrinsic qualities that it contains, rather than for its effectiveness as a symbol of some nonmusical relationship.

The distinction between aesthetic and symbolic meanings is seen in the varying reactions to the performances of different *anzad* players among the Tuareg. One performer, Ajo (Photo 5.4), was most highly praised.

> When asked why they thought her playing was superior to the others, they replied with such comments as, "Her playing has soul," "It has taste," or "It is like food with salt," implying that it contains an ingredient lacking in the others. Some commented also on her extensive repertoire and the clarity of her tone. All agreed that she has good technique, though not necessarily the best, and that technique alone, while important, is not the sole requisite for superior playing. Observation of my informants as they listened revealed that certain points in her music were particularly affective, notably passages with prolonged emphasis on the augmented fourth above the "tonic," or lowest and final pitch of the composition. During such a passage in "Chizabaten" [a particular song] . . . the listeners invariably sucked in their breath, threw back their heads, and released sighs of ecstatic pleasure.

5.4. A Tuareg woman, Ajo, playing the *anzad*, Agadez, Niger, 1977. (Photo by Caroline Card Wendt; used by permission.)

. . . Observation of Ajo in performance indicated that she is well aware of the effect of this device on her listeners and that she exploits it to the fullest extent. In doing so she does not break with tradition, but she utilizes the musical materials of her culture knowingly and skillfully. (Card 1982:88)

This case of enjoyment of the intrinsic quality of the music contrasts with other listeners who reacted to Ajo's style in terms of symbolic meaning. Since Ajo's style was modern, a young noble preferred another performer who used an older style. For him the old music represented the old way of life which he yearned for. Another *anzad* player did not like Ajo's playing because Ajo played like vassal women (who make a large sound), rather than like the noble women (who make a "light and delicate tone") (Card 1982:90). Reaction to the augmented fourth was aesthetic, involving appreciation of a feature of the intrinsic quality of the music. Reaction to the music in terms of yearnings or class distinctions comes from symbolic relationships of the music to various life experiences. When musical values like these have nothing to do with the intrinsic qualities in the music, it is confusing to refer to them as aesthetic. The young people of Macedonia, for example, "deal most often with what is 'in' rather than with what is beautiful and why" (N. Sachs 1975:276). What is "in" represents a value, but not an aesthetic value.

Establishing the basis of aesthetic response in other societies presents significant problems. Determining how much societies value the intrinsic qualities of music involves more than finding out what people say about them. The distinction between aesthetic discourse and aesthetic practice should serve as a reminder that while musical discourse is a characteristic of the Western world, many other societies may engage in complex and satisfying musical activities and scarcely talk about them at all. Aesthetic types of creativity and response may be entirely a feature of practical consciousness, indicating that they operate even though the researcher might not be told about them. Because many societies have not produced discourse regarding their musical values, it is incorrect to assume that the intrinsic qualities of music fail to produce affective responses simply because people are not talking or writing about them.

Certain clues often help the researcher discover the value system operating in a society. The fact that a rendition of music is marked as a performance indicates that the musical material being presented probably contains highly valued features. Although the value given such a performance might be due to qualities more closely related to symbolic or pragmatic uses of the music, it is also possible that something in the sounds themselves is also valued. The value given to various intrinsic qualities of music can sometimes be revealed as people discuss the relative merits of various musicians. This represents one of the important roles of the critic in understanding the musical value systems of different societies.

One problem in the cross-cultural study of musical aesthetics stems from the fact that researchers tend to begin with the Western idea of aesthetic qualities. These criteria include psychic distance, nonutilitarian goals, the presence of affect, and elements of design. It is not at all clear how much, if at all, these features relate to non-Western musical systems, but data from different places provide some indications. The first two of these need merely to be mentioned, but the last two are of major importance.

The element of "psychic or psychical distance" (Merriam 1964: 261) or contemplation may be more a feature of aesthetic discourse than of aesthetic experience. This type of behavior is essentially a matter of taking the time to note and enjoy the intrinsic qualities of things while the everyday commonplace meanings are minimized. Such behavior is not limited to Western society. For example, in the

Ekine masquerade dances among the Kalabari people in West Africa the performers wear masks so that instead of reacting to their fellow villagers, the audience may give their attention to the quality of the performance (Horton 1973:616–617).

Music often has utilitarian goals, but even so it is possible to add nonutilitarian elements. In the visual arts, aesthetic features of the artifact are considered those not necessary for the utilitarian purpose of the product. Such features are easier to perceive in relation to a water pot or basket than to a ritual dance. As will be seen in the next chapter, many societies perform music in order to influence spirits, display prestige, or achieve innumerable other goals. Qualities of a musical rendition that are over and above what is required for achieving its purpose might be considered aesthetic qualities. These qualities are very difficult to define, and even more difficult to quantify. Nevertheless, the addition of variations and increased intensity in a musical performance can serve as an indication that appreciation of intrinsic qualities is present even if people do not verbalize it.

Values and Affect

Another important feature of Western aesthetic philosophy is that the aesthetic experience causes an emotional or affective reaction. Such reactions are included in what d'Azevedo called the "enhancement of experience" (1958:706). In actuality, affect in music is related to its symbolic and pragmatic meanings as well as its intrinsic qualities. Symbolic meanings often depict valued things, which is particularly true when music is used for pragmatic purposes. When music is used in rituals for curing the sick or ensuring good crops, the emotions connected with success or failure in those enterprises are transferred to the music. From this perspective, emotion in music concerns the ways that music symbolizes whatever is highly valued, so that some of the analogical meanings relating music to the nature of society or of life in general can lead to heightened affect. Aesthetic types of affect are due to awareness of highly valued qualities intrinsic in the music. The same performance of music often has several concurrent meanings, some of which may be connected with the intrinsic quality of the music, while others are symbolic.

Questions of value are important to human affective responses because we tend to feel emotional about anything we value—particularly when it is achieved or denied. Many of the things we value are determined by society, so whatever we feel emotional about is closely related to our society's legitimized values. "Beauty"

5.5. Close-up of the buzzers on a xylophone from Ghana. (Instrument in William Hammond Mathers Museum, Bloomington, Indiana; photo by the author.)

has even been defined as that which elicits affect due to the achievement of valued goals determined by society (Newcomer 1979:225). Although the intrinsic qualities of music may result in affect due to basic human psychology, most of the affective features of music are determined within the sociocultural system. This difference in values is shown by the ideals of art in East Asia compared with Western civilization.

> The West believes in the personality. The East believes in the
> school. A work of art is evaluated in the West by its degree of
> independence and originality; in the East as a perfect specimen
> of a type. (Harich-Schneider 1973:547)

The intrinsic qualities of music that induce affect in some societies differ from those common in the Western world. For example, many societies value extraneous sounds that Westerners would call noise. Many groups in Africa carefully incorporate a buzzing sound into their music by attaching rattles or vibrating membranes to their traditional musical instruments (Photo 5.5). The buzzing is considered to intensify and prolong the sound, and the music is not emotionally satisfying without it. The Japanese value noise mixed with pure tone as a desirable intrinsic quality. Thus, the *shakuhachi* player often produces breathy sounds along with the pure flute tone (see Photo 5.1) (Kishibe 1984:80).

Another example of extraneous sounds is provided by the Suya of Brazil. They value musical performances that lead to a state of euphoria (*kin*), a kind of "high" (A. Seeger 1987:129). Since performances were staged with an emphasis on expressing social relationships, full participation was a key element leading to euphoria. "When everyone participated in a way appropriate to sex and age, the performance was beautiful and people were euphoric. When many remained silent or did not appear, it was considered ugly and emotionless" (ibid.:131). Seeger discovered that the full effect of Suya songs was not felt without the "shouts, cries, weeping, and animal sounds" that we consider extraneous to music (ibid.:77). The major value was social participation, but it was sensed through additions to the totality of sound.

The values given to intrinsic qualities of music are not limited to variations between societies or different ethnic groups. The taste publics characterizing high culture and popular culture in complex societies often value quite different features of music. Another significant difference in values exists between the **creator orientation** and the **user orientation** (Gans 1974:25). The creator orientation is the frame of mind of people who have the knowledge and practice to produce or create music or other forms of expressive culture. The user orientation characterizes those who enjoy the products and performances of expressive culture, but have little or no knowledge of how to produce them. This difference is indicated by a reference to performers in modern bands in northern India:

> As occurs with jazz and other instrumental music in the United States, those who are most aware and appreciative of proficiency and creativity are the bandsmen themselves. Often their artistry serves mostly to allay their own boredom; most listeners are aware only of the music's gross and spectacular features. (Henry 1988:223)

The difference between the creator orientation and the user orientation exists in most, if not all, societies. Whereas the high culture–popular culture distinction is irrelevant in nonstratified societies, the difference between creator orientation and user orientation is still significant. Applying this distinction to music, the musician as creator understands the problems of creating, and finds creativity interesting and exciting when those problems are solved well. Musicians can also apply their criteria to performances by other people. The user orientation characterizes the audience or consumer of music, who may be unaware of the thought and skill that go into the creative process, and may appreciate the lyrics and danceability of the music more than the creators do. This distinction is not clear-cut, since many people who are basically users may learn enough of the creative process to be able to understand and appreciate it. This is the purpose of such things as music appreciation courses.

> Music education in India is oriented toward teaching young men and women the rudiments of theory and practice so as to make them informed and sympathetic listeners, and in some cases teachers. (Neuman 1990:199)

Many creators also understand the perspective of the user, and create with the latter's values in mind. Even when most of the music in a society is communal, some people are still more talented and more interested in musical performance than are others. They are the ones who will tend to have increased affective reaction to various intrinsic qualities of the music.

The difference in these perspectives was apparent in relation to the mbira music of the Shona. Those who played regularly knew many different songs and many versions of each song. They could skillfully improvise variations over an extended period of time. They could discuss the relative merits of various players in terms of what they were doing musically. The users, who usually simply danced to mbira music, were unable to discuss the music itself, and the evaluation of various musicians was based on kinship or religious matters. The user orientation included those who were very impressed with the amateurish performance of the outside observer because they were unaware of the skill the great players required for their complex music.

In nonstratified small-scale societies the creator and user orientation may represent the only distinct difference in musical values within the group, but in stratified societies the different strata are likely to have differing values regarding many aspects of expressive culture, including music. Thus, the enjoyment of intrinsic qualities found in elite music, folk music, and popular music will differ among various taste publics. Music that has been legitimized by the elite is more likely to include a form of notation, a background of philosophical or discursive pronouncements, and some form of restriction on who can become a practitioner. Music that has not been legitimized as an elite type will nevertheless have intrinsic qualities that are enjoyed by creators and users of the various taste publics.

Differing values are seen in performance criteria. In Western music, producing the correct pitch is of utmost importance, and variations in rhythm are commonplace. In Africa the correct pitch is of much less concern than maintaining the rhythm without pause or break. Many musicians are concerned with producing the right timbre or tone quality, but societies differ as to what is considered correct. The differences in vocal tone between the pinched singing of Asia and the open singing of Europe and Africa is a good example of differing values concerning intrinsic qualities.

Sonic Design and Affect

In Western aesthetics, structure, or design, is considered a most important intrinsic quality. In all music, the meaning of one musical tone depends upon the tones around it, all of them becoming music only as they are somehow mentally related to each other. Thus sonic order is distinguished from noise. The intrinsic quality of music that is so important in Western aesthetics is **sonic design,** the deliberate arrangement of sounds to produce pleasing patterns. In other words, reference to sonic design serves to distinguish this creative element from the basic structural feature of all music, sonic order. One object of research in the study of world music systems is to discover the value given to sonic design in other societies in order to determine if the Western view represents universal human behavior or if it is culturally determined. The naive view assumes that matters of musical design are valued everywhere; the positivist view tends to assume that if people do not talk about sonic design, then it is of no value to them.

Several features of musical life indicate that appreciation of sonic design is indeed widespread. Some non-Western groups show an awareness of and positive value attached to features of musical design. The Kaluli, with their metaphor of singing and birds, place high value on moving people to tears through performances. Since their songs are based on social abandonment and death, this is not surprising, particularly when song imitations represent the birds as deceased loved ones speaking to the living. The anticipation and expectation involved in the performance context also contribute to affect (Feld 1982 : 180–81). However, it is not only the associations with the music that provide affect. The Kaluli "lift-up-over-sounding" (Feld 1988 : 76) referred to earlier is clearly a reference to quality of the sound patterns themselves. The Kaluli have also conceptualized the process of building "an aesthetic tension." They call it *halaido domeki* or "hardening" of a song (Feld 1982 : 36). The text of the song is "hardened" by increasing strength in the imagery of the text, particularly the verbs. Musical features are also "hardened," as in the growing intensity of the voice, the addition of a chorus, and the skill with which the singer improvises variations. In discussing Kaluli responses to a recording he had made of a performance of the sung weeping type of lament characteristic of *gisaro,* Feld noted that:

> Kaluli found its construction controlled, deliberate, crafted, and almost composed like song. Yet its delivery was spontaneous and improvised in immediate response to grief. It was this sense of an ability to articulate deeply felt sentiments within the constraints of an improvised form that Kaluli found so forceful and often led them to request its playback. (1982 : 129)

One feature of sonic design that may have a strong cross-cultural validity is the balance of unity and variety. Music that lacks unity and has too much variety is difficult to perceive as pattern, and is likely to be considered noise. Music with too much unity and not enough variety is likely to be boring, and not be used unless it has significant nonmusical meaning to assure its importance.

The drum dance songs of the Inuit have an interesting form that judiciously mixes variety and unity. Each stanza of a song begins and ends with a relatively free type of textual and rhythmic structure. In the middle of the stanza a chant is usually performed, which has a fixed text and a much stricter rhythm. Beverly Cavanagh notes that the shift from one section to the other has a strong aesthetic effect (1982 : 131). It is not quite clear from her writing whether this is her own reaction or whether it is recognized by the Inuit. Even though the Inuit may not recognize this feature verbally, it is interesting that although they have become westernized and have accepted many forms of Western music, the drum dance songs are still popular.

In Western societies the link between musical structure and the concept of musical aesthetics is related in part to the connection between music and mathematics that has existed since ancient Greek civilization. Both scales and rhythms were standardized in terms of neat mathematical relationships. Today we might look upon this concern with mathematics as an ancient attempt to seek legitimacy for musicians. Aesthetic music today is often considered to be more complex and require more training and skill on the part of performers and listeners than is required for other types of music, perhaps indicating the norms of the elite as they legitimize certain types of music. Discourse concerning structural values due to the prevalence of patronage is perhaps an important factor in leading to the Western aesthetic appreciation of features of musical structure as sonic design.

Although many of the affective qualities of music are based on culturally determined values, it is possible that some affective reactions result from the operation of universal human cognitive and affective processes. Some of the cross-cultural research in music involves searching for possible universal affective responses to intrinsic qualities of music. One useful theory of emotion in music has been developed by Leonard B. Meyer, in his book *Emotion and Meaning in Music* (1956).[4] His theory concerns affective reaction to the nature of the musical sound itself, without consideration of referents outside the music. According to his **theory of expectations**, affect is caused as a music performance progresses and the listeners experience uncertainty, particularly where the music fails to conform to what the listeners have learned to expect. The resolution of the uncertainty produces an affective reaction. As Meyer recognizes, this response to intrinsic features of music is not the only way in which music creates affect, but he considers it the most significant.

Meyer's theory is based on several features of the human mind. One of them is the propensity of humans to create structures and patterns from their experience. Humans have difficulty dealing with chaos, and actively seek to avoid it by creating organization. As infants grow, they develop mental images of the way things are in the world, including the norms of the musical style system they hear performed around them. Since perception and memory are not perfect, the mental models of a musical style tend to simplify the music, providing elements of continuity and completeness which are not necessarily present in the music. In performing and hearing music, the individual finds that the music is ambiguous, takes surprising turns, or generally fails to conform to the ideal mental models. When faced with uncertainty and frustrated tendencies, the natural human reaction is heightened emotion. Meyer points out that emotion is a generalized physiological state, and the differentiation of various kinds of emotion is dependent upon the nature of the stimuli. What makes music elicit a pleasurable emotion is the belief that the uncertainty is under control and will be successfully resolved. In music, such control is assumed when the musicians are competent; even incompetent musicians do not nullify the possibility of control, because experience has shown that control is possible.

From the perspective of the holistic approach to music, Meyer's theory is especially significant because it takes into account music traditions other than that of the West. Although Meyer's examples are mostly from Western art music, he is careful to show how his theory is applicable to other types of music. He speaks of melodic ornamentation in Asia as interrupting the continuity of the basic structures of the music. Traditions where improvisation is important emphasize the discontinuity and ambiguity inherent in creative variation. Meyer (1956: 236–239) cites ways in which the ensemble players of India vie with each other in appearing to abandon the basic raga and tala, and then eventually return to them in triumph.

This theory is also significant because it is not limited to the intellectual approach to music that characterizes many aesthetic pronouncements within the Western philosophy of music. Meyer maintains that affect resulting from delayed fulfillment or modification of expectations operates on an unconscious level, or what later terminology would call the practical consciousness. He distinguishes this affective level from the creator's orientation that involves the recognition of deviations from a stylistic norm and consequent appreciation of the skill with which problems of musical structuring are resolved. The question has often been raised about the aesthetic reactions of people in nonstratified and nonliterate societies with no tradition of intellectualizing about music (see Merriam 1964:260ff). The theory of expectation provides a basis for explaining emotional reaction to musical structures, even in those cases where no discourse about music structures exists.

Meyer specifically draws parallels between the course of life and the course of a musical performance. "Musical experiences of suspense are very similar to those experienced in real life" (1956:28). Although the process of affective response is based primarily upon suspense, it is highly possible that the analogical resemblance to life can add unconsciously to the emotional impact of a musical performance. Although much musical meaning requires enough perception of the sounds so that the hearer recognizes the identity of specific pieces, Meyer's work indicates that music can also carry meaning without involving perception of the details of the music.

The operation of expectations is seen in other societies.

Through years of playing or listening the gamelan audience in Java has come to associate certain melodic patterns, certain sequences of sound, with particular *pathet* [modal sequences]. The fulfillment of those expectations is part of the pleasure of listening to the music. A slight deviation from expectations may actually enhance the pleasure, but a radical departure from the norms of *pathet* will be likely to annoy the listener and interfere with his enjoyment. (Becker 1980:99)

Expectations play a part in musical humor. If the resolution of expectations is completely incongruous, the result is perceived as funny. The Blackfoot create humorous performances by mixing Indian and Western styles, so that expectations are met with incongruity (Nettl 1989:107–108). Distorted expectations form the basis of much of the work of Peter Schickele and his P.D.Q. Bach. In his performance of the *1712 Overture*, for example, one of the key humorous elements is using the French national anthem, as heard in Tchaikovsky's *1812 Overture*, and blending it with "Pop Goes the Weasel." Other forms of musical humor play with expectations by presenting unusually inept performances of well-known pieces.

Expectations and their resolution are related to the aesthetic idea of tension and release operating through a musical performance. Although different societies have various ways of creating tension and resolving it, the basic process is very similar to what Meyer has described.

The expectations created by some degree of musical consistency make it appear that sonic design is indeed important, and that the importance is not limited to "serious" or "art" music. Since the latter term often refers to the music of the elite establishment of professional musicians, another term is needed for music that may have solid qualities of sonic design, be the music tribal, folk, professional, or popular. Referring to such music as aesthetic avoids the association of musical terminology with elitism.

Another possible universal source of affect is the result of collaboration as interpersonal relationships develop through the act of performing music together. As long as a musical performance involves more than one person, some sort of coordination is required, and the resulting collaboration often results in strong emotional ties. One of the paradoxes in human life is the conflict between the desires of the individual and the good of the group. In most musical performances one is required to sublimate one's personal autonomy to the requirements of the group, which may account for the close social ties that develop. This aspect of musical performance has been noted in India: "Group singing and dancing are unique in the repertoire of human behavior in the way they join individuals in social relation through individual, psycho-physiological gratification" (Henry 1988:116). In many Indian villages much group singing, especially among the women, involves people of different castes and serves to overcome the caste barriers (ibid.:107). The effects of collaboration are not an analogy, but they represent a case of meaningful mental association resulting from a natural phenomenon. In terms of semiotic theory (Peirce 1960) this type of connection provides a rare example of an index operating in musical meaning.

Skill

Skill in creating and performing music does not play a large part in the Western discourse on aesthetics,[5] but it appears to be highly valued in many societies, perhaps universally. Appreciation of the possibilities of human achievement as seen in the skills of one's fellows often leads to heightened affect. The appreciation of skillfulness in musicians and other performers is found consistently throughout the literature on world musics. In the eighteenth century the predominant meaning of "art" was "skill" (Clifford 1988:233), and the word art can still refer to the skill shown by athletes and circus performers. Skill in music is often noted as showing off, for example, in such practices as dancing while playing a difficult instrument, playing interludes of particularly complex drumming patterns, or performing virtuosic feats on other instruments. It has been suggested that part of the appreciation of skill is that the expert performer is assuming the risk of looking foolish if the performance does not proceed as intended. It is a way of laying one's ego on the line (Herndon and McLeod 1979:90–91).

Skill is valued among the Tuareg. Players of the *tahardent* lute (Photo 5.6; Ex. 5.1) perform numerous variations of the pattern of twelve rhythmic pulses, especially in the instrumental interludes between verses.

They make much use of hemiola, transforming duple divisions into ternary and ternary into duple. The basic pattern is temporarily obscured by these hemiolic permutations, which create the effect of a suspension of metric values. Skills of this sort are among the more important criteria that establish a performer's reputation. (Card 1982:169)

The creator orientation often leads one to appreciate not only the skill of the performer who recreates music, but also how musical structures are manipulated in a gratifying way. In the Western world a person familiar with the creator orientation knows the criteria of

5.6. Hattaye eg Muhammed playing the *tahardent*, Agadez, Niger, 1977. (Photo by Caroline Card Wendt; used by permission.)

a good fugue or sonata form, and appreciates the techniques a composer has used to create such forms in their compositions. In improvisational traditions such as jazz the audience appreciates not only the skill in handling the instrument or the voice itself, but also how the sounds are related to the underlying structures. In all these cases the skill is often perceived as the ability to work creatively within a set of restrictions (Devereux 1971 : 194). Although the affective reaction to it may be universal, skill can often only be recognized within the framework of specific musical traditions. It is conceivable that showing appreciation of skill is simply another way of expressing pleasure at some of the intrinsic qualities that the skillful musician imparts to a performance.

When skill is recognized in a particular performance, the reaction to it is expressed in different socially determined ways. Steven Feld emphasizes the depth of emotion as he surveys the aesthetics of the Kaluli. Among the Kaluli a good singer is said to have a voice like a bird. When the singing at ceremonies moves the hosts to tears they take up firebrands and burn the backs of the dancers as a type of response to an affective situation (1982:6). In Buddhist music the voice of a good singer "shimmers like the sound of stone and metal" (Harich-Schneider 1973 : 308). The skillful player of the Shona mbira is said to sound as if several people were playing.

Conclusion

A close relationship exists between music as an aesthetic form and the social legitimacy of music as described in Chapter 3. Elite music circles tend to regard all music they have legitimized as somehow aesthetic and therefore aesthetically motivated. Distinguishing between legitimate music and aesthetic music raises the possibility that legitimacy and aesthetic quality are not necessarily the same, and that the music legitimized in a society might lack aesthetic qualities. Many people feel that highly experimental forms of "serious" music lack aesthetic qualities, even though they are innovative and expressive of the composer's feelings. Conversely, music that has not been legitimized by the elite might still be found to contain intrinsic qualities that are highly valued by many people. Thus, it is possible to look for aesthetic features in music—such as folk song, rock, and various forms of popular music, including rap—that is not necessarily legitimized by the elite in our own society. The same might be true for non-Western, nonstratified societies that have no overt concepts about aesthetic qualities, but might utilize them in their practical consciousness. This possibility should remove any reservations about looking for aesthetic qualities in the music of small-scale societies, even though those societies may have no concept of "beauty" or of "art" music.[6]

While legitimacy is a social phenomenon, aesthetic is primarily a quality of the music itself. Some societies legitimize certain music because it is thought to influence powerful spirits; other societies legitimize certain forms of music because they are profitable or prestigious. Thus, legitimacy can exist independently of aesthetic intrinsic qualities. One reason legitimate music might sometimes lack aesthetic qualities is that the rewards of recognition and financial success are given to those who operate within the social milieu of the legitimate form, even though factors other than aesthetic quality can determine success. Decisions about funding performances and publication can be made by people who act from nonmusical motivations or even lack musical understanding, but have money or other rewards at their disposal. This feature of the world of "fine arts" should make consumers aware of the possibility that some of the music produced in the "music establishment" may not be aesthetic. It is also important to recognize that high aesthetic achievement can go unrecorded and unrecognized if an individual's efforts lie outside the legitimate channels. A player on the musical saw can conceivably produce a performance that displays considerable aesthetic qualities, perhaps more than many performers of legitimate instruments, but the former will not receive commensurate recognition or rewards.

One test of the intrinsic qualities of music concerns the factor of time. The fact that music is performed long after it is new, even after its creators are dead, is a good indication that it is valued. Whether the values are symbolic, pragmatic, or aesthetic still remains in question. What frequently happens with a musical style is that highly skilled musicians add complexity to performances in what was originally a rather simple style. Jazz and rock, for example, both began in unsophisticated ways and developed from within until intrinsic qualities in the music became recognized and highly valued. This process can be limited, however, in societies that restrict musical variability.

The relationship between legitimate music and aesthetic music raises other theoretical questions. Does the fact that some music has been legitimized and its practitioners often have considerably more time at their disposal actually result in more aesthetically satisfying music? Is it really the actual structures of music that trained lovers of Western art music value so highly? Or is it the skill with which composers have solved problems of creating music under the restrictions imposed by the socially accepted criteria of good music? Is it possible that the aesthetic values in modern society are determined by commercialization and advertising more than anything else?

A related question concerning non-Western societies is whether the people practicing a particular musical tradition actually value the intricacies and nuances that musicological analysis can discover. Although the Kaluli, the Suya, and different subgroups of Western civilization have different values concerning what they appreciate in a musical performance, the fulfillment of those values is an important factor in providing music with its affective power. Probably the best conclusion that can be reached with the present state of knowledge is that sonic design is often a highly valued intrinsic quality of music, but it is not necessarily important everywhere. The values given to various types of music are determined by each society.

The aesthetic, as enjoyment of intrinsic qualities, is very different from emotional impact. Any type of meaning, whether symbolic, pragmatic, or aesthetic, can bring about emotional responses. Consequently, particular performances of music can be highly affective even though they may lack valued intrinsic qualities within the music itself. High culture and popular culture often show differences in the music appreciated by their taste publics. In both cases, however, it is possible that people with the creator orientation are likely to develop valued intrinsic qualities in their music.

The question of aesthetics looms large in the study of music because of interest in knowing whether universal aspects of aesthetics and musical affect exist and whether they can be discovered. This question is far from being satisfactorily answered. Evidence has indicated a few possibilities, however. One of these is the appreciation of high degrees of skill. A balance of unity and variety is another possibility. Tension and release are often considered a universal feature of music, and they appear to be closely related to the expectations and their resolutions, as suggested by Meyer. If universal features of musical meaning are to be found anywhere, they are most likely to be in the appreciation of skill, the development and manipulation of expectations, and the ubiquity of balancing unity and variety.

It has often been asserted that nonstratified societies have music that is "functional," whereas the stratified literate societies have music that is appreciated for its own sake. The pragmatic meaning given to music through its "function" in society provides essentially referential meaning. Among musically trained individuals in Western societies, the structural meaning of music is valued in the discursive consciousness. The structural meaning of music as emotional in the sense Meyer has described can apply to musically untrained individuals in our society as well as to members of societies that do not overtly teach the elements of musical structure. In other words, the emotional impact of musical structure, if Meyer is correct, can be a feature of musical meaning even in societies where value of music is expressed largely in terms of its use or function in the society.

CHAPTER SIX

Uses and Functions of Music

IT WAS MID-DECEMBER and the chapel was not well heated. Although rather small, it was elaborately ornamented. As people slowly arrived, the pews were completely filled, as were the chairs situated in odd corners of the room. Soon more people entered and remained standing in the center aisle until it, too, was full. Some of them appeared to be college students with traveling clothes and backpacks. The priests eventually entered and began conducting the Mass. Were it not for the fact that the chapel was in the palace of the former emperors of the Austro-Hungarian Empire, and that the featured singers were the Vienna Boys' Choir, the occasion might have been a typical Christmas Mass anywhere. The situation as it actually was, however, tended to raise questions about whether it was a Christian ritual, a tourist attraction, or a concert. Perhaps it had elements of all three.

This event indicates the essence of the issue of use and function of music. Why do people organize and conduct musical events? Why do people attend them? Do people's reasons have anything to do with the outcome? In the previous chapter, meaning was considered as the ways music and musical events impress themselves on people's attention and feelings. Meaning and use share the common characteristic of being the individual's subjective view of experience. Meaning essentially refers to a person's reaction to a musical event as it is experienced or remembered; use is the way meanings are incorporated into planning and realizing a musical event. The meanings people give to music are a part of their motivations; the creation of musical performances and musical sounds results from these motivations. This chapter emphasizes how musical meaning is transformed into individual and social action, and the consequences of that action in society. The issue of use and function concerns the sources of these motivations and whether or not they are satisfied.

The motivations and goals of the participant constitute the use of music. Whether or not the goals are realized is a matter of function.

In considering this issue, the distinction between the participants and the outside observer is especially significant. While the concerns of the participant are regulated by the dynamics of a specific case, the observer's motivations include a special kind of interest in the general consequences of musical behavior. Where the participants anticipate a musical event for what they hope to obtain from it, the observers are interested in viewing a musical event in retrospect to see what the results were or what effect it had on the situation. Many times the outside observer can infer intentions from noting the consequences. Whereas the participant's interest is individual and particular, the outside observer's interest is universal, to be achieved through study of the motivations in a variety of societies.

Music and Its Functions

The functionalist approach described in Chapter 1 was important in emphasizing the impact on human life of all aspects of culturally determined behavior. Since the development of this approach, the idea of social function has become widely accepted in Western thought. It has been necessary, however, to modify some of the earlier theories. The sociologist Robert Merton suggested that the school of functionalism had oversimplified the idea of function, and he made an important distinction between subjective dispositions and objective consequences (1949:27). He saw **subjective dispositions** as the personal motivations or feelings that lead people to certain behaviors. Merton limited the term function to the **objective consequences,** which he considered to be the results of behavior. Such consequences or functions were noted by an observer or inferred through analysis. Merton pointed out that some consequences are recognized and anticipated (manifest functions) while others are completely unknown or perhaps vaguely recognized (latent functions). In other words, manifest functions appear as discursive consciousness and latent functions as practical consciousness. Because Merton's major concern was function, he did not develop the idea of subjective dispositions. They refer to what are now called human drives or motivations.

The functions of most features of culture vary considerably, and many times several types of function are operating at once. The term **multifunctional** is used to indicate that the same performance, the same event, or the same music complex can serve a variety of functions. The multiple functions of music are exemplified by Blacking's interpretation of the *bepha* musical expeditions of the Venda of South Africa. These expeditions involve groups of singers and dancers who go from one chief's headquarters to another to perform traditional dances. One ruler will send an expedition to another ruler for any of several reasons. For example, performers are sent to express sympathy for the death of a member of the host's lineage. Another reason is related to the requirement that the host should kill a beast and feed the visiting performers. When the teams go to a subordinate headman, he is expected to send another beast to the chief, so that the performing team serves as a means of exacting tribute. Possibly not realized by the performers is the fact that when the members of the team go to a district that is far from their homes, they develop strong social bonds with each other through being outsiders together, eating special meat together, and performing music together.

> The pleasures of these associations . . . are enough to ensure that every ruler has a loyal and enthusiastic band of young ambassadors who can represent his interests, and in doing so grow used to the idea that these interests are of paramount importance in the district. In this way, the institution of *bepha* reinforces the solidarity of the rulers and their families, and their right to rule. (Blacking 1965:35)

The actual practice of sending the performers had a number of different functions, or consequences. The chiefs were aware of certain manifest functions, or purposes, for the various occasions when they sent out a group of dancers. The reasons given by the chiefs were not necessarily shared by the members of the groups, who were enjoying dancing and feasting. Probably none of the participants recognized that the practice of sending dance groups served the latent function of helping maintain the positions of the rulers.

Early functionalists emphasized how features of the sociocultural system function to maintain social harmony, an idea that has become widespread in Western thought. This early focus on social function may have distorted some of the findings in anthropological studies about music. Since the functionalist approach provided easy explanations of human activity in terms of social cohesion, it created a tendency to overlook other possible explanations. This tendency was particularly noticeable in relation to music. However, Robin Horton has provided an interesting case in which the function of a musical event appears to be related to religion and social status, yet he maintains that the event is basically an aesthetic experience. Horton analyzed the Ekine masquerade plays of the Kalabari people of Nigeria, which focus on dancing and involve costumes, masks, and drumming. The drums are important because their rhythms support the dancers, they symbolize particular spirits, and they provide the means by which people identify a particular play, "for every masquerade has its own characteristic set of drum-rhythms, beaten on a characteristic combination of drums" (1973:606).

Horton notes five functions or uses for the dances. The first is ostensibly religious, since origin myths relate the masquerades to a large variety of water spirits. Other functions involve recreation, the development of status symbols, and certain forms of governmental activity. He contrasts those functions with the aesthetic function, concluding that in this case art is not serving religion, as the functional approach assumes, but that religion is serving to validate or legitimize the art (1973:626).

Several factors in the performances indicate that the focus is not on the spirits but on the art itself, in spite of the superficial religious connection. In the ritual that precedes the plays, prayers are focused on the success of the performance rather than on general well-being of the community, as is the case with other rituals. Leadership in the social organization of the plays is based on the skill shown by the performers, rather than being based on an individual's status in the community. Whereas the performers for the Ekine dances rehearse, it is not customary for leaders of rituals to do so (ibid.:602–603).

Horton suggests that the general orientation of anthropologists to social function could very well lead them to define aesthetic performances in terms of social function simply because that is what they were looking for and expecting to find. The fact that a social function *can* be found for an art like the Ekine should not cause the researcher to ignore the possibility that other purposes and functions may exist and even surpass the social functions in importance. Horton says that the masquerade and the religious facade foster an aesthetic reaction to the performances because the audience is thus enabled to view the performers as something other than their relatives and friends.

Horton's work indicates that functionalism has not provided all the answers that its early proponents anticipated; nevertheless, it is a very useful and important concept which should be enlarged rather than thrown out. A widely used interpretation of the term function sees it as the contributions made by individual parts to the ongoing operation of a system. The early functionalists in sociology and anthropology were primarily concerned with society as a system that required some means of maintaining cohesive social ties. However, sociocultural systems involve more than social relations. Of equal importance are the two natural systems, the environment and the human nervous system. Both constantly impinge on human consciousness and require both individuals and groups to adjust their behavior to the requirements of the system. The term "function" must be extended to include not only the management of social relations but also the sociocultural techniques developed for adapting to the environment and to inborn human drives.

Music and Environmental Adaptation

The environment, seen as an ecological system, provides the resources from which all humans obtain the necessities of life. The study of ecological systems, that is, the interplay of humans and the natural world, has been the focus of ecological anthropologists. They have used the concept of adaptation as a framework for interpreting the data concerning human activity. This activity is conducted in relation to the environment, and it results in objective consequences. Music's impact on environmental adaptation is indirect, infrequent, and not widely recognized.

When music functions in relation to the environment it is usually associated with essential rituals. The song cycles of the Australian Aborigines have already been mentioned, especially how the songs recount the Aborigines' views of their past, and how their rituals provide reenactments of ancient journeys. These rites involve designs painted to symbolize aspects of the myths and song cycles containing songs that indicate the various places or events described in the Dreamtime myths. Each clan has its own myths, as well as its own traditional area for hunting and gathering, and the rituals reinforce each group's identification with its land. Strong identification with the land helps maintain an even distribution of the Aborigines over the land, so that depletion of the resources in any one area is avoided (Wild 1975:147–148). Moreover, in their traditional hunting and gathering life the Aborigines dispersed during the dry season, and collected in larger groups during the rainy season. They gathered where water and food were plentiful, allowing the natural vegetation in drier places to grow for a while without being subject to human use. The hope that the spirits of a group might grant more knowledge of the Dreamtime, including songs and rituals, provided motivation for the travel and hardships necessary for the annual clustering. The social obligation to serve as manager for the opposite moiety also increased the motivation to cluster (ibid.:39).

In Bali, temple rituals are related to the calendar in such a way that religious festivals indicate when the flow of irrigation water to the rice fields is to be opened or closed. By providing meaning and affect that motivate people to continue the rituals, music actually contributes to optimum yield from agricultural activities (Lansing 1983).

Individual Strategies and the Use of Music

Although music is sometimes connected to environmental adaptation, it plays a much larger role in the development of individual behavior and the ways human interaction develops into social norms. The human nervous system, as another natural system, not only requires physical nurture, but also some sort of meaningful integration of life's experiences on the part of each individual. The relationship between social life and the requirements of the human nervous system highlights the question of individual motivation and decision making. This question has been presented in several forms, variously known as symbolic interactionism (Blumer 1969), social exchange theory (Homans 1958), and generative theory (Barth 1966). More recently, the approach has been termed a theory of practice (Bourdieu 1977). The basic idea of these perspectives is that human beings are not simply automatons who react passively to the events surrounding them, but that they interact with each other to further their own satisfactions in life. These interactions develop into patterns that are then seen as social norms or cultural practices.

The interactionist perspective presents a model of the role of motivation and goals in determining human behavior. As children, humans are dependent upon the adults who provide them with care and instruction, but at an early age people begin to plot ways to influence events in order to increase the satisfactions in their own lives. As people become adults, music is one of the events in life which can be manipulated in terms of desired results. For example, at a funeral in Tikopia for an elderly unmarried woman, the mourners sang a dirge for a mother. The use of that type of song indicated the affection the people felt for the woman (Firth 1990:52). The types of manipulations that occur are called the strategies; the goals that are sought constitute the uses of music. The success with which music helps a person attain private goals varies considerably from one sociocultural system to another.

The actual consequences of choices determine the way music functions in psychological terms. The nature of these functions is not limited to an individual's conscious use of music. Many of the suggested social effects of musical activity, such as enhanced group identity, are brought about through people's feelings as they together sense similar types of affect. A person's conscious use of music for various purposes may be different from the actual result of the musical activity to that individual. Psychological functions range from the relief of stress through expressing frustration, to incitement to action through war songs, to the rhythmic response to music that results in dance.

Features of musical sound have functions of their own as they affect the listeners' perception of the music itself. The cues within a performance, as mentioned in a previous chapter, function to guide the performer or listener through changes in the music. However, the function of musical features is not limited to cues. In the classical ensembles of India, the main melodic performer is accompanied by a second instrument that functions something like an echo, and "fills out the spaces and hollows in the total musical performance" (Neuman 1990:137). Also in India, a type of "musical rhyme," where phrases have parallel or similar endings, functions to aid the listener in making transitions from one part of the music to another (Slawek 1988:85). The opening section (*alap*) of a classical Indian raga functions to introduce to the listener the sounds that characterize the particular raga being performed (ibid.:89).

As people seek to achieve their personal goals they also try to present their motives to other people in the best possible light. This factor is one of the major reasons for presenting the distinction between discursive and practical consciousness (Giddens 1984:7). The importance of this distinction for the study of music is that people often perform music as one technique of working out their personal strategies. This use of music is accompanied by the rationalizations that characterize the discursive consciousness of their society. The explanations that people use to justify their behavior to each other and to the investigator constitute their **rationale**, or rationalization. The actual motivations, i.e., practical consciousness, behind their activity might be quite different.

Although people can improvise their own personal rationale for their behavior, and they often do, it is more important in social science to investigate the types of rationale that characterize particular societies. The difference between discursive rationale and practical knowledge sometimes appears among music students. During a study of the activities connected with student recitals at an American college, a student researcher evidently detected signs of showing off among the music students. She ended her paper with the statement that the music students "learn to use music to communicate their skill, as well as use their skill to communicate music" (Long, unpublished manuscript). It appears possible that in Western society the idea of art for art's sake is sometimes a rationalization, an aspect of discursive consciousness. The knowledge of how to use one's musical skills to establish a career constitutes practical consciousness.

The process of rationalization occurs elsewhere. Horton's paper on the Ekine suggested that in Nigeria religious ritual served to justify music and dance. Ritual seems to serve a similar role among the Yirkalla Aborigines of Australia. "There are so many possible occasions for minor ceremonies that when, as often happens, a group simply wants to sing these songs a 'reason' can always be found" (R. Waterman 1971:172). Although the rationale can be different from the actual motivation, the two are often the same. The important point is that the thoughts expressed through a people's discursive consciousness should not be viewed as the only relevant facts.

Individual strategies often constitute the use of music in a particular situation. Regardless of whether the use of music is seen through forms of rationale or through the behavior of the participant, it is the personal motivations that lead to the organization and actualization of a musical event. The uses of music as motivations leading to a musical event must be carefully distinguished from function as the actual consequences of an event.

The significance of use, as distinguished from function, is shown by A. R. Radcliffe-Brown's understanding of the Andaman Islanders' reasons for engaging in the dance.

> If an Andaman Islander is asked why he dances he gives an answer that amounts to saying that he does so because he enjoys it. Dancing is therefore in general a means of enjoyment. It is frequently a rejoicing. The Andaman Islanders dance after a successful day of hunting; they do not dance if their day has been one of disappointment. (1922:247)

In determining why people behave as they do, one must both understand the account they give as to their motivations, and also interpret carefully what they actually do, as Radcliffe-Brown did when considering the Andaman Islanders.

To summarize the distinction between function and use, whenever the consequences or results of human action are involved, the term "function" is more suitable. When the question involves purposes and goals, "use" is the more appropriate term. In many cases the uses and functions of music overlap, as when music is used for communication, play, inducing trance, or easing the burden of work. In some cases the uses and functions are quite distinct. Differences are found in political songs where they fail to bring about desired political change, but function to give people an emotional release. Curing rituals are used as a form of medicine, but the view of most observers would be that the rituals are functioning to relieve anxiety.

Types of Uses and Functions

Musical activity may have consequences in any of the three components of the sociocultural system—the material, the social, and the expressive. Thus, a full understanding of the role of music in human life needs to observe how music is related to all of them. Although the relationship of music to ecological factors is indirect, and often not apparent, it should not be overlooked as a distinct possibility. The relationship of music to innate human drives is a much more pervasive issue, particularly as it leads to human decision making. In assessing the results of musical behavior it is most useful to use the term function to include the consequences of all musical activity, regardless of whether it relates to ecological adaptation, social relations, or personal integration.

The remainder of this chapter consists of a survey of the uses and functions of music as seen in various societies throughout the world. Although use and function are defined as distinct aspects of social behavior, the same behavior can often be interpreted in terms of both. Thus, the Andaman Islander mentioned by Radcliffe-Brown was motivated to dance in order to enjoy himself. However, the enjoyment, as an expected consequence of the dance, was also a form of manifest function. The element of social cohesion displayed in the dance was an objective consequence noted by the observer as a latent function. Both the enjoyment and the social cohesion were functions in the sense of the actual consequences of the act of dancing, even though the islander might not have had the latter consciously in his mind as a goal or use.

Certainly, no society will incorporate all of the uses and functions that music can possibly serve in human life. The variability of uses and functions of music is notable; even within the same society, some music complexes may perform one function while other complexes serve other functions. Because the functions of music are often unconscious, they are rather difficult to determine with any certainty. Enough research has been done, however, to give a general picture of the ways music affects human life, both in group endeavors and in meeting individual goals.

While it is possible that certain general functions of music occur everywhere, it is only in the building of advanced theory that one can consider the functions of "music in general." Thus, the following survey of possible roles of music in society will be organized by general topics rather than by a distinction between uses and functions. Such a distinction often depends upon the perspective of both the actors and the observers in a particular situation, and the perspectives of these people are not always possible to determine. In addition to that problem, the uses of music are often termed "function" by many writers. Many of the suggested uses actually do result in the desired consequences; others almost certainly do not.

The basic functions of expressive or taste culture have been described as art, entertainment, and information (Gans 1974:67). In terms of music these functions or uses are more usually referred to as aesthetic, play, and communication. The aesthetic was discussed in the last chapter. It, together with play and communication, join pragmatic uses as the major categories of uses and functions.

Music as Play

Of all the uses of music throughout the world, play is probably the most widely recognized. Considering music as a form of play might make it appear unnecessarily frivolous, but play has been taken seriously in studies of human behavior. Play not only includes the gamboling of young animals or young children, but also provides a possible basis for complex creativity in human life. Play seems to occur primarily in animals with slow maturation (Lancy 1980:475). The following definition of play can serve as a basis for discussing its relation to music:

> a voluntary activity or occupation executed within certain fixed limits of time and place, according to rules freely accepted but absolutely binding, having its aim in itself and accompanied by a feeling of tension, joy and the consciousness that it is "different" from "ordinary life." (Huizinga 1955 [1950])

Play is a part of expressive culture, since it incorporates all those forms of behavior that appear to lack practical purpose, particularly in terms of obtaining the material necessities of life such as food and shelter. It includes sports, games, and all the arts. Music is often a form of play, but it often serves other purposes as well.

Play can provide the major motivation for participation in music, even when some other reason is verbalized. In societies where obtaining the necessities of life is a struggle, musicians can be subject to criticism if they spend too much time practicing or playing music. As Horton suggested, possibly some of the ritual applications of music are basically an excuse for the performance of music as play. Connecting it with ritual provides an effective rationale for play. The Shona of Zimbabwe use music for many expressly religious purposes, particularly for spirit possession. However, the spirit possession songs are often sung in nonritual contexts, and if an ancestral spirit happens to appear through a medium in such circumstances it is greeted as a visitor and welcomed to join the fun. The terminology used by the Shona to refer to these rituals is significant. One of the Shona words used for a spirit possession ritual is *mitambo*, which comes from the word *kutamba*, meaning "to play." In Afghanistan, where men dominate the society, "the proliferation of ceremony surrounding weddings and occasions such as the birth of a son can perhaps be seen as female pretexts for recreation" (Slobin 1976:30). One of Mark Slobin's informants felt that ceremonial occasions in his village were often simply pretexts for making music.

A major question about play involves its function, that is, what consequences of play are so important that people will engage in such activities even if there is no material gain from them? One reason suggested for play is that such behavior results from an inborn drive or disposition in humans. The anthropologist Alfred L. Kroeber suggested that some human activities, including science and art, were rooted in a "play impulse" (1963:198–199). The possibility that play represents an innate disposition in humans is more likely in view of the fact that play behavior occurs in many mammals, especially primates. Studies in sensory deprivation have shown that primates tend to become psychologically unstable if they lack sufficient stimuli and interest in their environment. Without enough stimulation, many animals, including humans, tend to become bored and lethargic (Lancy 1980:479). Presumably, avoiding such a state is one of the reasons for engaging in play activity, including music.

Music, then, as a type of play, is one of the means humans use to provide themselves with additional complexity, as well as orderliness, in life. Such complexity is closely related to the structural or aesthetic component in music. Just as people must eat, and their society defines how it should be done, so must humans play with complexities, and the society determines if it will be in terms of language, music, painting, or other features of life. Thus, the ways of creating complexity through mental activity are another feature of life that varies from one society to another.

Play not only provides arousal in the form of complex mental activity, it also provides practice for later life. As children play at being adult, they learn how to fulfill adult roles and master adult skills. This practice for later life is relevant to music. Blacking has found that the songs sung by Venda children as they play are based on the structural principles underlying the music of adult Venda.

> The children's songs present Venda children with musical material which they can soon manipulate with confidence; they introduce them unconsciously to the basic principles of Venda music, reinforce lessons that they have already learnt, and demonstrate that all musical performances have their proper time and place, and may express both praise and criticism of the society. (1967:191)

Music also provides practice for adult life because it is a highly social form of activity. Music often involves the subordination of one's individual inclinations to the requirements of a group effort. It thus provides practice for a major feature of social life: that in real life one often cannot do as one pleases. Music helps the individual realize that the results of combining one's efforts with those of other people can be very pleasurable.

The performance of music facilitates control of one's physical responses, indicating another way in which music as play can serve as practice for mature behavior. One of the functions of music cited by Merriam is physical response (1964:223–224). He notes that music draws forth possession and crowd behavior and excites the hunter and the warrior. Skills of manual dexterity and control of the body are developed through music as well as through dance, which is perhaps the most notable physical response to music.

When viewed as play, music would seem to be separated from the idea of performance. However, the multifunctional nature of music means that it can serve as both play and performance. Whenever a performer signals a willingness or desire to be evaluated, the result is a performance; it is fully possible for both the performers and audience to enjoy the same experience as play. Some musical performances are definitely not play, particularly when associated with significant rituals. Because professional musicians have to perform at the demand of the patron or agent, whether they feel like it or not, the result may not be play. As with the professional athlete, what is widely considered play often becomes work.

Music as Self-expression

In Western society, music and the other arts are often considered to be a means of expressing one's self. Such expression is often related to the psychological needs and personal integrity of the individual. Many societies recognize the importance of this aspect of music. When music has a calming effect on individuals, enabling them to "get things off their chests," its function is called **catharsis.** This was one of the important uses and functions of songs sung by slaves. Many times the use of music in political situations does little to solve the political problems, but it does have a cathartic or safety-valve effect on the performers. Through their music and dance the Flathead Indians relieve the tensions of constant interaction with the dominant white culture (Merriam 1967:158). Catharsis is especially effective when music allows people to express the tensions they feel without fear of reprisal. At weddings in rural India, women sing obscene *gali* songs which ritually insult the guests. In these songs they are permitted to assert themselves by taunting and insulting the men (Henry 1988:31, 61).

The Koleda songs and rituals of Macedonia function as a type of cathartic ritual, even though they are determined by the calendar. In the week before Christmas the men build large bonfires and meet every night to sing around them. The use of ordinarily forbidden obscene language provides an outlet for repressed frustrations and desires. Even though the words may deride particular individuals or lineages with sexual innuendoes, the persons involved are expected not to take offense. Since each bonfire usually involves only men of the same lineage, it is valued as an expression of the strength and honor of one's lineage compared with others. This is the only ritual occasion when the traditionally oriented men mix with those who are transitional or acculturated. The ritual also fosters solidarity among men of different ages, of different degrees of modernization, and of various levels of the social hierarchy (N. Sachs 1975:293ff).

Songs of love or of sexual innuendo also serve a cathartic purpose by expressing forbidden thoughts or cloaking them in the defense of possible repudiation. Among the Tuareg of Niger a vassal woman can use *tende* songs for such things as stating in public her feelings for a man. Spoken openly, this type of statement is unthinkable and would cause untold embarrassment and criticism. Being sung makes it acceptable (Card 1982:134).

The expressive use of music enables people to raise their own self-esteem. The possibility of raising one's self-esteem through music is particularly important among individuals in subordinate or stigmatized social statuses. The Blood Indians of Alberta, Canada (relatives of the Blackfoot) have taken up European music as a way of saying something about themselves.

> To individuals suffering under the delusion of this inferiority complex, even a moderate level of accomplishment in white music (or the knowledge that some fellow-Blood have achieved this distinction) appears to provide a considerable boost to individual self-esteem, and in certain cases to ethnic self-esteem as well. . . . But when considering Blood involvement in white music-making from the point of view of "symbolic behavior" it seems evident that the desire to disprove stereotyped notions of Indian intellectual and academic ineptitude, and lack of patience and perseverance, has been an extremely important impetus to their attempted mastery of white music. (Witmer 1973:90–91)

Gaining prestige is certainly one of the important uses of music. In many societies musicians love to display their skill in front of others in what Nettl has called the "athletic view of music" (1983: 33). Virtuosity in musical performance is highly valued in many places, and success assures a degree of prestige, as well as a positive self-image. Prestige accrues not only to the successful performers of music, but also to individuals, organizations, and communities that sponsor highly esteemed performances.

Music as Communication

Music as a means of communication was examined in the previous chapter, but emphasis is given here to how music as communication is *used*. Music is sometimes performed specifically for the purpose of communication. A good example of this use is the lullaby, when a parent sings to express love, to entertain a child, and, it is hoped, to put it to sleep. Courtship songs provide another case of music used for a specific communicative purpose. Even when communication occurs, the use of a song for a specific purpose is not always successful, as demonstrated by the variable results of lullabies and courtship songs.

Some societies consider music to be a form of communication with the supernatural, as was already mentioned with the Blackfoot. In the South Pacific it was common for people to set forth on a sailing trip and never be heard from again. The Tikopia considered certain people to be spirit mediums who could provide news of missing persons through song (Firth 1990:186–187).

Music often results in communication even when people are not aware it is taking place. This principle guides the use of music in advertising and films. Elsewhere, such unconscious communication can take the form of defining various aspects of life for the individuals in a society. Among the Blackfoot, music helps people internalize the differences in gender roles (Nettl 1989:125). Music defines space among the Suya, with one type of singing for the village plaza, one for the house, and another for the forest. Time is shown by the use of dry season songs and rainy season songs. Probably the most important definition is that of social relationships. As a man sings his shout songs to his mother and sisters, he affirms his relationship to them in spite of the social norms that keep them apart physically (A. Seeger 1987).

One form of unconscious communication of music is that it often legitimizes other forms of activity. In northern India, women rarely make public appearances, but when musical events occur, their appearance in public is "licensed." They are thus able to make public statements concerning matters of importance to them (Henry 1988: 145). The public statements themselves represent uses of the music, whereas the legitimization through music is a pragmatic function. Because one of the functions of music is to legitimize other types of activity, it may legitimize forms of behavior that are socially disruptive. The texts of much modern rock music would appear to legitimize drugs, violence, promiscuous sex, and exploitation of women.

Music often serves for keying an event. Just as a musical performance is indicated by marking, so is the nature of an event sometimes indicated by the use of music. Among the Suya the presence of song serves to distinguish ritual behavior from ordinary behavior (A. Seeger 1987:6). At a ceremony for the dedication of a monument to the heroes of the liberation war in Zimbabwe, a wide range of musical styles was used. These styles appeared to be deliberately inclusive of all the different ethnic groups in the country, and their inclusion was a way of indicating that the ceremony, the monument, and the nation encompassed everyone.

Sometimes communicating through music is a way of publicly disseminating information. In rural India, wedding songs serve to make the whole community aware of the marriage (Henry 1988:33). The drums of West Africa, with their patterns based on language tones, are often used to communicate problems in a community.

Music often serves as an acceptable channel of communication in

a situation where open criticism or complaint would be unaccept-
able. Traditions of improvising music and lyrics enable performers
to make personal comments on events as they are occurring. This
practice occurs among the Tuareg, as heard in the performance of
one well-known singer of *tende* music at the annual Muslim Festival of the Sheep:

> she began by greeting her friends who were present, mentioning
> each by name. She commented upon their appearance and their
> camels and included bits of news about their families. She told of
> disputes among them and exposed small intrigues. She sang of
> herself and her longings to return one day to her native Mali. She
> also included a scornful comment about the tape recorders, mine
> among them, placed around her: . . .

> The tape recorder, O my soul, that of the Toshiba [a Japanese
>   brand name]
> I leave it to them, ya ya aya, the loafers!

(Card 1982:135, 137)

Through enhancing communication, music is often a way of
building and maintaining group identity. The identity of a group includes both the indication of boundaries separating one group from
others and the strengthening of solidarity within a particular group.
Boundaries with other groups are emphasized as members of a so-
rority or a fraternity sing their secret songs. Group solidarity is fostered in the industrial and business concerns of Japan by singing
company songs. This solidarity is believed to enhance the morale
and the productivity of workers (Reischauer 1981:131–32). Often
both boundaries and solidarity are involved. The people of Conima
in the Andes consciously compete with other communities in festivals, with each village striving to present the most popular musical ensemble. The groups vie in size, length of time on the plaza,
appreciation of their newly created songs, and qualities of their performance. This competition builds a strong sense of unity in each
community (Turino 1989).
Music often symbolizes the identity of different generations, especially in situations of rapid change. In a small Macedonian village
where the older people prefer traditional folk music, the young
people of today are into rock music and disco. Their *diskoklub* is
closed to older people, who are not interested in it, anyway. The
windows are covered, so that the young people not only diverge from

the musical tastes of their elders, but also from their sexual mores. The young people also refuse to take part in the rituals their elders have traditionally found meaningful. These activities make them feel free to pursue their goals of urbanization and upward mobility (N. Sachs 1975:321).

Music often serves to emphasize **ethnic identity,** or the principal characteristics of an ethnically distinct group within a larger society. This use of music is often found among Native Americans. The Flathead, for example, maintain a distinct identity of their own through their music, since it remains definitely Flathead, even though other aspects of life have become very westernized (Merriam 1967:158). The Blackfoot emphasize the stylistic features of their music that are most different from European music, namely, the way the voice is used and the way the vocal line is related to the rhythm of the drumming (Ex. 4.1) (Nettl 1989:107). In northern India the Ahir caste has a distinctive type of song called *khari biraha* (hollers) which gives that caste a particular image in a community (Henry 1988:154).

Another interesting case of the operation of ethnic identity is provided by the Tuareg, since some of them live in Niger and others in Algeria. Although the Tuareg are Moslem, they do not speak Arabic, but have their own language and their own identity. The Algerian government has an active policy of promoting the Arabic language and culture, which the Tuareg in Algeria are resisting. In Niger the government pursues a policy of recognizing cultural differences, so the Tuareg are not under pressure to change. Consequently, the typically Tuareg musical forms, such as the songs of the *anzad* (Ex. 2.5), are more carefully guarded from change in Algeria than they are in Niger because in the former they provide important symbols of Tuareg identity. Tuareg identity in Niger is not under such pressure, and it can be defined in other ways.

Ethnic identity often serves very practical purposes. In Alaska, the Inuit find it useful to maintain indigenous status because of advantages given to "Native" claims in land disputes (Johnston 1976:168; Cavanagh 1982:66). Elsewhere, as among the Suya of Brazil, status as an Indian brings not only recognition of land rights but also government assistance. In all these cases, one way of verifying Indian status is through the use of Indian songs and dances.

India is an interesting example of a society with strong linguistic and social divisions where music serves to provide a degree of unity. Indian music is broadcast by the government-owned All India Radio, and a large musical establishment that subsidizes musical activities is also sponsored by the state. The importance of music to national unity is often verbally expressed (Neuman 1990:213–214). Much of the concern with national unity is political.

Music as Politics

The group identities fostered through music do not always contribute to harmony and peace. Feelings of group solidarity can be used to mobilize one group against another, so that music easily becomes political. Politics is essentially a contest involving physical power, economic power, and power over forces of the universe as understood by the society. Gaining power over other people results in control of their time, labor, votes, or material resources. Because music has considerable power to mobilize the sentiment and action of masses of people, it becomes an important political tool. It symbolizes not only the conflicts that separate different groups, but also divisions occurring within the same group. Music serves these purposes in both nonstratified and stratified societies.

Political differences between ethnic groups are often resolved by war, so that war songs have been a significant use of music in many places. War songs function not only to mobilize sentiment in favor of war, but also to instill courage and enthusiasm in the fighters themselves. The Flathead performed war dances before going out to engage in battle (Ex. 6.1) (Merriam 1967:89). They also had a special song that was sung when a scout returned bearing news of the possible presence of enemies in the area (ibid.:102).

Music can indirectly symbolize political differences within the same community. This occurred during my research in Zimbabwe, when I found I was having difficulty obtaining information of musical events *before* they occurred. Eventually I discovered that I had inadvertently alienated the local people by focusing my work on a musician who represented a group of newcomers. Conflict within the community was symbolized by two different mediums who claimed to be possessed by the same spirit. Since each medium used a different musician to provide music for the possession ceremonies, the problems of knowing about musical events were considerably eased when I became more evenhanded in my approach to the various musicians.

Music is used not only to symbolize political differences, but also to help perpetuate them. Among the Warlpiri Aborigines, the older men practice polygyny, thus depriving younger men of eligible women. The ritual system, including the gradual teaching of rituals and songs to the young men, serves as an ideology maintaining the power of the elders to control marriages. The Warlpiri view the rituals as enabling the young men to build up eligibility for marriage. The outside observer noted that giving high value to the singing and rituals motivated the younger men to conform to the necessity of postponing their marriages, thus effectively giving power to the older men. When younger men arrange romantic affairs with the young wives of older men, they are subject to punishment by being refused promotions in the ritual system (Wild 1975 : 121).

Another political use of music is to control conflict. Settling disputes by song contests was formerly practiced among the Inuit of the polar regions, since violence connected with ordinary disputes could seriously endanger the whole community. Although today many Inuit are employed in defense installations or the oil industry, they were formerly hunters, a rather precarious mode of existence in the Arctic. The Netsilik people north of Hudson Bay had several interesting customs connected with music, including song contests. Unrelated men who belonged to different camps formed song partnerships, which frequently involved institutionalized forms of joking. Men would compose songs and teach them to their wives. In the large igloo used for winter ceremonies, a man would drum and dance and his wife would sing as they presented the song as a gift to the man's partner. The song partnerships also involved wife exchange, which was a common practice among many Inuit groups in traditional times. Sometimes sharing the wife with the song partner led to emotional tangles, causing dissension and fighting. In such cases the contestants prepared for a song duel by making new songs which they taught their wives. The quarreling men then faced each other in front of the assembled community, and drummed and danced while their wives sang the songs.

> The audience took great interest in the performance, heartily joking and laughing at the drummers' efforts to crush each other by various accusations of incest, bestiality, murder, avarice, adultery, failure at hunting, being henpecked, lack of manly strength, etc. (Balikci 1970 : 186)

By showing favor to the most biting and witty song, the reaction of the audience determined who had won the competition. Asen Balikci considered this an effective nonviolent method of handling conflict in a very small, closely knit society.

In Tikopia, dissension and personal grievances are often expressed in song. In order to be effective such songs must be performed by a group, so that the aggrieved individuals are required to obtain the support of other people for their performance. Such performances apparently do not result in satisfactory resolution of the conflict so much as in a cathartic effect gained through enlisting supporters for one's position (Firth 1990: 190–91).

Although music is related to political power in small-scale non-stratified societies, it becomes of even greater significance in stratified ones. When the upper classes in stratified societies use it as a symbol to mark their superior status, music becomes an expression of political power as well as group identity. One reason for the different patterns of legitimacy in high culture and popular culture is that the social distinctions themselves are legitimized through the statements provided by the symbols (Bourdieu 1984:7). The role of music as a symbol becomes a matter of control of the organization of musical events rather than the nature of the songs themselves. The power to organize and pay for musical events often rests with a society's elite. The employment of musicians and the staging of elaborate musical productions serve as important reminders of high social position. Instruments, such as trumpets and kettledrums, that are made of rare materials have often been employed to symbolize the wealth of the elite. Sometimes particular instruments are limited to the nobility. For example, the Tuareg had a large drum, called *ettebel*, whose use was restricted to the chief. It was considered to have a mystical power, and was played to summon warriors to battle (Card 1982:65).

Control of music by the ruling class has sometimes taken the form of forbidding the performance of certain types of music, particularly that which is considered subversive. During the struggle for independence in Zimbabwe, Thomas Mapfumo, a popular Shona singer, was detained by the police for singing anti-government songs (Zindi 1985:34). In Chile during the late 1960s, folk music was significant in bringing about the election of a socialist candidate, Salvador Allende. After his overthrow a couple of years later, the military government instituted a policy of favoring Western art music. Foreign instruments were cheap and easily available through installment buying. Chilean folk instruments were virtually impossible to obtain because it was not permitted to buy them on the installment plan, and stores considered it unwise to display them (Wallis and Malm 1984:63–64).

Political uses of music are not limited to symbolizing wealth and power or controlling music through force. Providing musical entertainment can distract the population so they lose interest in political matters. Governments often use music for indoctrinating a populace. Sometimes political messages are sponsored by the government itself. In 1959 the government in Ghana began to sponsor highlife bands, so called because they represented the kind of high living which Ghanaians aspired to achieve. Not only did these bands serve to communicate political messages, but the different government departments competed to produce the best bands (Coplan 1978:110).

Socialist countries have frequently objected to the communication through music of messages and ideas contrary to the prevailing ideology. Therefore, music was often put under close supervision of the authorities. Leaders in these countries object not only to the thoughts expressed in the music, but also to the fact that "bourgeois" (high culture) music is not understood by the masses. For example, in order to avoid undermining the egalitarian ideology, socialist countries commonly present operas in the local language so that more people understand the action. Where opera is more closely associated with the social elite, operas are performed in the language in which they were written.

The mental domination of subject peoples, often termed hegemony, has been facilitated by music. Sometimes conquered peoples or the powerless classes have been encouraged to perform certain types of music, thus symbolizing their inferior position and helping them to internalize their status. The use of European music in the era of colonial domination often had this effect. The Blood Indians cited earlier provide a case where success in foreign music was considered more prestigious than success in their own music. The acceptance of the superiority of European musical criteria has operated as Europeans attempted to "develop" or "regularize" the musical activities of subject peoples.

Music is used politically not only by the ruling class in a society, but also by the powerless classes. Abner Cohen (1974:67−68) has pointed out that where social groups are unable to formally organize themselves for political action, they can do so informally through symbols. Music has often been used in this way, as occurred with the spirituals of slavery days, or the more recent revival of powwows among Native Americans.

Music has often been highly effective in developing nationalist sentiments among people dominated by foreigners. On the island of Java in Indonesia, the gamelan was for centuries a symbol of power. Under the Dutch occupation the gamelan had been allowed to continue in the courts, whose leaders were cooperating with the Dutch, but orthodox Moslems and revolutionaries opposed it because they opposed the Dutch. After the Japanese conquered Indonesia during World War II, they encouraged the singing of a type of popular song called *kroncong.* These songs were Eurasian in style and were sung in the Indonesian language rather than the language of Java. The fact that they were not associated with the former Javanese rulers made them acceptable and even useful to the Japanese. However, when the Japanese themselves were perceived as exploitative colonial rulers, the Indonesians began singing *kroncong* songs against them. After the Japanese were driven out during the war, the songs were used against the Dutch. After independence the gamelan returned to favor and became a symbol of Indonesian identity (Wolbers 1985: 90–92). Indonesian composers have since written nationalist compositions using the gamelan combined with features of European music (Becker 1980: 39).

The Pragmatic Uses of Music

Not all uses of music are related to expressive culture. As noted earlier, music is sometimes intended to *do* something rather than simply *say* something, making it basically **pragmatic.**[1] Some of the political uses described above could be considered pragmatic. In many cases the multifunctional aspect of music means that it can serve as a means of communication with a real pragmatic purpose: courtship songs and lullabies again serve as an example. Work songs are often utilized to lighten the dreariness and exhaustion of hard labor; they can also serve to express dissatisfaction with the overseer, or personal problems in the community. The pragmatic uses of music include a wide range of activities, from disguising gaps in social events to drowning out the cries of boys at initiation rites in Africa.

The use of music is often widely influenced by economic factors. Some social scientists think that music is most properly studied as a feature of "taste" and "cultural consumption," since it involves the choice of alternate uses of time and resources (Bourdieu 1984: 6). This perspective is most useful in relation to pre-industrial stratified societies, where music was primarily a way of showing one's wealth rather than a way of obtaining wealth. The Navajo often spent large sums of money on rituals to the extent that they were practicing a type of conspicuous consumption (Kluckhohn and Leighton 1974: 230). Many musicians use their skill to assure themselves the necessities of life, like the musician at Hammoda's wedding described in Chapter 2. In India the *jogi* mendicant musicians (see Photo 2.2) use their singing to "establish a mood conducive to donations" (Henry 1988:186). Professional or semiprofessional musicians insert their names and locations within their songs to inform listeners how to make arrangements for future performances (ibid.:204). With the development of electronic media it has become possible for successful musicians to gain considerable wealth themselves, and for their agents to do the same. The tremendous money-making potential of music may blind people to the effects of promoting socially disruptive forms of behavior.

One of the most important pragmatic roles of music is the didactic, that is, music used as a tool for teaching other things. According to Jomo Kenyatta, a trained anthropologist and the first president of independent Kenya, an early "constitution" or agreement among the Kikuyu people about the policies of their pre-colonial government was put into song, since the society at that time had no system of writing (1965:185–86). In India the government adopted songs that were already popular and had them performed throughout the countryside with words designed to emphasize the importance of family planning (Bonnie Wade, cited in Hood 1971:356). The song cycles of Aboriginal rituals teach the performers geographical details of a wide area, even when the people have never been there.

The didactic use of music is particularly important in transmitting ideologies from one generation to the next. Many of the folk songs of rural India contain Hindu teachings, even those sung at weddings for entertainment (Henry 1988:135). References to the *Ramayana* epic are particularly common. Other songs teach role expectations, such as informing a bride about the situation she is going to face in her husband's home (ibid.:35). Some songs contain detail of rituals, so that as they are sung they help worshipers learn the rituals in which the songs are included (ibid.:92).

Related to the didactic use is the mnemonic use of music (i.e., using music as an aid to memory). This use is seen as children learn the alphabet by singing it to the tune of "Twinkle, Twinkle Little Star." One Navajo singer was found to have forgotten one of the old chant myths. Although he had forgotten the plot, he was able to recall part of it because he remembered some of the songs (Reichard 1950:283). Many of the nonliterate societies of the world have maintained their histories in oral tradition through the performance of a song form called the **epic.** This was the basis of the ancient Greek *Iliad* and *Odyssey* before they were finally written down, and some people of Eastern Europe today still sing their epics. In West Africa the *griot* is a singer who performs the epic stories of the various ethnic groups; it was a *griot* performance of a group's history that gave Alex Haley a clue to the African background of his own family (1976).

Music, Ritual, and World View

The close association between music and various aspects of religion has already been noted. Earlier chapters emphasized the impact of world view and rituals upon musical behavior. This section considers how musical activity might affect religion. The views of the Navajo people of the Southwest concerning power in music have already been noted. As might be expected, music is an integral part of nearly all Navajo ceremonies, which are performed to ensure good health and a plentiful life for the members of the community (Ex. 6.2). When seeking help for someone who is ill, the Navajo will consult a diviner, a person who can provide information through supernatural means. The most common form of divination is by "hand-trembling," a method in which a song is used to invoke the spirit of a gila monster that is believed to move the hand of the diviner to provide the information. The diviner determines the cause of the illness, thus indicating which of the various ceremonies should be performed. For example, if the sickness is caused by people of the spirit world, the Holy Way chant is performed; if it is caused by ghosts of the dead, the Evil Way chant will be performed. If the ghosts of foreigners are involved, the Enemy Way chant is required (Kluckhohn and Leighton 1974:220).

Each of the chants involves several days of singing, dancing, and performing rituals. Most of the songs are very sacred, and only a specialist singer will be called upon to perform them, for fear that having them sung wrong would not only nullify the effect, but might also prove dangerous. Some of the rituals, particularly the Enemy Way and the Night Way, have songs which are felt to be less powerful, and are sung by the participants in the ceremony. The curing rituals involve not only songs, but also drypaintings. Powdered minerals are placed on the floor on a background of sand, creating designs depicting the Navajo mythological beings. This process is accompanied by singing. When the picture is finished, the sick person is placed on it, and the body areas where the symptoms of illness appear are symbolically connected to the same body areas of the supernatural beings (Kluckhohn and Leighton 1974:213, 219).

Curing illness is not the only use of music in Navajo society. Songs are considered to "break the resistance of the gods" (Reichard 1950:286). The Blessing Way is a series of chants that are designed to assure general well-being. Songs are also used for assuring safe journeys or for making rain.

Navajo rituals often involve other kinds of latent functions. The aura of festivity at large assemblages provides the community with a change of pace and release of emotions. The fact that the organization of the rituals necessitates a large outlay of resources to provide food and pay the musicians ensures that the organizer will receive a great deal of prestige. The task of the singer involves considerable memorization, which leads to gaining additional prestige from a successful performance. "The Singer who knows one nine-night chant must learn at least as much as a man who sets out to memorize the whole of a Wagnerian opera: orchestral score, every vocal part, all the details of the settings, stage business, and each requirement of costume" (Kluckhohn and Leighton 1974:229).

When music is used as a form of power, most people with a scientific orientation are likely to find that the purpose or use is not the same as the consequences or function. Even though music may not in itself have the power to heal, it has several latent functions, or objective consequences. While the curing rituals may not actually restore health, they do improve the mental attitude of the patient, since they express the concern of the family and eliminate a feeling of hopelessness. This process helps the patient and the concerned family to overcome tension, thus eliminating at least one significant barrier to improvement in health.

Music is often used in rituals even though it is not considered to have power in itself. In rural India special songs called *sohar* (Ex. 6.3; see Photo 2.4) are sung at the birth of a son not only to express gladness, but as a type of good omen or auspicious act, "a kind of mild magic" (Henry 1988:64) to assure the child of longevity. The same songs are also used when reference to bearing sons is important, especially for women who have not yet had a son. Music in general is often used to praise and entertain the gods or goddesses so they will not bring harm (ibid.:111).

In many areas of the world the supernatural use of music is associated with altered states of consciousness, commonly called trance. In a comprehensive study of music and trance, Gilbert Rouget finds that although music and trance are often associated, music is not necessary for the trance state. He defines trance as "an altered, transitory state of consciousness conforming to a cultural model," and gives primary emphasis to the cultural expectations (1985:56). Many factors can induce these altered states in humans, including sensory deprivation, hallucinogenic drugs, and physical or psychological stress, as well as music. Whenever such states are considered a special manifestation of the supernatural, music assumes an important part in religious observances. Among the Plains Indians, the vision quest was traditionally undertaken by young men who deliberately made themselves suffer from sleeplessness, hunger, cold, and sometimes cutting off fingers. One of the results of this experience was a hallucinatory trance when men heard songs, which they interpreted as their own gift from the supernatural. The songs were thereafter performed exclusively by their owners (Merriam 1967).

In African and African-American societies the possession trance is very common, and it is usually brought about by music. In Haiti followers of the *vodou* cults believe that mediums ("horses") are "mounted" by the spirits of various gods (*loa*). This process is brought about by drumming, singing, and dancing at ceremonies organized by the priest (*hungan*) of a shrine. Once possessed, the medium is considered to be acting and speaking as the *loa* itself. Erika Bourguignon graphically describes the kind of experience that takes place:

> Suddenly Ida, one of the women dancers, begins to tremble and sway on her feet. Several times she seems ready to fall, but each time one of the bystanders catches her, and she continues dancing. The others have stopped and all attention is on the woman who is entering trance, or, in local parlance, is being "mounted." Ibo-Lélé is possessing her, in response to the drums, the songs, the dances and the food, all calling him. Ida now dances more and more rapidly, with greater control over her movements. Now she is dancing more and more still-limbed, sometimes with her eyes closed. As she circles the center pole ever more closely, several women rush in to snatch away the dishes of sacrificial food that have been set out at the base of the pole, and which risk being turned over as she whirls about seemingly blindly. Finally, she falls on a mat at the edge of the structure, where several women are sitting, the *hungan's* wife among them, who catches Ida in her arms, as she lands on her knees. At that moment the drums stop and the possessed woman remains motionless. (1979:237)

The exact nature of altered states of consciousness has not been determined with any certainty. To some it appears as a type of hypnotic state. To others it seems to be a form of hysteria involving dissociation or multiple personalities. In the types of altered states called possession trances, the person involved does not remember what occurred during the trance period. If the trance is a form of hypnotism, then the music that causes it serves simply as a means of associating the individual with a former hypnotic experience. If the altered state is a form of hysteria, then the role of music may be more pervasive as the intensity and/or the complexity of drumming contributes to a psychophysiological reaction.

Even where music is not considered to possess supernatural power itself, or where it is not used to activate religious trances, it still plays an important part in religious ritual because of its recognized power to call forth emotional responses. Thus, the Mbuti Pygmies not only express their group unity in song, but devote their singing to "rejoicing the forest," expressing their thanks to the forest for providing them the necessities of life.

In many societies, rituals are guided by a hierarchy of religious specialists. Presumably instilling devotion in the faithful is a major reason for using music, but it may also provide entertainment and serve as part of a spectacle that will attract people to the ritual. Thus, religion often plays an important part in the organization of musical life through legitimizing musical activity and sponsoring musicians and musical performances. The music, in turn, may have a profound effect on religion by attracting adherents to a faith and providing their beliefs with strong emotional foundations.

Conclusion

As people use music to further their own satisfactions in life, it is important to be aware that unintended consequences or functions may result. Humans make decisions about their strategies on the basis of information they have received and incorporated into their internal model of reality, or schemata. Reasons for particular decisions can include clear goals with well-tried methods, or the presence of social pressure and a disinclination to flout it. Many times the real reasons lie in the practical consciousness, and various forms of discourse are used to validate the behavior. Whatever the reasons for a choice, its consequences are not based on the information as understood by the individual, but rather on the nature of the realities of the world at large. If the information on which a decision is made is faulty or incomplete, then the consequences are likely to be unanticipated, unrecognized, or even unwanted. Unless the uses and functions of music are carefully examined, it is always possible that the consequences of a musical performance will not be what is intended, but might well be inconsequential or even detrimental to one's own goals.

One weakness of the early functionalist view of society was its assumption that function is always positive. The functions of music are more often positive than negative, since music, as an optional activity, can be discontinued once any negative effects are perceived.

However, the negative functions of a social practice are overlooked if they are outweighed by positive factors. When musicians and their promoters profit from songs promoting antisocial behaviors and children innocently enjoy them, then the public needs to be aware of potential negative effects.

The use or function of music can make a difference in the form the music takes. If music is to enhance the opulence of a court, it tends to become elaborate. As Stephen A. Wild has pointed out concerning Aborigines, music for magical purposes requires correctness, while for commemorative purposes it requires affective response (1975:144).

As noted earlier, many writings on world music have included the generalization that music in most of the small-scale societies of the world is "functional," but in complex societies it is not. Such a statement is preposterous when function is considered to be the consequences, since all human behavior, including music, must have some sort of consequences. What *does* characterize small-scale societies is the use of pragmatic values to provide the rationale for performing music; in modern society the aesthetic and symbolic values provide the rationale. However, just as small-scale societies often exhibit aesthetic and expressive functions in their music, so do modern societies frequently reflect pragmatic functions. The amassing of wealth or achievement of renown is as much a pragmatic function of music in some societies as is curing illness or broadcasting social criticism in others.

CHAPTER SEVEN

Change and Continuity

AS THE PRECEDING CHAPTERS have shown, music throughout the world displays a wide diversity. However, what will happen to this diversity in the future is uncertain. One is occasionally surprised in ethnic recordings or films to hear a song such as "Clementine" being performed in the middle of Africa or on some Pacific Island. No less startling is a piano glissando in the midst of an Oriental pentatonic piece. Changes in music occur not only in exotic places, but also in music systems all over the world, all of the time. Nor is change entirely a result of the world turning to Western musical styles: note the Beatles' utilization of idioms from India, or the modern use of the bongo drum. Changes in music are not limited to the way music sounds.[1] Changes also occur within the systems of cognitive understanding and behavior related to music. In some societies change is very extensive, while in others it proceeds slowly. The purpose of this chapter is to explore the factors that determine differences in the rate and the extent of change in musical practices.

Change in music is often interpreted in terms of historical development, assuming that what is being done today is the result of what was done in the past. However, simply describing the results of musical activities of the past is not as helpful as exploring the processes that produced those results. Many forms of historical treatment still leave untouched the question as to *why* certain innovations are integrated into the musical life of a society and others are not, or why certain musical idioms disappear and others remain. An important question concerning music change is how individual behavior that is subject to social pressures can still lead to new sociocultural norms. Examining these processes of change can substantially increase the range of explanations offered for present forms of music activity.

Music and Anthropological Views of Change

Understanding music change today depends on noting general views of sociocultural change as well as unique features of the relationship between society and music. A major view of sociocultural change in the nineteenth century was evolution, applying to society the idea of biological evolution. The view of social evolution as inevitable progress was a dominant perspective well into the twentieth century, and it still influences popular thinking today. From prehistoric times, change has occurred in societies and presumably in musical systems, so that the ways music is related to the concept of evolution has been a significant issue. Scientific studies have shown that the human organism did evolve gradually, and that human societies have indeed evolved in relation to size, complexity, and technological sophistication. However, the assumption that changes toward modern industrial society invariably constitute progress is becoming increasingly questioned.

The applicability of the evolutionary perspective to music has often been assumed, but such a view has no basis in fact. One result of this erroneous attitude is that some musics have been disparaged and labeled "primitive." There is no evidence to indicate that the simplest music found in the world today resembles in any way the music of prehistoric humans. The application of evolutionary theory to music must be dealt with very carefully. Many scholars of music during the early part of the century, such as Curt Sachs, amassed huge amounts of interesting and significant information about the musics of the world, but many of their works are not highly relevant today because of outmoded evolutionary interpretations.

Obviously, many modern musical instruments involve highly skilled technology to build; however, improvements in technology cannot be assumed to constitute "advance." Indeed, some tribal people have musical instruments requiring little technology to make, but this fact is not necessarily correlated with the simplicity or complexity of the music itself. Highly complex rhythms and tunes can be performed with a very simple musical bow (Ex. 7.1). Moreover, technologically imperfect instruments may have valuable musical qualities that could easily be overlooked. For example, the gourd resonator used with the Shona mbira has an irregular shape, so that inserting the instrument into the resonator differently for each performance produces a variety of overtone possibilities. The manufacture of a perfectly round resonator will make the overtones the same all the time, thus reducing the variety of sounds available to the musicians. Traditional mbira resonators used pieces of shell to provide the buzzing sound favored by Africans, but today bottle caps are used for the same purpose. Because of their random sizes, the shells vibrate with many different pitches; the bottle caps, being the same size, tend to vibrate with some pitches more than others.

In many cases musical styles do evolve over time, as has happened in Western music with the use of the tempered scale over the last three hundred years. This fact does not mean that musical evolution necessarily continues indefinitely, nor does it mean that more recent or more complex forms are better. Although an increase in technological complexity is seemingly unlimited, that does not appear to be the case with complexity in music. Increasing complexity in a musical idiom that has existed for a long time may have exhausted the possibilities of creative innovation, so that new idioms are sought. The human brain can handle only a limited amount of cognitive input. When music becomes so complex it can no longer be organized in the mind, it then becomes mere sound or noise. The sounds produced by elegantly patterned computer programs do not necessarily sound like music to persons trying to understand the sounds aurally. New idioms are being sought today, as musicians experiment with new scale systems or exotic rhythms. Music undoubtedly evolves when a simple style attracts talented people who experiment with it and create complexity. This has happened with jazz and appears to be happening with rock and roll. Evolving in this sense is very different from continuous evolution viewed as constant and inevitable progress.

In the first half of the twentieth century, social scientists were seeking to explain society in terms other than evolution. Sociocultural systems were still viewed as a mysterious force that somehow swept people along in spite of themselves. These relatively fixed forms were thought to have served the small-scale societies of the world for hundreds, perhaps thousands, of years, and were now being unraveled by the impact of Western civilization. This idea of the continuity of ancient traditions was also considered to apply to music. Early ethnomusicologists were eager to record as much non-Western music as possible before it succumbed to the domination of Western music. It was considered especially important that the non-Western music be authentic, i.e., free of Western influence.

While change in the rest of the world was seen as a departure from normal conditions, Europeans viewed their society as changing purposefully because of the alleged importance of reason and progress in the conduct of their affairs. Since World War II, scholars have come to see that change in all societies, large and small, is a normal condition in which modifications are naturally introduced as the system is replicated. Clarification of the process of change is a matter of understanding the dynamics by which a system is replicated, sometimes without notable change, and sometimes with drastic modifications. This view of constant change has modified ideas of authenticity so that it is much more common today to find current musical idioms being studied by scholars who are no longer bound by the view that such trends are somehow defective.

Research has indicated that change did indeed occur in non-Western music systems even before the coming of Europeans. Thomas F. Johnston, for example, has found that the music of the Shangaan-Tonga people of southern Africa includes music borrowed from several neighboring peoples before European domination (1973). Frances Densmore, an early ethnomusicologist among Native Americans, noted that "there are contrasts in the various classes of songs within a tribe as well as differences between the songs of certain tribes. In some instances the songs of one class resemble those of the same class in another tribe whose music, in other respects, is quite different" (1926:62). Such a pattern of differences and similarities indicates the strong possibility of inter-tribal borrowing of songs in the past. The enjoyment and use of new kinds of music apparently existed all over the world long before the arrival of Europeans.

Earlier concepts of culture as a relatively fixed entity were accompanied by a theory of change often called the **innovation-acceptance theory** (Barnett 1953). This theory basically states that change occurs as a new idea, called innovation, is presented to a society or subgroup, whose members then either accept or reject it. The innovation can be either a totally new concept originating with a member of the society (invention) or it can be some new idea from outside the society (diffusion). The innovation was not considered a part of culture until it had been accepted by the people in the group. Innovations that were not accepted did not result in culture change. This theory, while accurately describing what often occurs, is nevertheless an oversimplification. For one thing, it emphasizes the acceptance of the new, and virtually ignores the decline of the old. Another weakness is that it does not take into account the many cases where unwanted change is literally forced onto a group of people, so that invention is stimulated by the need to adapt to particular situations.

The belief that innovations are a normal part of everyday life and that humans are naturally inventive has led to the modern generative or interactionist views of cultural processes mentioned earlier.

These views are based on the idea that people everywhere engage in strategies designed to provide themselves with the greatest possible degree of satisfaction. These strategies involve choices between possible courses of action, related to values as diverse as kinship obligations and stock market speculation. People's choices tend to develop into patterns, since many people prefer acting in ways already tried by others rather than striking out on their own. These patterns of choices are what the analyst views as norms, culture, or social structure (Barth 1966). Whereas the innovation-acceptance theory focuses almost exclusively on introduction of the new, the generative theories focus on decisions among various courses of action, some of which have been customary for generations and some of which are new. When new courses of action predominate over the old, change in culture is quite rapid.

Changeable Features of Music

Changes occur both in the sounds of music and in its meanings, uses, and functions. Changes in the sound are essentially changes in **style,** a rather broad term that consists of several features. The most widely recognized area of style change is modification in the **structures** of music performed in a given society. This type of change includes such things as the use of chordal techniques, modifications in the standard scale tones, or changes in rhythmic patterns. For example, women's contemporary folk songs in India are often characterized by the tempered scale and more regular rhythms, partly because the women create new words for tunes from films (Henry 1988:112). Closely related to structural modifications are changes in **performance practice** that occur as larger ensembles become more prestigious, or new ways of playing instruments are learned. Foreign vocal styles are often adopted, as when the acculturated people in Macedonia use "more vibrato, less nasality and less epiglottal constriction" than the traditional singers (N. Sachs 1975:276). Another aspect of change in style is a gradual change in the **repertoire** or repertory, terms which refer to the totality of musical pieces that are customarily performed in a society, in a particular music complex, or by an individual. Changes in repertoire frequently occur as changes in the relative number of times that certain types of music are performed. The changing rates of performance are perceived by a younger generation as a new norm, and as a change in style if the new repertoire is very different.

Changes in the sounds of music are related to musical instruments as well as style. Technological improvements in musical instruments are important features of change in this area, because it is through musical instruments that technology has historically had the greatest impact on music. Changes in instruments have often included the substitution of new materials for old purposes. Today in some places the *tende* drum is being replaced by a jerry can, a type of tall narrow gasoline can (Card 1982:121–122). The Shona now often make rattles of tin cans filled with corn or pebbles, rather than using gourds as in the past (Photo 7.1). Musical instruments frequently pass from one area to another, sometimes without knowledge of the commonly accepted ways of playing them, or with changes in the names given to them. This process of diffusion will be dealt with in the next section.

Changes in style and in instruments produce changes in the sounds directly; changes in the system of cognitive understanding and behavior related to music lead to changes in the sound indirectly. Music change often takes the form of a change in the use or meaning of music. The Flathead now use their war dances as entertainment, but they combine the fun with economic benefit by charging admission and dividing the proceeds among the performers (Ex. 6.1). They no longer use the old traditional war songs, but songs they have made up (Merriam 1967:90). In Java, according to old beliefs, the gamelan was a representation of royal powers that were related to the power of nature. Modern views of the gamelans are changing the emphasis from their power to their aesthetic values. Consequently, the gongs of the gamelan are being tuned with more definite pitches, since they no longer represent the sounds of nature (Becker 1988).

A common type of change in meaning today is from ritual music to music as an expression of ethnic identity. This change is particularly important to people who find their life-styles changing drastically in the face of modern industrialized society, yet who value the bonds which tie them together as a community. Frequently, older traditional music and dances which have become ritually irrelevant assume importance as a symbol of a group's distinctive culture. Performances of traditional musical idioms affirm an individual's membership and pride in the group. The widespread use of a pan-Indian musical idiom in modern powwows helps Native Americans retain their sense of identity with their heritage. The festivals of South Pacific music bring many ethnic groups together, and performing their ancient music affirms their identity.

The use of music for ethnic identity has been a factor in the "marginal survival" of certain musical idioms (Malm 1977:29). When people emigrate from their home area, they often value their tradi-

7.1. Shona tin can rattles in use with *jocho* dance, 1972. (Photo by the author.)

tional music very highly, whereas those who remain behind are often quite willing to change it. The Chinese who came to the United States continued to perform traditional Chinese opera while in mainland China music became oriented to socialist themes (ibid.:169). Many old folk songs that have disappeared in England have been rediscovered among the people of Appalachia in the United States.

Change in use or meaning involves change in patterns of legitimacy. This is most clearly shown in the changes after the 1917 Bolshevik revolution in Russia. Where legitimacy was formerly shown by performance at court or in cathedral, today it often comes from being heard on the radio or television. This change has occurred in Afghanistan, where Moslem views of music discourage its performance by members of the higher social class. By the 1960s and 1970s, performance by upper-class individuals had become legitimate because of radio presentations (Sakata 1983).

Legitimacy can change even when different social strata are not a factor, as indicated by the role of the flute among the Tuareg. By tradition, the flute has been used by herders to entertain themselves and to help in controlling the animals. It was never used for performance in social gatherings. However, Radio Niger has recorded flute players from time to time, and occasionally broadcasts the music, which is beginning to cause interest among the people at large. A flute player was given a recorder by a tourist, and he now plays it in an ensemble with several friends using various instruments (Card 1982:64–65). The legitimacy of flute music seems to be increasing.

Sometimes changes in legitimacy have developed from the need for ethnic or national identity. Even though many of the leaders in Zimbabwe prefer African or international popular music for their own entertainment, they recognize the importance of the mbira as a national symbol. Consequently, it has become a legitimate form of music, although it was once looked down upon as an amusement of the untutored, superstitious country dweller.

A common change is the shift of folk music into the realm of art music, a case of folk music becoming legitimized by the elite. This change has often characterized Western music. For example, Bach, Mozart, Schubert, and many others incorporated folk music into their compositions. The Hungarian composers Béla Bartók and Zoltán Kodály are noted for their collections of Hungarian folk songs and subsequent utilization of many of them in their works. Similar shifts have occurred in other societies. The performers at Japanese festivals (mitsuri) were originally chosen at random from among the populace because the music was considered a type of folk music; today, performers are engaged as specialists by the organizers of the festival. In Macedonia the urban composers and arrangers of popular music rely heavily on music from the rural areas (N. Sachs 1975: 190–191).

The interplay of art music and folk music operates the other way also. Bartók and Kodály found that the songs of Hungarian peasants were of different types. One type retained certain musical characteristics of Central Asia, whence the Hungarian people had originally come. This music was notable for its use of melismatic singing, the pentatonic scale, and a form in which the first phrase of a tune was repeated at the distance of a fourth or a fifth from the original line as the tune proceeded. These features are thought to represent the very oldest type of Hungarian folk music, since they are also found in the music of the Cheremis people of Russia, whose language is similar to Hungarian. These musical features are not found in the musics of the European peoples whose languages are Indo-European (Kodály 1960:24–25). A second type of folk song became popular in Hungary in the eighteenth and nineteenth centuries as the Hungarians freed themselves from foreign domination and began to develop their economy. Some of the folk songs showed signs of having developed from "art songs," a term which in this case means songs that were published. Kodály cites the case of a song recorded in the early twentieth century in rural Hungary. "The singer . . . could only tell me that his grandmother . . . had learnt it from the village miller. He had no idea that it was a verse of a work by János Bodó Szentmártoni . . . published in 1636" (1960:98). During the latter half of the nineteenth century, when Hungary was becoming conscious of nationalism and feeling the effects of the Industrial Revolution, folk song traditions incorporated a wide range of foreign songs, including hymns and non-Hungarian folk songs (Manga 1988).

Part of the reason that art music works its way into folk traditions is because of the growth of economic differentiation in a society. Kodály pointed out that the presence of a folk music tradition does not mean that the people involved are all on the same economic level or living by the same set of values. In such a situation people try to raise their own self-esteem by symbolically relating themselves to the wealthier and more influential members of society. One way of doing this is by using the same music preferred by the wealthy. When the wealthy have been trained in music notation and the poor have not, such music is incorporated imperfectly into the body of folk music.

Kodály notes that the art songs hastened the disappearance of the old-type songs and also contributed to the performance of less ornamentation in the singing. He attributes these changes to the fact that the art songs were considered "new and fashionable" (1960:68). Hungary in the nineteenth century was highly concerned with strengthening its ties with Europe, which may account for the introduction of European-type songs.

The status of musicians also changes, often in relation to legitimacy. Players of the *sarangi* in India were originally folk musicians often living as wandering minstrels (see Photo 2.2). More recently, many of them have become players of accompanying instruments in the classic ensembles, replacing the vina players, whose instrument had become acceptable for solos. In both cases the changes brought a rise in status for the musicians (Neuman 1990: 135). The sweeping changes brought to India by the British in the nineteenth century caused the rapid growth and development of *gharanas*, which served to enhance the status of the musicians (ibid.:90). In spite of many changes in the status of musicians, Indian music has not undergone change in the basic sounds (ibid.:202).

Changes in one feature of music often lead to changes in other features. For example, the classical music of India includes delicate nuances of intonation. However, many musicians in North India use the Western harmonium, a kind of organ with reeds, that has the tempered scale. The advantages of the harmonium seem to outweigh any concern for the traditional Indian scales (Henry 1988: 207–208). Brass bands in rural areas of India often play music based on ragas. Although conforming to many characteristics of the classical raga performances, the brass bands sometimes introduce different melodic phrases, and they perform with a shorter *alap*. They also pass the solo part back and forth between each other (ibid.:222). Whether the use of these Western instruments will eventually change the tonal norms of Indian music remains to be seen.

Processes of Change in Music

Music change is basically seen today as variation in the replication of cultural norms as they pass from generation to generation. A major feature is the way that children as new members of a society experience life around them. As described in Chapter 2, musical experiences are largely determined by the society, and involve the teaching of musical skills as well as the value system related to the use of music. Once people become adults, they find that music can be used to enhance life or further their own goals. The ways individuals seek to do this affect the replication of the norms for following generations. The individual's musical behavior is heavily influenced by society through incentives and constraints, which are imposed by circumstances. The incentives and constraints may be determined by the natural environment, common human psychological motivations, internal social factors, and contact with other societies.

The natural environment is not generally considered to be a major factor in musical activity, but it does represent one important set of incentives and constraints. Although obtaining necessities of life from the natural environment is an inevitable feature of human life, it is often rather peripheral to music. The environment is important to music primarily as it influences the nature of musical instruments. In central Africa, trees are not large enough in circumference to make deep-sounding drums, so the people add a small patch of rubber to the center of the drum head to lower the pitch. In the savannah area in West Africa, elephant tusks were formerly used for trumpets, but they became scarce, so trumpets of wood were made to take their place (A. Schaeffner, cited in Zemp 1971:63). Aside from instruments, the major impact of the environment on music is the way economic arrangements of specific societies affect the livelihood of musicians, their audiences, and their agents, as described in Chapter 2.

Common human psychological motivations have often been over-emphasized as reasons for change or stability in music. Many anthropologists consider individual drives and motivations to be outside the realm of social science. Even if they are considered to occupy a legitimate place, the means of conducting research into such questions involves serious problems. Nevertheless, the consideration of psychological human drives has provided useful hypotheses regarding human social action, and suggestions concerning the impact of such drives upon music making are here presented in those terms.

While humans appreciate the security of continuity, they also crave the excitement of variety. Many changes that occur in musical behavior can be attributed to a desire to escape boredom or simply to play with sounds. Meyer's theory of expectations suggests that creative and striking changes in music are necessary in order to provide new types of resolutions to expectations. People learn a new song because it pleases them, or they take up a new instrument because it has a rich sound that appeals to them. The consideration of music as play, which has been discussed as one of the functions of music, involves a great deal of postulated psychic motivation. Probably seeking variety in play is an important incentive for inserting new materials into musical performances.

An innate need for variety may also serve to explain the phenomenon of rising and waning popularity in music. The rise and fall of styles of musical fashion occurs in many societies. J. H. Kwabena Nketia cites a case from West Africa. "In many places in Ghana new forms of music and dancing based on the old indigenous style come in vogue and gradually disappear as new ones are created, or old ones are revived" (1959:32). The rapid spread of Christian hymns in Polynesia has been generally attributed to the shortsightedness of the missionaries, who customarily forbade indigenous music. However, the Polynesians seemed to adopt European hymns wholeheartedly, and it appears that the missionaries may have been simply accelerating the natural process among the Polynesians of seeking new and interesting styles (McLean 1986:34). The Flathead used a Round Dance for social dancing up until about 1900, then replaced it with a Gift Dance, which was later replaced with the Owl Dance (Merriam 1967:75).

Some of the motivations for changing fashions of music are apparently due to factors other than a need for variety. Frequently the music of young people differs from that of their elders. In the early 1970s in Zimbabwe several old people remembered songs from pre-European times. Among the songs were several types they had sung as young people for recreational dancing. They remembered songs called *njore, dembe,* or *pfonda*—all of which were used in ways similar to the songs of modern young people, but none except the elderly knew them. Middle-aged people were dancing to *jocho* (see Photo 7.1), while young people in the 1970s were performing *jiti.* Each generation seems to have had its own songs. Perhaps the young are motivated to develop new styles in order to symbolize their distinctiveness and independence in relation to older people.

An individual's attraction to a certain type of sound may account for some of the borrowing that happens as people see and hear the musical practices of other social and ethnic groups. Some borrowing of European musical styles seems to have occurred simply because of the attraction of the sounds of the music and the instruments. The sound of chords, a characteristic of European music, has been copied extensively throughout the world. I have seen African students become very excited over the sound of sung chords performed as a vocal exercise. When Europeans arrived in Japan in the middle of the sixteenth century, their music apparently took the country by storm. This may have been due partly to the new sound of polyphony as well as to the fact that European music was not tied to guilds or other social restrictions. Church music was a great force for conversion of many Japanese people to Christianity. In fact, it is possible that the very popularity of European music contributed to the fears of the government that it could not control the people. Consequently, it ruthlessly wiped out Christianity and isolated Japan from the rest of the world in the early seventeenth century (Harich-Schneider 1973:445–486).

Sometimes European instruments were borrowed because their sounds were pleasant and they were more resonant or more versatile than the indigenous instruments. The guitar has become very popular in Africa because it is louder than the plucked lamellophone (mbira) or stringed instruments it replaced, and it also has a wider range. The violin has become a major instrument in India. The absence of frets on the fingerboard enables the player to perform microtonal embellishments, and being a bowed instrument, it contrasts nicely with the many plucked string instruments of India.

Prestige is an important factor leading to change in musical behavior, particularly when use of the musical idiom of the ruling classes is involved. In rural Java the gamelan formerly included instruments of bronze (see Photos 3.1, 4.12, and 4.15), but due to limited economic resources the ensembles were considerably smaller than those in the urban courts. With the rise of prestige of the urban gamelan, social pressure caused the rural communities to seek larger ensembles, even if the instruments had to be made of painted iron rather than bronze to reduce costs (Becker 1980:9). In rural India, wedding music is changing because it is prestigious to hire musicians with amplification equipment (Henry 1988:112).

The strategies of individuals can include changes in discourse. Once a feature of music is understood, discourse about it can easily be invented, a fact which can make the task of the researcher more complicated. So-called ethnographic information is an example of the kind of discourse that can be created by people for their own purposes. Merriam witnessed an occasion when a Flathead musician arranged groups of Native American singers and dancers to perform for outsiders. The program, which was provided by the leader, had extensive information about Flathead customs, most of which was newly invented (Merriam 1967:140ff). Merriam had enough experience with the music tradition to know that he was witnessing a case of entertainment music becoming an important symbol for group identity.

Social Incentives and Constraints

Individual motivations are a key element in decisions affecting the course of action, but individuals must work within the framework of the group in arriving at decisions involving public performance. Group decisions are an area where levels of interaction are important. Although the musician might be able to make decisions about what pieces to play, it can be up to the community to decide about specific musical events. Small group decisions are often made by consensus, but as groups grow larger and become communities such unanimity is not always possible. At levels of interaction higher than the community, decisions are often made by powerful individuals or groups within the larger social unit. Questions of power and politics thus become important in matters concerning music change. Understanding the processes of music change requires investigation of the incentives motivating people to choose new courses of action, as well as the constraints that motivate them to do things the customary way.

Where music is concerned, the social aspects of a sociocultural system are considerably more important than the environmental and the personal factors. The nature of the rewards a society provides for musical behavior constitutes a major incentive for people to perform music. The values of a society can also provide incentives for introducing innovations in musical performances. A society also provides constraints in the form of penalties or social disapproval for those who innovate too much. This interplay between the individual and society is not always possible for the researcher to observe, but a revealing case on the island of Malta was described by Marcia Herndon and Norma McLeod (1979). A guitarist named Indri Brincat was noted for his performances of Maltese folk songs. He valued the folk heritage and refused to participate in inauthentic popular idioms. At the same time, his creative abilities led him to invent creative changes in his guitar playing, including performances without a singer. These changes represented exciting musical developments to him, but the community considered him to be departing from the norms of folk music.

> Mr. Brincat, recognized as the greatest of the living Maltese guitarists, was chastised indirectly and later ostracized because the other musicians felt that he was no longer playing traditional Maltese material. In their criticisms of his playing the other musicians revealed quite clearly the boundaries of traditional Maltese folk music. By following the ideal statement rather than the practice, Brincat had broken another set of rules and, in changing the musical form, had encountered a high degree of resistance. (Ibid.: 65)

This ostracism was a factor in a dispute over a contract for performing, and led Brincat to become unsure of his role as a folk musician. The difficulty was finally resolved when he decided to conform to expectations in public performance, and do his creative innovations by himself (ibid.: 78). Although individual motivations and decisions eventually lead to formation of norms, it is the rare musician who will accept social ostracism due to inappropriate musical or behavioral innovations.

It is not possible to determine from the broad types of social organization the particular course that musical activity will take. However, the nature of the values concerning social organization is often of major importance, and it differs widely from society to society. Japan, for example, is widely recognized as one of the world's leading industrialized countries, yet its musical life does not follow the pattern of any other industrialized society. According to Chie Nakane (1970), the basic arrangement of Japanese society is vertical rather than horizontal. This means that life in that country does not emphasize the social strata, but rather the relative autonomy of each family, company, or professional association. Thus the world of music, as well as other arts, is organized into innumerable groups or types of guilds that the Japanese call *ryu* (Harich-Schneider 1973). The term has been translated as guild or school, although sometimes the term family-school is used. Membership in the groups is usually determined by family relationships, but in many cases teacher-student relationships also determine membership. The term *ryu* is related etymologically to the idea of flow or flowing, so the guild in a sense represents the flow of a tradition through time. The importance of the "schools" can be seen at performances of *kabuki* theater, where it is customary for members of the audience to shout the family-school names of actors as a form of applause.

The reason the term "school" is often attached to these groups in English is because each one maintains its own musical traditions, with emphasis on guarding them against change. Thus, the ancient traditional music was preserved in spite of drastic modernization because the various groups had much to lose, both materially and in the sense of prestige. This system consequently is more conducive to continuity than to change because competition forces each group to regard its repertoire with jealous care. Although this form of organization provides incentive for continuity, it could also inadvertently cause change. For example, when a particular *ryu* was proscribed by the government or died out, its knowledge and musical practices disappeared with it.

Some anthropologists have suggested that the course of music change is affected by the nature of sponsored music complexes or patronage. E. R. Leach (1954:37) notes a similarity in art styles between the Northwest Coast Indians, the Maori of New Zealand, and Victorian England. He attributes their ostentatious style to the fact that all these societies have a strong hierarchy as well as socially competitive people. Ostentatious or showy music could very well be caused by similar forces. Where governments are not centralized, music tends to become more diverse, as the leaders of relatively small political units compete with each other for prestige. Blacking noted processes of this type taking place among contemporary Venda, as well as in eighteenth-century Germany (1965 : 51). The operation of music in courtly competition is exemplified in Java.

One of the duties of a king was to put on the best, the most magnificent performances of the traditional arts, *wayang kulit, wayang orang,* and so forth. If some other nobleman staged more grand performances than he (hardly likely in view of his tremendous financial advantage), there might be doubts as to his right to be the monarch. It has been suggested by several Javanese scholars that the great flowering of artistic activity at the two major courts of Surakarta and Yogyakarta from the mid-nineteenth through the mid-twentieth centuries was because both courts were rendered politically impotent by the Dutch and therefore transferred their innate hostility and competition from the political to the artistic sphere. In any event, the finest performances were given by the princes, who although largely neutralized politically, still kept and maintained the trappings of power. (Becker 1980:29–30)

It is not only the values concerning social organization that provide incentives and constraints affecting music change, but also the concepts about the meaning and value of music. Merriam (1964:63) cites these concepts as important variables in music change. The belief in supernatural origins of music often inhibits innovation and creativity in music.

Also significant is the relative value a society gives to innovation and to maintaining the old. The Japanese concept of *kata* indicates the importance of this factor. *Kata* refers to the ideal pattern or the way things should properly be. This ideal is used in many areas of life in addition to music. Japanese buildings were formerly all built of wood, and since they were often destroyed by earthquake, wind, or fire, a replacement was often built on the same site with the same plan. Because it was the same *kata* it was considered the same building (Hozumi, personal communication, June 25, 1987). *Kata* appears in Japanese music not only as the proper sounds produced during a performance, but also as the many standardized and exaggerated movements involved in singing, acting, and playing instruments. The importance of conforming to the *kata* of one's school or guild makes innovation and change very difficult. The only way to make a significant change in the music one has learned is to break away and begin a new guild. When young Japanese went to Europe to study in the latter part of the nineteenth century after Japan opened

up to the outside world, they learned Western music as it was performed in Paris, Vienna, or London. Upon returning to Japan they
formed groups similar to the *ryu*, each based on the music of the
particular European style that they had learned (Harich-Schneider
1973:548–549). This value given to *kata* is a major reason that ancient Japanese music has retained its characteristics for hundreds of
years.

[Many times music is drastically affected by nonmusical values,
especially those linked to religion. Music accompanies both festive
processions and the words of prayers. In many societies it leads to
possession by spirits.] Some writers have suggested that music
changes less frequently when it is connected with religion (Herndon
and McLeod 1979:43; D. Olsen 1980:388). In many societies the
music of rituals is under severe constraints because it must be performed absolutely correctly every time or it will be ineffective. In
some situations, however, religious beliefs seem to provide incentives for change. Among the Shona, considerable change has taken
place in the repertoire of songs used in ancestral spirit possession
ceremonies. The songs that are actually used are believed to be the
favorite songs of deceased ancestors, so songs from the whole range
of traditional repertoire are incorporated into the body of ancestral
spirit songs. This may simply be a result of the desire to continue
using favorite songs from the past that would otherwise be lost.

Music change is often drastic when nonmusical values determine
decisions affecting music that are made by powerful groups in the
society, particularly government or large commercial concerns. Japan provides an example of this factor: the institution of the Imperial Music Department is a part of the government. When the Japanese government decided to westernize the country in the latter part
of the nineteenth century, the imperial court musicians were told to
learn Western music, and they had no choice but to do so (Harich-
Schneider 1973:535). Central authority also provided for the inclusion of Western music in the educational system.

The strength of subtle coercion arises both from the government
itself, and from agencies sponsored by government. A clear case of
purposeful government influence was shown in the Soviet Union,
where composers were subject to varying degrees of pressure from
the Communist Party after the revolution of October 1917. This
pressure took the form of requiring musicians to communicate socialist ideals, to make their music accessible to all the people, and
to create music distinct from the music of the West. Similar goals
were imposed on all the arts; their implementation was known as
socialist realism. The requirement to communicate the goals of so-

cialism was much more difficult to implement in music than it was in literature, theater, and art because the latter could represent verbal or visual images and music could not. The effect of socialist realism on composers was to encourage them to create works with texts that could present the message, or to give their works programmatic titles that would enable the hearer to perceive some sort of message. Purely musical works, such as orchestral pieces or chamber music, were often labeled formalist, indicating that the structure of the music itself overshadowed any meaning that might be given to it. By persistently writing such works, some of the great composers of the twentieth century, like Prokofiev and Shostakovich, were often in trouble with the authorities. Making the music accessible to workers and peasants meant that composers had to avoid complex structures that required musical training in order to understand the music. A major concern was that *"all* art must be understood by *all* the people" (Schwarz 1983 : 245). The political revolution in Russia came at a time when European composers were experimenting with forms of musical style that no longer relied on the system of key relationships that had guided Western music for three centuries. This kind of music did not appeal to Russia's political leaders, particularly Josef Stalin, and the use of too much dissonant or atonal music by Soviet composers was considered a sign of decadence. Dissonant music sounded like conflict, which the socialist system was supposed to eliminate from society. Such music indicated a lack of concern for communicating musically with the people; nevertheless, talented composers resisted the demand that their music should sound like that of everyone else.

The goals of socialist realism were pursued through the Union of Soviet Composers and its relationship to the Communist Party and the government. Composers who did not stray from the prescribed criteria continued to receive their support from the Union. Occasional failures to conform were condemned, and most musicians simply amended their work in order to conform. Some composers continued as performers, and either did not compose, or did not present their compositions for performance. Opinion as to whether this system improved or hindered the development of Soviet music is divided. The composers were not allowed to produce music in an ivory tower atmosphere, catering to a small coterie of followers. On the other hand, the government role made it possible for less talented musicians to obtain power by political means over other musicians. In short, composers had to choose between creating music they considered simplistic or forgoing a musical career. The fact that some of them reduced their output of compositions could be cited as weakening or slowing the development of Russian music. Clearly, the arrangements between Soviet composers and the government played a substantial role in determining the direction in which Russian music developed.

One of the goals of the Bolshevik revolution was to enable Russia to break away from the political, economic, and cultural domination of Western Europe. The socialist government not only influenced Russian composers of "serious" music, it also was active in promoting the presentation and dissemination of the traditional music of non-Russian peoples in the Soviet Union. Soviet leaders were eager to avoid not only the unaccustomed sounds of Western Europe's avant-garde composers, but also any tendency to imitate Western music or show any servility to the West. Many types of music, particularly jazz and rock, were condemned as decadent, foreign, and bourgeois (Schwarz 1983).

In stark contrast to this situation is capitalism, where economic factors are extremely important and decisions concerning music events are often determined by the possibility of producing profits. The economy, as the portion of the sociocultural system that offers goods and services, provides important incentives or constraints to change. In the days before music was electronically reproduced, it was provided by musicians under the patronage system as a form of service. Thus, as we have seen, musicians were often treated the same as gardeners, cooks, barbers, and others who catered to the wealthy. With the introduction of records, tapes, and compact discs, music has become a commodity, and consequently an opportunity for making profit. Although live music continues to exist as a form of service—for example, in the form of a band hired to play at a wedding—the commercialization of music as goods is especially conducive to music change.

An important feature of music change is that it occurs on many different levels, and comparing change or change processes in different societies must take these levels into account. The levels of change are similar to the levels of musical behavior discussed in Chapter 1. Changes often occur in a certain piece or a specific performance, but they are not necessarily going to result in changes to the musical norms. Changes occur in the work of individual musicians, but they too can be idiosyncratic, unless the individual is highly influential. The community is a level at which many significant musical changes can occur. In many cases, change in the musical culture or musical tradition tends to result from changes in the nature of music events and music complexes rather than any striking innovation of an individual. Often it is the community that abandons rituals containing music. Change frequently occurs as a result of the decline of a music complex, or by the adoption of one from neighboring peoples. Other important levels of music change are the ethnic group and global levels, as mentioned earlier. Much of the controversy in theoretical discussions is due to different researchers failing to consider that they are focusing on different levels in their analyses.

Some general features of sociocultural change often occur in relation to music. Not all changes in music are equally noticeable. Some occur so gradually that people are unaware of them until they look back over a long period of time. Such changes are called "drift" in linguistics and anthropology (Herskovits 1948:581). This term aptly describes similar changes in music. Drift can be caused by purposeful minor changes, as well as by lapses in socialization, where members of a new generation reinterpret or misunderstand the activity of their elders.

One of the major processes that occurs in music is syncretism, which occurs when idioms from two societies or musical cultures are combined, thus forming a new type of idiom. Syncretism is the basis of African-American music, which often combines the leader-response form of Africa with the harmonies of Europe. Musicologists have suggested that syncretism is more likely to occur when two musical styles have sufficient musical features in common to provide compatibility (R. Waterman 1952:207; Merriam 1964:314; Nettl 1985:20). Others maintain that nonmusical features can contribute equally or even more to syncretism (Kartomi 1981:240). Possibly the high prestige value attached to accomplishment in features of Western music is more important than similarities in style (Wachsman 1961:147). The cases used in this controversy are often comparisons of African and Native American musics. African music seems to share more common features with European music than does that of the Amerindians. Africans, who often eagerly embraced European civilization, perhaps created combinations of their music with European music because they did not, at least at first, foster the resentment felt by Native Americans at the loss of their land and cultures to outsiders. Moreover, African music was basically improvisational, and was never required to be absolutely correct in performance, as was much Amerindian music.

Although Japan often maintains distinct separation between its traditional music and music of the West, syncretism still occurs. *Kayokyoku* music blends European harmonies with features of Japanese music, including the pentatonic scale, voice production, and duple meter (Kitahara 1966:271). Syncretism is also represented in more recent forms of popular music, such as *enka,* which combines the use of European instruments with an Asian singing style.

Much of what has been happening in the art music establishment throughout the world is basically syncretism. A type of international music has developed in which non-Western instruments are used with Western orchestras, or vice versa. Ravi Shankar has composed concertos for sitar and orchestra. The Japanese koto has been used with an orchestra in some works. Lou Harrison has composed music for the gamelan, with French horn or viola as solo instruments.

The opposite of syncretism, **compartmentalization,** exists when the musical idioms of different backgrounds are kept separate, with both being used but not mixed. Compartmentalization is a social as well as a psychological phenomenon. In Japan, the society has maintained traditional music and also adopted wholeheartedly the music of Western civilization, but few, if any, Japanese perform in both traditions.

Compartmentalization sometimes occurs when individuals are able to perform in two musical idioms, using whichever is appropriate. In a case from southern Africa:

> Bushmen girls could imitate European music with simple harmonies that they had in all likelihood heard on farms and outside the church at the Kuruman mission. And they were able to sing in the European diatonic scale without prejudice to their own very different mode. In fact they kept the two styles completely distinct. (Kirby 1971:245)

The Inuit of Greenland and Alaska also have compartmentalized their musical experience.

> East Greenlanders are managing to separate the two basic kinds of musical expression, which means that the occidental style does not influence the traditional style and vice versa. . . . The normal reaction to occidental music has been to accept it or to reject it, but not to combine it with the traditional music. (P. R. Olsen 1973:32, 35)

In the Americas, one reason for compartmentalization by Native Americans is so they can enjoy modern idioms but still use traditional music as a means to lay claim to Indian status for the purpose of obtaining land (Johnston 1976:168).

One pattern of change that has often been ignored is the gradual decline or abandonment of old forms of musical behavior. When the activity requiring a particular musical complex is no longer relevant in a changing social situation, people often choose not to take the time or effort to perform the music involved. Unless such music has intrinsic qualities of its own, or takes on some new form of meaning, it is likely to be forgotten. Among some Shona groups the songs formerly used for rituals connected with the chiefs began to decline as the chiefs lost autonomy under the rule of the European invaders. A few of the particularly well-liked songs either became symbols of resistance, or were related to various ancestor spirits and performed in that context. In Micronesia in the Western Pacific, certain music and dances were related to the widespread custom of tattooing, but as that practice declined in popularity, so did the music and dances connected with it.

Although social processes are primarily accountable for determining the existence of music events, it is mainly the cognitive processes of individuals that determine the musical forms themselves. However, the choice between an ancient local idiom and a modern foreign one often is based also on nonmusical factors. Just as some people refuse to perform the music of an oppressive ethnic group, so do others deliberately choose to perform music of their own ethnic group. In Zimbabwe, during the liberation war, the Shona musical idiom was used to develop national identity and to affirm commitment to the liberation forces. After the war the use of other idioms was commonplace, and many young men returned to the guitars they had previously enjoyed. It is very possible that when people live in the midst of upheaval they will retain a large amount of their traditional symbolism; when the society is relatively stable, people will be freer to venture into new and different areas of musical expression.

Culture Contact and Music Change

Although social and ideological factors within a society are important in determining the balance of change and continuity, by far the greatest incentive to change in music has been contact between societies. These contacts have included the wanderings of occasional traders, conquest, and long-term political and economic domination. These contacts commonly result in a process referred to as diffusion or borrowing. **Diffusion** is often used to refer to this process as it occurred in the past, whereas **borrowing** refers more to contemporary activity. It is also useful to note that whereas people borrow, it is cultural features that diffuse. Culture contact not only presents new ideas and artifacts, but also causes social, political, and economic changes that require adjustive reactions in the life of the society. Music is affected by both of these processes.

As far back as data are available, musical cultures have changed by borrowing new instruments, repertories, and even uses of music from other societies. The musical traditions of Indonesia are the result of an influx of Hindu musical practices superimposed upon a basis of native beliefs and rituals. Subsequently, Islam swept over the islands, creating yet another layer of cultural and musical norms (Kartomi 1980). China represents another example of diffusion, since it has received cultural and musical influences from central Asia throughout its history. China, in turn, has profoundly affected musical practices in Korea and Japan.

Diffusion is particularly significant in relation to musical instruments. They diffuse fairly easily and rapidly, either as the instruments themselves are taken from one area to another, or as people migrate from one place to another and take with them the knowledge of how to construct the musical instruments of their cultural heritage. Diffusion of musical instruments has occurred throughout human history. The continual warfare that took place in antiquity in southwestern Asia ended "the exclusively national character of musical instruments" (C. Sachs 1940:87). The practice of taking slaves helped spread musical instruments. Even more significant in terms of scope were the Moslem conquests beginning in the seventh century:

> The Kurdish spike fiddle then was found in the Balinese gamelan as well as in the hands of the Egyptian bard; the old Semitic frame drum was struck by the Arabian as by the Spanish girl; the Persian oboe was blown by the Dayak in Borneo as in Morocco. (Ibid.:246)

The widespread diffusion of musical instruments throughout Europe and Asia is an important chapter in musical history, and it is still occurring today. The borrowing of instruments has included the use of trumpet, violin, and accordion by the rural Macedonians, replacing the use of bagpipes and flutes (N. Sachs 1975:206). The Gypsy musicians who are hired there to play on special occasions now mix Western and Eastern instruments with Eastern rhythmic patterns and Western harmony (ibid.:208).

This diffusion involves more than the instruments themselves. The names of instruments also move from place to place, and one cannot assume that the names always stay with the same instruments. The expression **floating terms** has been used to indicate that

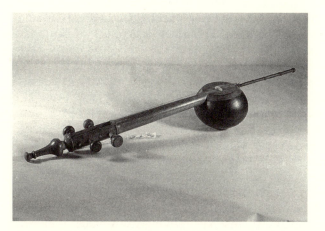

7.2. The *kemenche*, a spike fiddle, 37″ long, from Iran. (Instrument in William Hammond Mathers Museum, Bloomington, Indiana; photo by the author.)

instruments, when borrowed by one society from another, are sometimes given new names; in addition, names that diffuse with certain instruments can later be given to different instruments (Malm 1977:31). An example is the spike fiddle, which is a type of lute where the stick supporting the strings pierces the resonator and extends below it (Photo 7.2). The spike fiddle was originally played by holding it upright on the ground or on the lap, much like a cello is played today. The Arabic form of the spike fiddle had come from the short lute of Persia, which in the tenth century became bowed instead of plucked. The Arabs called it *rabab*, a generic term for a bowed instrument. As the instrument spread, it became known as a *rebab* in Indonesia and a *ribab* in Morocco. When it arrived in the Philippines, through the agency of Moslems, it was called the *gitgit* (Malm 1977:30). In Byzantium it was given a new name, *lura*, which later became lyra, and the instrument changed considerably. In Europe it was originally called the *rubeba*, and later became known as a *rebec* (Marcuse, 1975:432). After undergoing numerous modifications, both to the form of the instrument and to its playing technique, it became known as the violin and its related instruments.

Such changes characterized many other instruments. The *nay* was an early Arabic generic term for a woodwind instrument. In the Near East it referred to a long end-blown flute, but the term was also widely known as referring to the shawm, a double-reed instrument (see Photo 4.7). In Iran today the shawm is called a *surnay*. In Turkey today *nay* is the generic term for flute, in the Punjab (India) the term refers to a shawm, and in Rumania it refers to panpipes (Marcuse 1975:360–361).

The Persian word for string, as on a chordophone, is *tar*. Derived from this are the terms *dutar*, a two-stringed instrument, and sitar, a three-stringed one (C. Sachs 1940:256–257). Even though additional strings were later added to the sitar, the name remained the same. Persian and Greek are both Indo-European languages, and it is interesting to speculate on a possible relationship between the Persian *tar* and Greek word *kithara*. The latter word is the origin of both the words "guitar," a form of lute, and "zither," a form of chordophone in which the strings are placed over the resonator.

The spread of musical instruments has not always depended on the instruments themselves moving from place to place; it has occurred through diffusion of the techniques used in constructing them. The plucked lamellophones of Africa (mbira) are indigenous to no other areas of the world, except for South America today. The lamellophone was taken there in the minds of African slaves, through their knowledge of its construction techniques. The slaves were stripped of everything they owned, but the knowledge went with them.

Another important aspect of instrument diffusion is the playing technique. Some musicologists of African music surmise that the mbira was taken from central Africa to West Africa, since some West Africans play the instrument with the prongs or keys facing away from the body rather than toward it. In China, some stringed instruments are bowed, with hairs of the bow inserted between the strings and the resonator (Photo 7.3), while others are played with the bow above the strings; the latter is the technique that spread from Europe and West Asia via Islam.

Musical changes result not only from borrowing, but also because of adjustments to the music system brought about by adaptation to a new situation, particularly conquest by outsiders. Conquest has long been a factor in human history, and it has often had a significant effect on musical behavior. Political activity is one of the most important areas where decisions can involve music, since music is often seen and used as a symbol of political identity and political aspirations. The social anthropologist Abner Cohen (1974) points out that when people are not permitted to organize political groups to protect their own interests, they often express themselves politically through symbols. Certain types of musical events decline simply because performing them symbolizes acquiescence in un-

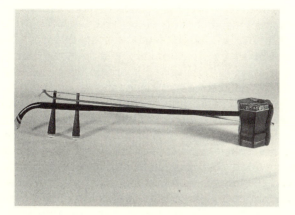

7.3. A Chinese *er-hu*, a chordophone that is played with the bow under the string. This one is 32" long. (Instrument in William Hammond Mathers Museum, Bloomington, Indiana; photo by the author.)

popular political situations. Karl Signell (1976:76) cites the backwardness of the old Ottoman Empire as a reason why traditional Turkish music, including classical court music, was no longer played when Turkey became a republic. Blacking (1973:37–38) notes the South African oppression of the Venda as an explanation for the fact that the latter do not choose to perform European music. This situation contrasts in an interesting way with Zimbabwe. There, the elite prefer Afro-European–style music, even though they recognize that African-style music is preferred by many of the peasants, and would be a more suitable national symbol.

Sometimes conquerors have simply outlawed or banned certain forms of music. For many years Canada forbade the presentation of potlatch feasts by the Kwakiutl and other Native American groups because they were considered a waste of time, effort, and resources. This proscription applied also to the music and dance that were an integral part of the feast (Spradley 1969:82). African drumming was banned in colonial Angola ostensibly because it disturbed the Portuguese settlers.

Sometimes banning is an attempt to prohibit symbolic communication among subject people. In Papua New Guinea during World War II the Japanese forbade slit-drums of the Papuans because they did not want the instruments used for reporting troop movements. They also inadvertently destroyed the Papuans' skin drums, which were used for different purposes. This mistake caused resentment among the Papuans and of course interfered with their music (Ryan 1972:819). The African hymn "God Bless Africa" was often banned in African countries by the colonial powers. At one time during the English domination of Ireland and Scotland, bagpipes were banned because they served as nationalistic symbols.

Changes in social conditions due to culture contact have produced indirect change in music. India has not widely adopted the sounds of Western music, but it presents a clear picture of the impact of social change on musical practices. One of these social changes was the loss of power of the maharajahs and other aristocrats. The decline of power meant that fewer musicians, if any, were employed at court, so performances of the classical court music had to be arranged in other ways if the musicians were to continue practicing their skills. Associations were formed for the purpose of organizing public concerts. In order to accommodate people who worked during the day, concerts were offered only in the evenings, which meant that the leisurely improvised nature of the performances had to be curtailed in order to present more than one raga before the public transportation closed down for the night. Evening concerts also meant that the significance of the ragas in terms of appropriate times of day came to be increasingly irrelevant, especially in South India (Higgins 1976). Similar changes have occurred elsewhere. Music of the *tahardent*—the three-stringed plucked lute—was originally popular among the western Tuareg of Mali (Ex. 5.1). The vassal caste performers formerly played this music at the chiefs' courts, but due to the abolition of slavery and the weakening power of the nobility, the bards now perform on a contractual basis. This music, which has spread to all Tuareg areas, has become urban music that appeals to individuals who are particularly interested in modernization and urbanization (Card 1982:179–180). *Tahardent* music appears to combine an Arabic modal system with sub-Saharan principles of rhythm and meter (ibid.:174).

Western Influence on World Musics

By far the greatest amount of music change in the last 150 years has been due to the spread of Western culture. As the industrial revolution drove Europeans to look for raw materials and markets all over the world, they gradually spread their own views of music and musical styles everywhere.

Much of the European expansion was military, and music was used to impress people with the pomp and power of European armies. As armies and police units were organized in the colonies, they were provided with bands based on the European model. In many parts of the world Western control depended not only on armies, but also on the psychological domination engendered by the ideology of European superiority. Music played its part in maintaining this ideology. Europeans sent missionaries to convert and educate the indigenous peoples. Being steeped in unquestioned ethnocentrism, these missionaries not only emphasized European music, but also condemned traditional local music as either primitive, or sinful, or both. Many groups, such as those in Polynesia, assimilated Western music to such a degree that older people forgot the original forms of local music, and young people never learned them.

Western educational "experts" have sometimes made attempts to "develop" or "systematize" various music traditions. Some people have tried to "regularize" the asymmetrical rhythms of India and the Balkans. Such undertakings may have represented good intentions, but they certainly helped undermine self-esteem among the recipients. Moreover, one must not overlook the possibility that many such cases may represent efforts by the ruling classes to control the musical expression of the conquered peoples.

In many different areas schools and music teachers introduced music notation. Its use in other countries has had unforeseen consequences for the music systems where it was adopted. For example, the use of notation in Javanese gamelan music is profoundly affecting that music. Because it is seen as a feature of Western civilization, the use of notation carries considerable prestige; thus, it tends to be used excessively. Notation is often used to accelerate the learning process, since industrialization has brought about a situation in which musicians have less time to devote to their art. Notation is "the most pervasive, penetrating, and ultimately the most insidious type of Western influence" (Becker 1980:11). The use of notation has made it possible for people in the rural areas to learn to play the gamelan the way it is played in urban courts, resulting in a decrease in the variety of styles used in different parts of the island. A major problem of notation is that Javanese gamelan music is basically an improvisational tradition. When the notes to be played are written down and come from an authoritative source, an idea of right and wrong versions results. This attitude decreases variety in performance by inhibiting the musicians' freedom to improvise (Becker 1972:3–4). Notation also affects Javanese music through the learning process. Gamelan music has been conceptualized traditionally as a pattern of sounds, not a linear sequence. The pattern of sound within each of the cycles has been of major importance. The training of the musician has emphasized orientation to the whole ensemble while gradually increasing the concentration given to his own part. The use of notation inevitably involves thinking in terms of lines rather than cycles or patterns, so that the performer begins to think of his own line rather than the totality of effect of the entire ensemble (Becker 1980:23).

The effects of bands, churches, and schools are insignificant compared to the more recent effects of the music industry. Popular music has been characterized in earlier chapters as a kind of commercial successor to folk music, that is, the music of modern popular culture. It emerged as a part of the industrial revolution, first as a result of widespread publishing and later as the production of **phonograms**—records, tapes, and compact discs. The music industry aimed to provide music to a mass audience, and its purpose, as with other capitalist enterprises, was to produce a profit (Wallis and Malm 1984:29).

The international music industry today is a part of the worldwide socio-economic system. At the time Roger Wallis and Krister Malm did their study of the effects of the music industry on small countries, they found that the world music industry was dominated by five transnational companies, all based in the core countries of the world system (1984:49). These companies produced phonograms primarily for sale in the wealthy countries of Europe and North America. The records that sold well in those areas could then be marketed in the peripheral countries for pure profit. The production of phonograms for the small countries is less profitable because of production costs and the small market. In some cases the large companies have discovered profitable talent in the peripheral countries, and produced phonograms for sale to the worldwide market. This practice has occurred primarily with reggae in Jamaica, calypso in Trinidad, and East African popular music. This system has affected the countries of the periphery because while it has subjected them to the musical norms of international music, it has largely ignored their own. It is extremely difficult for musicians, either alone or in groups, to counteract these powerful influences. "It is only on a governmental level that we find decisions that can possibly match decisions made within the transnational music corporations" (ibid.:18).

Some of the problems caused by the power of the transnationals are financial. When small countries buy copies of phonograms produced in Europe or North America, or play the music on these copies, they are expected to pay royalties, which are locally viewed as an excessive drain of foreign exchange. When local artists are recorded they are often paid a token lump sum so that any large royalties that may result go to the company's profits (ibid.: 150). When a folk song is recorded, all of the royalties go to those who arrange and perform the song for the music industry, with little or nothing going to the original creators. This often happens even when the composers are known, since the mechanism for returning royalties is so cumbersome and corrupt that very little is returned to them. People in small countries who may wish to begin a recording company find that they are undersold by the large companies or overcharged for use of production facilities (ibid.). The transnational music industry represents another way in which the core countries are exploiting the periphery; instead of taking iron ore or mahogany, they are taking cultural materials.

The problems caused by the music industry are not just economic ones; many are musical. A major factor in marketing phonograms is to make the public aware of them, which is most effectively done through broadcasting on the radio. Various methods, including money, sexual procurement, exotic vacations, and free phonograms, are used to bribe radio station managers and disc jockeys to play the numbers that are being promoted by the companies (ibid.:243). Since the international hits are the most profitable, they are the ones most often pushed, leaving local musicians and local styles with fewer opportunities to be heard. The music industry not only emphasizes foreign styles; by creating and marketing music with the widest appeal, it tends to focus on music in which the desirability is based on the text or its danceable qualities. Hearing these performances affects the types of musical styles that appear most natural. People learn to prefer whatever they hear most often, even if it may not be of high quality (ibid.:247).

The buyers of phonograms become accustomed to hearing a studio product, which is difficult to reproduce with live performance.

> Jamaican reggae is an example. It is only in the sophisticated recording studios of Kingston that the reggae sound the world has learnt to recognize is created. Live performances of reggae are extremely rare since the demands on equipment are so great and the finances of all but the top reggae artists are so poor. Reggae can be heard live in Jamaica only at major events such as the Sunsplash Festival or the newly instigated Rockers Magazine awards show. On the other hand, giant discothèques dominate where the spontaneous performance would be by disc jockeys who often improvise lyrics ("toasting" or "rapping") over reggae rhythm tracks ("dubs"). (Wallis and Malm 1984:278–279)

One result of the music industry, then, is to discourage the development of musical skills through performance, as well as to reduce opportunities to hear live performances.

The impact of the music industry on expressive culture in general is extensive. Where the major meaning of a piece of music is conveyed through the text, people become weary of hearing songs in a foreign language. The felt need for recorded music in a local language has often led to the founding of music industries in small countries. The success of such enterprises depends partly on support of the local government and partly on building a cooperative relationship with one of the multinational corporations. The latter course of action works well unless the sales of the smaller company begin to cut the profits of the large one. In such cases the transnational might buy out the local company. This happened in the case of WEA (Warner, Electra, Atlantic) in Sweden.

> WEA, who bought up their Swedish distributor, Metronome, in 1979 (indicating at the time that Metronome's policy of supporting local releases would continue), sold out their studio in 1983 to an employee. The Swedish Council for Cultural Affairs was asked to provide the necessary funds to "look after" the cultural heritage embodied in the company's unique tape library of Swedish music recordings. Such experiences are understandable and can be expected to be repeated many times in the future—obviously the global interests of any transnational must go before the national cultural interests of any one small nation. Otherwise, they would not be in business. (Wallis and Malm 1984: 317–318)

The need for local languages is accommodated in several ways. Sometimes major companies distribute recorded background music, so that the lyrics may be added locally (ibid.: 55). This practice permits use of a local language, but still imposes a musical idiom from outside. The development of inexpensive cassette tape recorders has made it possible for people to record favorite musicians performing their own musical idiom, and then exchange them with each other (ibid.: 270). Where recorded music is restricted on the public media, it is often broadcast from taxis or buses (ibid.: 256). Even though the music industry is contributing to the homogeneity of world music, many people are not content to give up their own expressive culture for a foreign one. "A country which lacks its own culture is no more than a collection of people without the spirit that makes them a nation" (Julius Nyerere, quoted in Wallis and Malm 1984: 218).

The development of cassettes means that in the remotest and poorest areas of the world people have access to worldwide popular music, as well as diverse musical traditions in their own areas. In Java the recording and broadcasting of music in the urban styles has led to imitation of those styles, contributing, along with notation, to the eclipse of regional styles (Becker 1972:4). A similar situation exists among the Tuareg in Algeria, who cannot hear their music over the radio. However, they do purchase tapes for readily available tape recorders, and exchange them with their friends. Thus, they consistently hear their favorite performers and pay less attention than formerly to the local players. If new players begin to imitate the favorites, the result may be less variability of styles in the future (Card 1982:187).

The effects of the music industry are not limited to the sale of phonograms. Technology from the West has also had an impact on music throughout the world, particularly the effect of amplification on performance practice. In Java, gamelan music was originally an interplay between the gamelan and a solo instrument or singer. Placing a microphone in front of the solo performer suddenly emphasizes that part, thus reducing the role of the gamelan to simply providing accompaniment. It is not only the sound that has changed, but the whole idea of interplay of the parts, so that the meaning of the music is now different (Becker 1972:4–5). In India the use of the microphone has meant that inferior equipment often makes the subtle nuances of vocal technique and ornamentation less clear than they were before. It has also enabled singers to sing at a lower pitch and still be heard, thus providing a change in the overall vocal effect (Higgins 1976). Although amplification enables more people to hear a performance, technological problems often distort the music (Neuman 1990:74).

The results of Western technology are not always inimical to the traditions involved. The changes brought about in *juju* bands in Nigeria provide a good example. Originally, these westernized instrumental groups were small, consisting of four performers: one played a banjo and sang, another also sang and sometimes played cymbals or triangle, and two performed on tambourines or the "bottle-gourd rattle." Electronic amplification suddenly made it possible to combine these instruments with traditional Yoruba drums and compensate for the different degrees of loudness of the various instruments. Adding Yoruba instruments, particularly the hour-glass drum, made it possible not only to add more performers, but also to emphasize some of the essential features of Yoruba music. The result of this technological innovation was actually less westernization in the bands, enabling them to serve more effectively as an expression of ethnic identity (C. Waterman 1990:84).

The tourist industry has also made an impact on the musical practices of people throughout the world. Whereas the music industry has taken Western music to the rest of the world, the tourist industry takes wealthy people from North America, Europe, and Japan to exotic places, where they expect to be entertained. The forms of entertainment are often specially arranged events in order to accommodate the short time the tourist is present, and to make sure that what the tourist sees is most profitable (Wallis and Malm 1984:293). Both the musical idioms and the meaning of the music are often modified or improvised to suit the tastes of the outsiders, which eventually results in changed norms for the local people.

The impact of the tourist industry is expressed by a man who was formerly an official of the Ministry of Culture in Sri Lanka.

What is offered to the tourists at many hotels is just a fake. As a practising musician and dance choreographer, I feel sorry that this sort of muck is being shown to the foreign people—many carry home the wrong impression . . .

We once called the hoteliers together, and told them that much of the stuff that was being put out was trash. Most of them get hold of one person who knows a little bit, tell him to bring along six or seven who can jump around. Then there will be a lot of drum-beating and fire eating, with the least amount of art and the most amount of gymnastics and "magic." And the tourists go home thinking this is the culture of Sri Lanka.

We offered to put on a proper show. Of course we had demands— we had to get paid. And we refused to perform in hotels when people are munching their chicken and drinking their beer. We will perform if they come to sit down and appreciate our show. Take it between seven and eight, and then let the people disperse. No hotelier would take it that way. (Wallis and Malm 1984:293–294)

Tourism is not always under the control of the hotelier or tour guide, since communities sometimes arrange to present their own traditions. Among the Kwakiutl of British Columbia, the use of music has changed because of tourism. Music was originally used with the dances accompanying the potlatch ceremonies, where chiefs would proclaim their status by giving away gifts to the participants. The presence of white settlers in the village of Alert Bay led to the hospital committee presenting Kwakiutl dances as a European-type benefit concert. This meant that instead of giving goods away to the audience, they were asking the audience to pay. Later the village built a community house and presented dances to people from the tourist boats that stopped there in the summer. These performances again required an admission fee; dancers and singers were paid for their performances and profit went to the community. Performances that had at one time taken all night and had been conducted in terms of social relationships were now performed during the day for pay. Long dances were shortened so that a variety could be performed during the amount of time boat passengers were ashore (Spradley 1969).

Tourism does have its positive features. In many situations people would be inclined to discontinue their traditional forms of expression once they no longer served their original purposes. The need to have some sort of unique presentation for tourists has provided motivation for continuing the traditional songs and dances. Such events can provide both economic benefits and a positive image of one's cultural heritage. The nature of the impact of tourism depends to some extent on whether it is under local control or whether the whole system is forced on people by outsiders.

Recent studies have shown that although Western music is very popular the world over, it by no means dominates the musical life of all societies. In many areas people inadvertently change Western music, or combine it with their traditional idiom to create something new. Non-Western peoples seem to be continuing to create new forms of musical expression, with or without Western influence. Nettl, in fact, suggests that the spread of Western music throughout the world will actually *increase* the world's musical diversity (1985:3).

Conclusion

It has been customary for people interested in the diversity of human culture and human musical systems to deplore the gradual westernization of so many societies throughout the world. Western musical styles and technology are usually considered to cause a permanent loss of musical diversity as they make their imprint on hundreds of local and regional musical styles. Although the loss of any musical idiom is a diminution of the human heritage, the picture is not as bleak as it sometimes appears. In many areas people are returning to the musical traditions of their ancestors, particularly as they see the need for maintaining some sort of ethnic identity.

Moreover, a decrease in musical styles does not necessarily involve a decrease in musically skilled people, so that the interplay of cultures may eventually result in even wider musical possibilities. In India "there has probably been a *decrease* in the diversity of performance styles. At the same time there has been an *increase* in the variety of musical experiments and forms that musicians perform" (Neuman 1990:229). One must not forget that in the formerly isolated corners of the world people are experiencing the introduction of new and exciting musical possibilities. One question that remains for the future is whether the development of music will be guided by people in their own societies or whether it will be left to those whose interest is motivated by personal profit.

CHAPTER EIGHT

Music in Modern Life

THIS SURVEY OF MUSIC from the holistic and scientific perspective should have given the reader a wider and fresher view of what music is all about. Although some people consider anthropology to be the study of the exotic, it is basically the study of all humans, including those in modern complex societies. Studying the role of music in diverse societies should clarify the role it plays in one's own. One reason the sociocultural matrix has such a profound effect on music everywhere is that people become accustomed to things as they are, and tend to be unaware of the forces operating around them. The scientific and holistic study of music is designed to increase awareness of those forces.

As with any form of science, social science has an applied side, as well as a theoretical one. The applied form of the study of music is usually considered to relate to the performance of music itself, and in the case of worldwide music systems, it would involve the playing of a diverse range of world music. However, when science deals with the relationship between music and the society in which it develops, the applied form logically is directed toward using the findings of the study to provide intelligent and informed decisions about organizing musical experiences in society. Effective decisions regarding musical performance and enjoyment require awareness of the sociocultural forces that are constantly at play around us.

Some of the decisions concerning music are purely personal, and include one's choices about the music one will choose to play or listen to. Individuals should become aware of whether they are reacting to the words, the usefulness, or the intrinsic qualities of music, or perhaps to a combination of these. One should try to understand and appreciate the intrinsic qualities of musical styles that are at present unfamiliar. The greater the variety of music that one can relate to, the greater the amount of enrichment it will provide to life. One should be aware of the possibility of missing something valuable musically if one's taste is limited to danceable music or songs that depend primarily upon appealing lyrics.

Modern Society

Many characteristics of modern industrial society have profound effects on musical activity. One of the most important of these is social stratification. Although some egalitarian societies once existed, they have been swallowed up in modern nation-states to the extent that it can truly be said that everyone on earth now lives in a stratified society. Even societies with an egalitarian ideology are divided between the well-educated and the poorly educated—those who control the basic decisions regarding the society and those who have little or no voice in those decisions. The different social strata are reflected in the ways music is used to symbolize class distinctions, particularly through differences between high and popular culture. Social stratification also appears as differential opportunities for people to pursue careers in music.

Stratification exists not only within national societies, but also in the world system. In this case the status differences tend to be expressed as ethnocentrism or ethnic distinctiveness, often reinforced by musical practices. In some cases ethnic groups retain their ancestral music as a means of struggling against the mental domination of outsiders. In other cases ethnic musics serve to highlight the status of people whose position in the world system is clearly subordinate. In either case, the study of distinctive musical traditions should reveal them as valid and often unique forms of expression. Noting the skill and intrinsic qualities of such musical expressions ought to lead to greater respect for the people who create them.

Another characteristic feature of modern industrial societies is individualism, which develops as people are required to move about in search of employment. Individualism is particularly noticeable in America, where it was considered a necessary quality for taming the wilderness. One result of individualism is to minimize the interactional aspects of music performance and stress the competitive ones. This occurs, for example, as performers are urged to compete with each other for first chair in a band or orchestra, or when groups of performers see their efforts as competition with other groups. Individualism is also fostered by the widespread use of earphones with portable tape players. The music industry fosters individualism when it promotes the cult of stardom because of the lower cost of marketing recordings of widely known and popular performers. Developing a following for new performers is costly and reduces profits. Individualism emphasizes self-expression more than it does communication. Much so-called "art" music seems to be produced to satisfy the expressive impulse of the creator rather than to communicate anything to an audience.

Western society is not only stratified and individualistic, it is also highly materialistic. In the modern capitalist system it is necessary to foster a sense of materialism in order to encourage the marketing of products of industrial production. In terms of music, this emphasis leads to the use of resources for larger and more ornate opera houses and concert halls, or more and bigger loudspeakers both at performances and in private homes. The essential features of music are not material, and the focus on material aspects of musical products can undermine recognition of qualities of the music itself. This materialistic orientation has been fostered by many approaches in anthropology, and is one of the reasons music has been considered peripheral to the important aspects of life.

In modern industrial society, one of the major features of music is that it has become a type of commodity to be bought and sold. The effects of this trend have often gone unrecognized. In order to be commercially successful, a commodity must be constantly improved, or at least presented as a new version, in order to stimulate sales. This practice has resulted in valuing novelty for its own sake in Western society. This high value on novelty has been transferred to music, so that new or different effects in text, content, and musical features are more highly regarded than anything else. The need to create as large a market as possible has resulted in simplification of forms. As a result, much commercial music is based on the novelty and appeal of the texts and a pulsing dance beat. A trend toward diminished importance of complex musical features also appears to be taking place in much commercial music.

The prevalence of phonograms has caused musical behavior to shift from actively producing music to passively listening. Consequently, many of the benefits obtained from musical performance are missed. These benefits include the esprit de corps that often develops from performance and the pleasure from mastery of physical movement required for performance. In many places it reduces the possibility of singing in one's own language. Music education, in the sense of teaching children performance skills, is considered relatively unimportant. The appreciation of individual or group skill is lessened when the performance is not live. Listening to phonograms can develop a taste for live performances, but this is frustrated as studio technology produces sounds that cannot be replicated easily in a live performance.

Functions

People in Western society today are blissfully unaware of some of the basic functions of music. The propagation of profitable forms of music has contributed to the perception that music is merely a form of entertainment. As a result, many people engage in musical behavior without considering the real functions of music. Function in this sense refers to the consequences of musical experience, whether they are intentional or not. Many of these functions are operating even when the music is viewed primarily as entertainment, and the functions can be either negative or positive. One of these functions is to legitimize other areas of activity, and this has a negative effect when popular music appears to legitimize the use of drugs, violence as a solution to problems, and a view of women as sex objects.

A better understanding of the various uses and functions of music should lead to considerations as to whether or not some of the potential positive functions of music might add something to life in one's society. One feature of music as play is that it serves to develop in children a sense of cooperation. This sense is also reinforced in adults through group performance of music. Excessive individualism can nullify this very important feature of musical activity. Music helps a society as it fosters the cooperation that can counteract the antisocial effects of individuals who act exclusively on their own impulses. Musical participation can also serve as a means to develop skills in evaluating various courses of action and making decisions accordingly. Such skills are essential to effective participation in the life of complex societies, and the arts provide opportunities to practice them in an area that is not likely to be disastrous if a mistake is made. Music also helps a society adapt as it provides a means of reducing boredom by increasing mental challenge and variety in life's experiences. To the degree that music is simplistic and inane, it fails to function in this way. The stimulus of producing music in a group may serve to counteract feelings of alienation and aimlessness that permeate much of our society today. The quality of life in a society depends upon awareness of what is happening, including the consequences of various forms of musical activity. Society needs to discourage musical behavior that produces negative effects and encourage behavior that results in positive ones.

Musical Values

The function of music as a form of aesthetic experience has often been overlooked or misinterpreted. The standard definition of the term aesthetic relates it to beauty, or to intrinsic quality, as the word has been rephrased for cross-cultural comparison. Perhaps one reason intrinsic qualities in music and the other arts are valued less today is because of the rejection by many people of bourgeois values in general. During the 1960s, reaction against the established power structures led many people, especially youth, to question and reject the value system of the elite. Although many of the old values may have needed rejection, one should not assume that this is necessarily true of artistic values. The rejected values have included those related to beauty or the intrinsic qualities of music and the other arts. Western values regarding music now emphasize innovation and the requirement that something be expressed, with attention focusing on emotion. None of these things necessarily involve beauty in the sense of appreciation of intrinsic qualities of finesse, skill, and structure.

Perhaps the focus on innovation and expressiveness is a reflection of the profitable or prestigious uses of music. The values given to arts within a society are determined by interaction within that society. Music as a commodity and as a symbol of prestige is important in modern society, and both require high degrees of innovation. When music is primarily a commodity, its profitability is enhanced by the constant input of new material. When the elite promulgate music primarily as a symbol of class distinction, they seek endless innovation to assure, perhaps unconsciously, that ordinary people will not obtain it easily or cheaply. Commercialism and prestige are both forces that lead innovation to become more important than beautiful intrinsic qualities.

Expressiveness is more closely related to the referential than the aesthetic meanings of music, but because the feelings expressed are often emotional, the term aesthetic has been applied to them. It is much easier to produce for the market if expressiveness is limited to the text. Truly artistic music combines profound expressiveness with skillfully produced intrinsic musical qualities. The requirement for uniqueness creates a problem in that musical tones can only be combined and understood in limited ways. Concern with aesthetic musical qualities would tend to limit the amount of new material created, and would probably narrow the potential market.

An apparently unavoidable feature of a stratified society is conflict of interest between the ruling class and the majority of the people. This disparity is often expressed as differences in the expressive cultures of the two groups, with one group being accused of elitism and the other of mediocrity. Having different types of musical life and musical preferences sets the classes apart. Before the development of electronic reproduction of music, the distinction between music for the elite and music for the masses was probably unavoidable, since opportunities for hearing music were limited. Any kind of music requires high familiarity for people to appreciate its intrinsic qualities. Much folk music had such qualities, as did much music of the upper classes. But the music that resulted from full-time music professionals was not heard by most people because of the cost and exclusiveness of performances. Due to the availability of a wide range of music on records and tapes, attitudes of elitism concerning music need not persist. The issue of elitism has been a concern of many socialist countries, some of whom have chosen to deal with it by forcing musicians to simplify their work. A truly democratic society would find a much more effective approach by providing better music education in schools. Thus, all students would have the opportunity to hear good recordings and learn to perceive and appreciate a wide range of intrinsic music qualities. Quality of life in a society would be enhanced if music were a unifying factor, rather than a divisive one.

It is important here to recall the distinction between legitimized music and aesthetic music. Aesthetic music must be distinguished from the music legitimized in high culture, since the latter is often used as a way of symbolizing class differences. Much high culture music does have aesthetic qualities, but one must not assume that this is true for all of it. Nor can one assume that other music lacks these qualities. Aesthetic qualities are found in many types of popular culture music. People who are talented and musically sensitive take part in popular music performance, and they should be given recognition when their ability leads them to include interesting and affective intrinsic qualities. Although many non-Western societies do not have forms of discourse about aesthetic values, denying any aesthetic interest to the music of non-Western people could well be a form of claiming superiority over them. The fact that aesthetic qualities are not talked about does not mean they are absent. The appreciation of complex mental activity in life is apparently a universal human trait, and musical complexity, as one aesthetic form, seems to be valued in many societies. Aesthetic music is not simply a matter of complexity, but also of fitting expressive communication into restricted forms. It certainly has played an important part in Western civilization over the centuries. The skill involved in meeting such a challenge has been valued in many societies, and has been an important feature of Western music.

An important consideration for the future is whether the empha-

sis on novelty and expressiveness means freedom or meaninglessness. The fact that people all over the world have tended to structure
their expressive activities in some way would seem to indicate that
overcoming restrictions in order to create meaningful art or music
provides additional challenge for the creative person's skills. Instead
of using the arts to express the meaninglessness of modern life, the
artist might do better to use the arts to instill meaning into life.

The Future

An important reason for studying the processes of change is to discover how positive change can be brought about creatively. If the
situation needs improvement, what can the individual do to bring
about positive changes? Wallis and Malm refer to enthusiasts as
"people who feel motivated to work hard, often for unimpressive
salaries, for the sake of creative activity they feel is important to
themselves and to those with whom they associate" (1984: 120). Enthusiasts are a type of nonprofit entrepreneurs of music whose activities are significant. They are the people who at the local level
work for better music education, sponsor performances, or promote
the opportunities for unrecognized performers to be heard.

Few individuals have the power to counteract the way the transnational corporations dominate the music scene. However, enthusiasts can work to bring about changes through government, which
does have power to counteract the influence of transnational companies. Governments can pass laws restricting detrimental activities of such companies, or requiring certain types of beneficial activity, such as recording local musicians.

Governments can be a positive influence on music through subsidies of the arts, including music. In many countries, governments provide such subsidies, sometimes in relation to government-sponsored
radio and television. Subsidies are also provided for performances of
many types of music, especially ensembles whose costs preclude existence on ticket sales alone. Arts subsidies are sometimes a contro-
versial issue, since critics ask why public money should be used for
programs that interest only a small fraction of the population. However, dependence upon wealthy donors tends to make the arts even
more elitist. If schools would do more to foster appreciation of music and the other arts, the subsidies would be appreciated by greater
numbers of people, and the arts would become less elitist. If the
potential functions of music were understood and valued, then the
arguments in favor of subsidies would be enhanced.

Another area where governments, under pressure from musical enthusiasts, can make a difference is in education. Since the perception of more subtle aesthetic features of music often requires a certain amount of experience, its appreciation often depends upon schooling. Making such training available to large numbers of children would counteract the tendency toward musical elitism. The fact that society considers music as somehow peripheral leads educational leaders to put it on the fringes of the curriculum, often cutting it when financial problems appear. Helping school leadership view music as a means of producing sensitive, well-adjusted citizens might help them see musical programs as an important part of the curriculum. Improved music education would help music fulfill more of its potential in making life interesting, and perhaps decrease the role of drugs and vandalism. Perhaps it is the fault of society that music which could provide intellectual stimulation in life for many young people is simply not appreciated.

The nature of the transnational music industry leads to a final question about the future of music: How is a potentially worldwide musical idiom related to the expressive culture of people in many diverse linguistic and cultural groups? Because music is minimally dependent upon the natural environment, few obstacles would seem to impede the growth of worldwide musical idioms. One reason for concern among musicians is the possibility of what Lomax called a "cultural grey-out" (1968:4)—that the world will become homogeneous musically, with the loss of extremely interesting types of musical expression. Another concern is that many people in smaller sociocultural systems will be left without songs in their own language as a means for expressing their own life experiences. Probably some people will always want to express their political frustration through music. These issues, plus the fact that music is an important indication of ethnic identity, will probably keep the music industry from completely homogenizing the world.

As the world becomes one socio-economic system, it is slowly developing international forms of expression, which are probably necessary for developing mutual understanding. A worldwide musical system is one way to develop a type of common experience. Learning to appreciate new musical idioms is certainly much easier than learning another language. One can only hope that the popular music being disseminated internationally by the music industry today will not be the only music available. Expecting other people to take up the music of the West, while the West ignores their music, is not the course to wider understanding. Africa has made a contribution through jazz and jazz derivatives, such as rock music. So has the international world of "serious" music, with its input from India and Japan. International forms of music are certain to increase, and it is to be hoped that some of the less widely known musics of the world will eventually make their contribution.

Notes

1. "Sciencing" about Music

1. "Musical segment" follows the usage of Maquet (1979:56), who refers to the "aesthetic segment" as those aspects of technology, social structure, and ideology that have to do with producing art objects.

2. "Etic" comes from the term "phonetic," which refers to all of the sounds an analyst can determine as being used in a given language. "Emic" is derived from "phonemic," which refers to the particular sounds that carry meanings known only to the speakers of the language. Merriam (1964) referred to this difference by distinguishing the analytical evaluation from the folk evaluation.

3. The distinction between practical and discursive consciousness, or practice and discourse, reflects the distinction often emphasized by Charles Seeger (1960) between making music (music-rationale) and talking about it (speech-rationale of music). Practical consciousness includes the skills necessary for listening to and evaluating music.

4. Bauman speaks of keying or framing in referring to language performances, and Maquet (1979:12), who makes a similar distinction in relation to art objects, uses the term "art framework."

5. The term "performance" has been used not only to distinguish creative from casual behavior, but also to distinguish between behavior and the mental competence serving as the basis of behavior. This distinction was developed by Noam Chomsky, the linguist, to distinguish the knowledge of language forms from the actual spoken language as influenced by factors of a particular situation, such as being tired or intoxicated (1965). Some studies of music have utilized this distinction, so that performance simply means the sounds actually resulting from a particular rendition. The sounds might be influenced by nervousness, intoxication, or a severe cold, none of which would have been part of the intention. The competence refers to the knowledge, both discursive and practical, which the performer used in various renditions; the term practical consciousness covers much of what is meant by competence.

6. Nettl (1965:12–24) presents a clear, concise history of ethnomusicology.

2. The Sociocultural Matrix: Social Factors

1. Henry (1988:6) uses the term "music institution" to refer to what is here called the music complex. Both of these concepts are derived from Anthony Wallace's idea of cult institutions (1966:75 ff).

2. This instrument is often called the Jew's harp, but that term reflects an unnecessary ethnic connotation.

3. Basongye is also written Songye, the "Ba-" being a prefix indicating the plural of the Songye people.

3. The Sociocultural Matrix: Conceptual Factors

1. Although legitimate as an adjective has only one form, the related verb has three forms: legitimate, legitimize, and legitimatize. Many writers prefer to use legitimate, but because that verb form is the same as the adjective, legitimize seems less confusing for the nonspecialized reader; legitimatize seems unnecessarily cumbersome. The two noun forms legitimation and legitimization are interchangeable.

2. Merriam (1964:141–142) presents an interesting description of the position of jazz musicians in the early twentieth century.

3. Since the author who first formulated this idea wrote in French (Gennep 1960), the actual terms for these three stages vary somewhat when discussed in English.

4. The terms socialization and enculturation are often used interchangeably, with socialization used more by sociologists and enculturation preferred by many anthropologists. A small difference exists between the terms, with **socialization** referring to the qualities instilled in a child through interaction with other people, and **enculturation** specifically including learning through symbolic means.

4. Musicianship

1. The terminology regarding pulses and beats is inconsistent, particularly when dealing with African music. In the usage here, pulses are rapid and of an equal length; beats, on the other hand, can vary between long and short in additive rhythms.

2. The 3 + 3 + 2 pattern   ♩ ♩ ♩   sounds very much like a pattern of five: ♩ ♩ ♪   It is possible that in some of the literature the two have been misrepresented in notation.

3. Pantaleoni (1985:141–143) presents an example of a Bulgarian song in which the second is considered a highly desirable consonant sound.

5. Meaning in Music

1. The degree of resemblance between sign and referent varies when iconicity is involved. This type of relationship is referred to in the literature on music as analogy, metaphor, coherence, correspondence, and homology.

2. The word emotion is often used synonymously with affect, but because psychologists have used "emotion" to refer to such measurable physiological changes as rage, affect seems to be a better word for referring to the more subtle feelings resulting from a musical experience.

3. Bourdieu (1977:166) notes the coherence between "objective structures" of experience and the "internalized structures" that result from growing up in a particular society.

4. Pantaleoni (1985:33–34) deals with expectations and meaning from the perspective of psychology.

5. Skill is not included in Merriam's summary of the Western aesthetic of music (1964:259–270).

6. This idea is related to the view of Jacques Maquet (1979:9), who has suggested that since the concept of art does not exist in many non-Western societies, it would be more objective to define art in terms of its place in Western culture, which *does* use the concept. Thus, he suggested that art exists where an art market is to be found, that is, the buying and selling of art objects as a commercial venture. He also suggests that the term "aesthetic" be used as a term distinct from "art," and that it be recognized as the non-instrumental forms of an object, or as features of an object that call forth contemplation.

6. Uses and Functions of Music

1. In the anthropological literature the nonexpressive goals are often called "instrumental." However, in discussing music, the use of the term instrumental can cause confusion because the word also refers to musical instruments. Thus, the term instrumental is avoided here in favor of the terms "pragmatic" or "utilitarian."

7. Change and Continuity

1. The term "musical change" is often used in reference to studies of change in music that focus on the sounds themselves. Since some important elements of change do not involve sounds at all, at least directly, the term "music change" is used here because it is more inclusive.

Glossary

Acculturated: Influenced by an alien culture.

Aerophone: A musical instrument that sounds by causing an enclosed portion of air to vibrate.

Aesthetic: Meaning or function of music in terms of its intrinsic qualities without reference to anything else.

Aesthetic locus: The form of aesthetic activity that is most prevalent and most important in a society or social group.

Affect: Delicate feelings or emotions.

Agent: A person who instigates and organizes musical events without necessarily taking part.

Analogy: A type of thought process whereby the mind perceives similarities between various aspects of experience.

Association: The basis of meaning, whereby experience is related to memory in the mind.

Bilateral: Refers to societies without clans or lineages, so that the males and females are equally important in determining ancestry.

Binary opposition: The organization of experience in terms of opposites.

Borrowing: The adoption of cultural features, including musical instruments and musical ideas, from other societies.

Calendrical rituals: Rites that occur at particular times through the year, such as the new year or harvest.

Call and response form: The type of music in which a soloist sings a line and a group responds; characteristic of African and African-derived music.

Canon: The performance of the same music by two parts, one following the other.

Caste: Groups whose members can only marry others in the group, and whose occupations are restricted.

Catharsis: A form of behavior that relieves anxiety and tension.

Cents: A system of measuring intervals in music by assigning the equivalent of one hundred cents to each semitone of the equal-tempered scale.

Chord: Several notes sounding simultaneously or perceived as a unit.

Chordophone: A musical instrument that produces sound by a vibrating string.

Circular breathing: In playing aerophones, the practice of using the mouth as an air chamber to maintain a steady flow of sound while inhaling through the nose.

Clan: A large group of people believed to be descended from a common ancestor in the distant past.

Coda: An extended ending to a piece of music or a performance.

Cognition: The activity of the brain related more to concepts than feelings.

Coherence: A postulated relationship between certain musical forms and forms of society or human life.

Commercial: Music events or complexes organized primarily for profit by an agent.

Communal: Music events or complexes organized and conducted by a group of people without a musical specialist.

Communication: Putting one's thoughts or feelings into a form that conveys them to someone else.

Compartmentalization: The practice of a society or individual when maintaining distinct separation between different idioms, rather than combining them.

Connotative meaning: Meaning given to music by the participants and audience through their own largely subconscious input.

Consumer: The people for whom music is created; the audience or the buyer of recorded or printed music.

Contractual: Music events or complexes for which a musician is procured on a short-term basis.

Creator orientation: The perspective of the person who has the skills needed to engage in creative activity, including music.

Crisis rites: Rituals intended to deal with difficult circumstances, particularly illness.

Critic: A person who provides evaluation of the musicians' work, usually reflecting the norms of the community.

Cross rhythm: Conflicting metric patterns occurring at the same time.

Cyclic form: The structure of pieces of music that contain a repeated pattern with variations.

Denotative meaning: Meaning purposefully inserted into music by the creator.

Didjeridu: An aerophone of the Australian Aborigines, consisting of a long wooden tube into which the performer blows or sings.

Diffusion: The passage of cultural features from one society to another.

Discursive consciousness: That part of an individual's knowledge which can be verbalized or explained.

Drone: A tone held constant through a piece of music while other parts vary.

Egalitarian society: A nonstratified society that does not limit access to prestigious positions, except by gender.

Electrophones: Instruments in which the sounds are electronically produced.

Emic: The meanings and perspectives of the participant in a group where research is being conducted.

Endogamous: Referring to a community or group (lineage, class) in which marriage with outsiders is not permitted.

Epic: The extensive history of a people presented in a poetic form, usually with music.

Ethnocentrism: The tendency to view all human behavior from the value system of one's own society, often including the view that other practices are inferior and misguided.

Etic: The meanings and perspectives of the outside observer.

Expression: Putting one's thoughts or feelings into a form, regardless of whether the message is received by someone else.

Fieldwork: The study of music that is carried on among the people who produce it, rather than in an office or studio.

Floating terms: The names of musical instruments that seem to diffuse separately from the instruments themselves; thus, the same term becomes associated with different instruments.

Free rhythm: A rhythm that lacks meter.

Fundamental: The lowest of the complex vibrations of a tone. It usually provides the basic pitch.

Genre: Refers to one of various categories of musical or verbal performances that occur in a society.

Gharana: The guilds formed by musicians in India.

Harmony: The patterns formed by successive chords as sets of prescribed tones.

Heptatonic: A basic scale having seven different pitches.

Hexatonic: A basic scale having six different pitches.

Hocket: A melodic pattern formed by the coordination of various pitches played by individuals successively.

Holistic: Refers to the inclusive and integrative view that things seen in their entirety are different from the sum of their parts.

Icon: A sign whose meaning is shown through resemblance or analogy. Iconic refers to meanings carried through perceived resemblances.

Idiophone: Instruments that vibrate without any particular tension, using the material of the instrument itself.

Index: The kind of sign operating through a physical connection between the sign and its meaning.

Individualistic: Refers to music events whose major feature is the motivation of the performer.

Informant: The person in a research situation who provides information to the researcher. It is important to distinguish this word from "informer."

Innovation-acceptance theory: The view that change involves the introduction of new features into a group, with subsequent acceptance or rejection.

Interval: The difference in pitch between two different tones.

Jaws harp: An instrument consisting of a plucked prong resonated in the player's mouth. Also known as Jew's harp.

Lamellaphone: An instrument formed of a series of reeds or iron prongs that are played by plucking.

Legitimacy: Recognition that certain forms of activity are valued in a society.

Lineage: A group of people descended from a common ancestor only a few generations back.

Linear form: The structure of musical pieces whose beginning and ending are definite and established.

Marking: An indication that a performance is to occur, and that evaluation is expected.

Matrilineal: Referring to societies where membership in clans and lineages is determined through females.

Melody: Combination of successive pitches to produce patterns of sound.

Membranophone: Instrument that produces sound by a vibrating membrane, often of leather.

Metaphor: A metaphor occurs when the meaning of one symbol becomes another symbol with an additional meaning.

Metric rhythm: The movement of music within regular patterns of stress, accent, or rests.

Mode: Standardized forms of tonal orientation involving the emphasis given to various tones within the pitch inventory.

Multifunctional: Relating to the characteristic of cultural features, including music, that enables them to serve several functions at once.

Multipart music: Performances in which different voices or sections of a group perform different musical patterns simultaneously.

Multivocalic: Relating to the presence of several meanings in the same symbol.

Musical segment: Those aspects of technology, social organization, and expressive culture that are related to making music.

Music complex: A set of music events having the same goal and the same conceptual basis, and performed by the same social group.

Music establishment: Those groups or individuals who exercise control over musical activities, either through economic, political, or ideological means.

Music event: Any occasion at which music is performed, heard, or talked about.

Noh: A type of Japanese theater with very restricted, stylized movement.

Objective consequences: The actual results of behavior.

Overtones: Those higher vibrations of a tone above the basic pitch that provide different forms of tone color or timbre.

Participant observation: Research conducted among human groups when a researcher takes part in the activities of the group.

Patrilineal: Refers to a society where membership in a clan or lineage is determined through males.

Pentatonic: A basic scale consisting of five pitches.

Performance: A specialized meaning of this term refers to an individual's expectation that a creative act will be evaluated by others.

Performance practice: The socially standardized ways of performing music in a given society.

Phonogram: The format used for distributing recorded music, such as records, tapes, and compact discs.

Pitch inventory: All the tones within the octave that are used in a particular musical tradition or a certain piece of music.

Polyrhythm: The practice of performing two or more rhythms or metrical patterns at the same time.

Practical consciousness: An individual's knowledge of how to deal with a particular situation, even though that knowledge cannot be put into words.

Pragmatic: Referring to forms of behavior that are intended to accomplish something practical or utilitarian.

Professionals: Musicians who make a living from their music.

Raga: A configuration of distinctive tone relationships and stylistic devices that serves as the basis for melody in the music of India.

Rank society: A transitional form between a nonstratified society and a stratified one where leadership roles are restricted but access to resources is not.

Rationale: Explanations used to justify behavior.

Regularities: Basic principles that might have exceptions, but are used for explaining social phenomena.

Repertoire: The totality of musical pieces that are customarily performed in a society, in a music complex, or by an individual. Also called repertory.

Repudiability: The ambiguous quality of the arts that permits the denial of meaning if it appears troublesome.

Rites of passage: Rituals performed to symbolize the passing of an individual from one social status to another, as in birth, puberty, marriage, and death.

Sarangi: A bowed lute type of chordophone used in India.

Situational meaning: Significance given to music through the context in which it is first experienced.

Socialist realism: The view of socialist societies that the arts must serve to express revolutionary ideology and be accessible to all the people.

Socialization: The process of learning the techniques, values, and symbols of one's society.

Social role: The socially acceptable ways of behaving according to one's relationships in a society.

Societal: Another term for social, with definite reference to society at large, rather than to socializing.

Sociocultural matrix: The environment of technological skill, social relationships, and cultural understandings in which music is produced.

Sonic design: The deliberate arrangement of sounds to produce pleasing patterns.

Sonic order: The relationships between tones that give them meaning and distinguish them from noise.

Specialists: People who are recognized as particularly good musicians, but do not make their entire living from music.

Sponsored: Referring to those music events or complexes where musicians are maintained over a long period of time, as in patronage.

Strophic form: The structure of pieces of music that consist of repeated verses or stanzas.

Subjective dispositions: The personal feelings or motivations that lead people to certain behaviors.

Symbol: A sign that calls attention to something beyond itself, sometimes limited to arbitrary meanings. Symbolic meanings and functions of music exist when music refers to other aspects of experience.

Syncretism: The result of combining features of two or more different societies into one new form, usually related to religion or the arts.

System: A group of things so closely related that a change in one will bring about change in others.

Tala: The patterns of beats, often irregular, serving as the rhythmic basis of the music of India.

Taste public: People who share common musical or expressive values.

Tende: The Tuareg drum made from stretching leather over a mortar; the term also refers to music using that instrument.

Theory of expectations: The hypothesis that emotion in music is due to the interplay between what one anticipates musically and what one actually hears.

Timbre: The particular quality of a sound caused by different combinations of frequencies in the sound waves occurring at the same time.

Tonal language: A language in which the pitch of a syllable distinguishes between meanings of words or grammatical features.

Tonal orientation: The overall impression of a particular pitch inventory determined by the way the various tones function in creating sound patterns.

Totem: A concept or an object, often an animal, used to symbolize a clan or a lineage.

Unconscious: Those human drives and motivations of which people are not aware.

User orientation: The perspective of the person who enjoys the creations of others, but does not have the skills to create.

Vina: A plucked lute from South India, similar to the *bin* in North India.

Vocables: Syllables that are sung but have no linguistic meaning.

References Cited

Anderson, Richard L. 1979. *Art in Primitive Societies.* Englewood Cliffs, N.J.: Prentice-Hall.

Balikci, Asen. 1970. *The Netsilik Eskimo.* Garden City, N.Y.: The Natural History Press.

Barnett, H. G. 1953. *Innovation: The Basis of Cultural Change.* New York: McGraw-Hill.

Barth, Fredrik. 1966. *Models of Social Organization.* London: Royal Anthropological Institute, Occasional Paper No. 33.

Bauman, Richard. 1977. *Verbal Art as Performance.* Prospect Heights, Ill.: Waveland Press.

Becker, Judith. 1972. "Western Influence in Gamelan Music." *Asian Music* 3(1):3-9.

———. 1980. *Traditional Music in Modern Java: Gamelan in a Changing Society.* Honolulu: University Press of Hawaii.

———. 1988. "Earth, Fire, *Sakti,* and the Javanese Gamelan." *Ethnomusicology* 32:385-391.

Berliner, Paul. 1978. *The Soul of Mbira: Music and Traditions of the Shona People of Zimbabwe.* Berkeley: University of California Press.

Blacking, John. 1965. "The Role of Music in the Culture of the Venda of the Northern Transvaal." *Studies in Ethnomusicology* 2:20-53. New York: Oak Publications.

———. 1967. *Venda Children's Songs.* Johannesburg: Witwatersrand University Press.

———. 1973. *How Musical Is Man?* Seattle: University of Washington Press.

Blumer, Herbert. 1969. *Symbolic Interactionism: Perspective and Method.* Englewood Cliffs, N.J.: Prentice-Hall.

Boiles, Charles L. 1967. "Tepehua Thought-Song: A Case of Semantic Signaling." *Ethnomusicology* 11(3):267-292.

Bourdieu, Pierre. 1977. *Outline of a Theory of Practice.* Cambridge: Cambridge University Press.

———. 1984. *Distinction: A Social Critique of the Judgement of Taste.* Translated by Richard Nice. Cambridge, Mass.: Harvard University Press.

Bourguignon, Erika. 1979. *Psychological Anthropology.* New York: Holt, Rinehart and Winston.

Card, Caroline. 1982. "Tuareg Music and Social Identity." Ph.D. diss., Indiana University, Bloomington.

Cavanagh, Beverly. 1982. *Music of the Netsilik Eskimo.* Ottawa: National Museums of Canada.

Chomsky, Noam. 1965. *Aspects of the Theory of Syntax.* Cambridge, Mass.: M.I.T. Press.

Clifford, James. 1988. *The Predicament of Culture.* Cambridge, Mass.: Harvard University Press.

Cohen, Abner. 1974. *Two-Dimensional Man.* Berkeley: University of California Press.

Columbia World Library of Folk and Primitive Music (SL 212). 1949. *Venezuela.* Edited by Juan Liscano. Recording by Pierre Gaisseau.

Coplan, David. 1978. "Go to My Town, Cape Coast! The Social History of Ghanaian Highlife." In *Eight Urban Musical Cultures,* edited by Bruno Nettl, 96–114. Urbana: University of Illinois Press.

Cudjoe, S. D. 1953. "The Techniques of Ewe Drumming and the Social Importance of Music in Africa." *Phylon* 14(3):280–291.

Cunnison, Ian. 1960. "The Omda." In *In the Company of Man,* edited by Joseph B. Casagrande, 309–331. New York: Harper & Row.

d'Azevedo, Warren L. 1958. "A Structural Approach to Esthetics: Toward a Definition of Art in Anthropology." *American Anthropologist* 60: 702–714.

Densmore, Frances. 1926. *American Indians and their Music.* New York: The Woman's Press.

Devereux, George. 1971. "Art and Mythology: A General Theory." In *Art and Aesthetics in Primitive Societies,* edited by Carol F. Jopling. New York: Dutton. (Orig. in *Studying Personality Cross-Culturally,* edited by Bert Kaplan. Evanston: Row Peterson, 1961.)

Elkin, A. P., and Trevor A. Jones. 1958. *Arnhem Land Music.* The Oceania Monographs, No. 9. Sydney: University of Sydney Press. (Reprints from *Oceania* 1953–1955.)

Feld, Steven. 1982. *Sound and Sentiment.* Philadelphia: University of Pennsylvania Press.

———. 1988. "Aesthetics as Iconicity of Style, or 'Lift-up-over Sounding': Getting into the Kaluli Groove." In *Yearbook for Traditional Music* 20:74–113.

Firth, Raymond. 1963. *We, the Tikopia.* Boston: Beacon Press. (Orig. 1936.)

———, ed. 1990. *Tikopia Songs.* Cambridge: Cambridge University Press.

Fried, Morton H. 1967. *The Evolution of Political Society.* New York: Random House.

Gans, Herbert J. 1974. *Popular Culture and High Culture.* New York: Basic Books.

Geertz, Clifford. 1973. *The Interpretation of Cultures.* New York: Basic Books.

Gennep, Arnold van. 1960. *The Rites of Passage*. Translated by Monika B. Vizedom and Gabrielle L. Caffee. Chicago: University of Chicago Press. (Orig. *Les Rites de Passage*, 1909.)

Giddens, Anthony. 1984. *The Constitution of Society*. Berkeley: University of California Press.

Haley, Alex. 1976. *Roots*. Garden City, N.Y.: Doubleday.

Harich-Schneider, Eta. 1973. *A History of Japanese Music*. London: Oxford University Press.

Henry, Edward O. 1976. "The Variety of Music in a North Indian Village: Reassessing Cantometrics." *Ethnomusicology* 20:49–66.

——. 1988. *Chant the Names of God*. San Diego, Calif.: San Diego State University Press.

Herndon, Marcia, and Norma McLeod. 1979. *Music as Culture*. Norwood, Penn.: Norwood Editions.

Herskovits, Melville J. 1948. *Man and His Works*. New York: Alfred A. Knopf.

Higgins, Jon B. 1976. "From Prince to Populace: Patronage as a Determinant of Change in South Indian (Karnatic) Music." *Asian Music* 7(2):20–26.

Homans, George C. 1958. "Social Behavior as Exchange." *The American Journal of Sociology* 62:597–606.

Hood, Mantle. 1971. *The Ethnomusicologist*. New York: McGraw-Hill.

Hornbostel, Erich M. von, and Curt Sachs. 1961. "Classification of Musical Instruments." Translated by Anthony Baines and Klaus P. Wachsmann. *Galpin Society Journal* 14:4–29. (Orig. "Systematik der Musikinstrumente." In *Zeitschrift fur Ethnologie* 46:553–590, 1914.)

Horton, Robin. 1973. "The Kalabari *Ekine* Society: A Borderland of Religion and Art." In *Peoples and Cultures of Africa*, edited by Elliott P. Skinner, 600–627. Garden City, N.Y.: Doubleday/Natural History Press. (Orig. *Africa* 33(2):94–114, 1963.)

Huizinga, Johan. 1955. *Homo Ludens: A Study of the Play-Element in Culture*. Boston: Beacon Press. (Orig. 1950.)

Johnston, Thomas F. 1973. "The Social Determinants of Tsonga Musical Behavior." *International Review of the Aesthetics and Sociology of Music* (Zagreb) 4(1):108–130.

——. 1976. *Eskimo Music by Region: A Comparative Circumpolar Study*. Ottawa: National Museums of Canada. Canadian Ethnology Service, Paper No. 32.

Kaemmer, John E. 1975. "The Dynamics of a Changing Music System in Rural Rhodesia." Ph.D. diss., Indiana University, Bloomington.

——. 1980. "Between the Event and the Tradition: A New Look at Music in Sociocultural Systems." *Ethnomusicology* 24:61–74.

Kartomi, Margaret J. 1980. "Musical Strata in Sumatra, Java, and Bali." In *Musics of Many Cultures*, edited by Elizabeth May, 111–133. Berkeley: University of California Press.

——. 1981. "The Processes and Results of Musical Culture Contact." *Ethnomusicology* 25:227–249.

Kauffman, Robert A. 1970. "Multi-part Relationships in the Shona Music of Rhodesia." Ph.D. diss., University of California at Los Angeles.

Kenyatta, Jomo. 1965. *Facing Mt. Kenya.* New York: Vintage Books. (Orig. 1938.)

Kimberlin, Cynthia Tse. 1980. "The Music of Ethiopia." In *Musics of Many Cultures,* 232–252. See Kartomi 1980.

Kirby, Percival R. 1971. "The Changing Face of African Music South of the Zambezi." In *Essays on Music and History in Africa,* edited by Klaus P. Wachsman. Evanston, Ill.: Northwestern University Press.

Kishibe, Shigeo. 1984. *The Traditional Music of Japan.* Tokyo: Ongaku no Tomo Sha Corp.

Kitahara, Michio. 1966. "*Kayokyoku:* An Example of Syncretism Involving Scale and Mode." *Ethnomusicology* 10:271–284.

Kluckhohn, Clyde and Dorothea Leighton. 1974. *The Navaho,* rev. ed. Cambridge, Mass.: Harvard University Press. (Orig. 1946.)

Kodály, Zoltán. 1960. *Folk Music of Hungary.* Translated by Ronald Tempest and Cynthia Jolly. London: Barrie and Rockliff.

Kroeber, A. L. 1963. *Anthropology: Culture Patterns and Processes.* New York: Harcourt, Brace & World, a Harbinger Book. (Orig. 1948.)

Lancy, David F. 1980. "Play in Species Adaptation." *Annual Review of Anthropology* 9:471–495.

Lansing, John S. 1983. *The Three Worlds of Bali.* New York: Praeger.

Leach, E. R. 1954. "Aesthetics." In *The Institutions of Primitive Society.* Glencoe, Ill.: The Free Press. (Lectures on the Third Programme, BBC.)

Li, Charles N., and Sandra A. Thompson. 1987. "Chinese: Dialect Variations and Language Reform." In *Languages and Their Status,* edited by Timothy Shopen. Philadelphia: University of Pennsylvania Press. (Orig. 1979.)

Locke, David L. 1978. *The Music of Atsiagbeko.* Ph.D. diss., Wesleyan University, Middletown, Connecticut.

Lomax, Alan. 1968. *Folk Song Style and Culture.* Washington, D.C.: American Association for the Advancement of Science, Publication No. 88.

Long, Tracy. 1977. "The Essence of Music: An Ethnography of Student Recitals." Unpublished MS.

McAllester, David P. 1954. *Enemy Way Music.* Cambridge, Mass.: Peabody Museum. (Papers of the Peabody Museum of American Archaeology and Ethnology, Harvard University, vol. 61, no. 3.)

———. 1984. "Native America." In *Worlds of Music: An Introduction to the Music of the World's Peoples,* edited by Jeff Todd Titon. New York: Schirmer Books.

McLean, Mervyn. 1986. "Towards a Typology of Musical Change." *The World of Music* 28(1):29–42.

———. 1990. "The Structure of Tikopia Music." In *Tikopia Songs,* edited by Raymond Firth. Cambridge: Cambridge University Press.

Malm, William P. 1977. *Music Cultures of the Pacific, the Near East, and Asia.* Englewood Cliffs, N.J.: Prentice-Hall.

Manga, János. 1988. *Hungarian Folk Songs and Folk Instruments.* Translated by Gyula Gulyás, Cynthia Jolly, and David Skuse. Budapest: Corvina. (Orig. 1969.)

Maquet, Jacques. 1979. *Introduction to Aesthetic Anthropology*. 2d ed. Malibu, Calif.: Undena Publications.

Marcuse, Sibyl. 1975. *Musical Instruments: A Comprehensive Dictionary*. New York: W.W. Norton.

Mead, Margaret. 1968. *Growing Up in New Guinea*. New York: Dell Publishing Co., Laurel Books. (Orig. 1930.)

Merriam, Alan P. 1964. *The Anthropology of Music*. Evanston, Ill.: Northwestern University Press.

————. 1967. *Ethnomusicology of the Flathead Indians*. New York: Wenner-Gren Foundation for Anthropological Research.

Merton, Robert. 1949. *Social Theory and Social Structure*. Glencoe, Ill.: The Free Press.

Meyer, Leonard B. 1956. *Emotion and Meaning in Music*. Chicago: University of Chicago Press.

Morgan, Harry T. 1942. *Chinese Symbols and Superstitions*. South Pasadena, Calif.: P.D. and Ione Perkins.

Nakane, Chie. 1970. *Japanese Society*. Berkeley: University of California Press.

Nettl, Bruno. 1964. *Theory and Method in Ethnomusicology*. New York: The Free Press.

————. 1983. *The Study of Ethnomusicology*. Urbana: University of Illinois Press.

————. 1985. *The Western Impact on World Music*. New York: Schirmer Books.

————. 1989. *Blackfoot Musical Thought: Comparative Perspectives*. Kent, Ohio: Kent State University Press.

Neuman, Daniel M. 1990. *The Life of Music in North India*. Chicago: University of Chicago Press. (Orig. 1980.)

Newcomer, Peter Jay. 1979. "The Production of Aesthetic Values." In *The Visual Arts: Plastic and Graphic*, edited by Justine M. Cordwell, 221–228. The Hague: Mouton.

Nketia, J. H. Kwabena. 1959. "Changing Traditions of Folk Music in Ghana." *Journal of the International Folk Music Council* 11:31–36.

Olsen, Dale A. 1980. "Folk Music of South America—A Musical Mosaic." In *Musics of Many Cultures*, 386–425. See Kartomi 1980.

Olsen, Paul Rovsing. 1973. "Acculturation in the Eskimo Songs of the Greenlanders." *Yearbook of the International Folk Music Council for 1972* 4:32–37.

Pantaleoni, Hewitt. 1987. "One of Densmore's Dakota Rhythms Reconsidered." *Ethnomusicology* 31:35–55.

————. 1985. *On the Nature of Music*. Oneonta, N.Y.: Welkin Books.

Peirce, Charles S. 1960. *Collected Papers of Charles Sanders Peirce*, vol. 2, book 2, chapter 3. Edited by Charles Hartshorne and Paul Weiss. Cambridge, Mass.: Harvard University Press, Belknap Press. (Orig. 1930.)

Picken, Laurence. 1957. "The Music of Far Eastern Asia." In *Ancient and*

Oriental Music, edited by Egon Wellesz. New Oxford History of Music, vol. I. London: Oxford University Press.

Purcell, William L. n.d. Jacket notes on Nonesuch Record H72012.

Radcliffe-Brown, A. R. 1922. *The Andaman Islanders.* Cambridge: Cambridge University Press.

Ranger, T. O. 1967. *Revolt in Southern Rhodesia 1896–1897.* Evanston, Ill.: Northwestern University Press.

Reichard, Gladys A. 1950. *Navaho Religion.* Princeton, N.J.: Princeton University Press.

Reischauer, Edwin O. 1981. *The Japanese.* Cambridge, Mass.: Belknap Press.

Rouget, Gilbert. 1985. *Music and Trance.* Chicago: University of Chicago Press. (Orig. *La musique et la transe.* Editions Gallimard, 1980.)

Ryan, Peter, ed. 1972. *Encyclopaedia of Papua and New Guinea.* Melbourne: Melbourne University Press in association with the University of Papua and New Guinea.

Sachs, Curt. 1940. *The History of Musical Instruments.* New York: Norton.

———. 1962. *The Wellsprings of Music.* New York: Da Capo Press.

Sachs, Nahoma. 1975. "Music and Meaning: Musical Symbolism in a Macedonian Village." Ph.D. diss., Indiana University, Bloomington.

Sakata, Hiromi Lorraine. 1983. *Music in the Mind: The Concepts of Music and Musician in Afghanistan.* Kent, Ohio: Kent State University Press.

Schieffelin, Edward L. 1976. *The Sorrow of the Lonely and the Burning of the Dancers.* New York: St. Martin's Press.

Schwarz, Boris. 1983. *Music and Musical Life in Soviet Russia,* enl. ed., 1917–1981. Bloomington: Indiana University Press.

Seeger, Anthony. 1979. "What Can We Learn When They Sing? Vocal Genres of the Suya Indians of Brazil." *Ethnomusicology* 23:373–394.

———. 1987. *Why Suya Sing: A Musical Anthropology of an Amazonian People.* Cambridge: Cambridge University Press.

Seeger, Charles. 1960. "On the Moods of a Music-Logic." *Journal of the American Musicological Society* 13:224–261.

Signell, Karl. 1976. "The Modernization Process in Two Oriental Music Cultures: Turkish and Japanese." *Asian Music* 7(2):72–102.

Slawek, Stephen M. 1988. "Popular *Kirtan* in Benares: Some 'Great' Aspects of a Little Tradition." *Ethnomusicology* 32(2):77–92.

Slobin, Mark. 1976. *Music in the Culture of Northern Afghanistan.* Tucson: University of Arizona Press. (Viking Fund Publications in Anthropology, No. 54.)

Spradley, James P., ed. 1969. *Guests Never Leave Hungry.* New Haven: Yale University Press.

Stevenson, Robert. 1968. *Music in Aztec and Inca Territory.* Berkeley: University of California Press.

Stone, Ruth M. 1982. *Let the Inside Be Sweet.* Bloomington: Indiana University Press.

Turino, Thomas. 1989. "The Coherence of Social Style and Musical Creation Among the Aymara in Southern Peru." *Ethnomusicology* 33:1–30.

Turnbull, Colin. 1961. *The Forest People*. New York: Simon & Schuster, a Touchstone Book.

———. 1965. *Wayward Servants*. Garden City, N.Y.: Natural History Press.

Turner, Victor. 1967. *The Forest of Symbols: Aspects of Ndembu Ritual*. Ithaca, N.Y.: Cornell University Press.

Wachsmann, Klaus P. 1961. "Criteria for Acculturation." *Report of the Eighth Congress of the International Musicological Society*, pp. 139–149.

Wade, Bonnie C. 1979. *Music in India: The Classical Traditions*. Englewood Cliffs, N.J.: Prentice-Hall.

Wallace, Anthony F.C. 1966. *Religion: An Anthropological View*. New York: Random House.

Wallerstein, Immanuel. 1983. *Historical Capitalism*. London: Verso Editions.

Wallis, Roger and Krister Malm. 1984. *Big Sounds from Small Peoples: The Music Industry in Small Countries*. New York: Pendragon Press.

Waterman, Christopher. 1990. *Juju: A Social History and Ethnography of an African Popular Music*. Chicago: University of Chicago Press.

Waterman, Richard A. 1952. "African Influence on the Music of the Americas." In *Acculturation in the Americas*, edited by Sol Tax. Chicago: Proceedings of the 29th International Congress of Americanists, vol. 2, 207–218.

———. 1971. "Music in Australian Aboriginal Culture—Some Sociological and Psychological Implications." In *Readings in Ethnomusicology*, edited by David P. McAllester. New York: Johnson Reprint Corp. (Orig. *Journal of Music Therapy* v:40–49, 1955.)

White, Leslie. 1949. *The Science of Culture*. New York: Grove Press.

Wild, Stephen A. 1975. "Walbiri Music and Dance in their Social and Cultural Nexus." Ph.D. diss., Indiana University, Bloomington.

Witmer, Robert. 1973. "Recent Change in the Musical Culture of the Blood Indians of Alberta, Canada." *Yearbook for Inter-American Musical Research* 9:64–94.

Wolbers, Paul. 1985. "National Music." In *The Western Impact on World Music*, Bruno Nettl, 90–92. New York: Schirmer Books.

Wolf, Eric R. 1982. *Europe and the People Without History*. Berkeley: University of California Press.

Zemp, Hugo. 1971. *Musique Dan*. Paris: Mouton.

Zindi, Fred. 1985. *Roots Rocking in Zimbabwe*. Gweru: Mambo Press.

Additional Resources

Periodicals

The following publications customarily deal with the music of societies all over the world. Large research libraries, as well as many smaller libraries, will have these periodicals in their collections:

Ethnomusicology is the journal of the Society for Ethnomusicology.

The World of Music is the journal of the International Institute for Comparative Music Studies and Documentation in Berlin. It is related to UNESCO.

Yearbook for Traditional Music is published by the International Council for Traditional Music.

Books

The following books complement this work by providing full descriptions of the musical practices of selected ethnic groups. The following two books are collections of descriptions written by the people who did basic research among the groups concerned:

May, Elizabeth, ed. 1980. *Musics of Many Cultures: An Introduction.* Berkeley: University of California Press.

Titon, Jeff Todd, ed. 1991. *Worlds of Music: An Introduction to the Music of the World's Peoples,* 2nd ed. New York: Schirmer.

The next two books together provide a survey of the music traditions of the world. They are written by ethnomusicologists with wide experience in the study of world musics:

Malm, William P. 1977. *Music Cultures of the Pacific, the Near East, and Asia,* 2nd ed. Englewood Cliffs, N.J.: Prentice-Hall.

Nettl, Bruno et al. 1990. *Folk and Traditional Music of the Western Continents,* 3rd ed. Englewood Cliffs, N.J.: Prentice-Hall.

The following book has descriptions, historical data, and line drawings of musical instruments from all over the world.

Musical Instruments of the World: An Illustrated Encyclopedia by the Diagram Group. 1978. New York: Facts on File Publications.

Recordings

The cassette available from the University of Texas Press includes examples of many of the groups mentioned in the book. No examples of the music of India or Japan were included because their music is widely available commercially.

It is difficult to recommend specific recordings because many of them tend to be on the market for a very short time. The world music section of large record shops will have many recordings from around the world. Many record shops will be willing to place special orders. Readers who prefer older traditional forms of world music rather than the more recent popular forms should look particularly at the following series:

Smithsonian/Folkways, distributed by Rounder Records.

UNESCO productions, including Auvidis/UNESCO, Le Chant du Monde, and Ocora, distributed by Harmonia Mundi.

Nonesuch Explorer Series.

Lyrichord Traditional World Music.

Index

Aborigines (Australia), 31; Arnhem Land, 38–39, 59–60; didjeridu, 38; Dreamtime, 31, 46, 63; music and environment, 146–147, 164; songs, categories of, 59–60; song cycles, 63, 112–113, 146, 164; Yirkalla, 48, 117, 149. *See also* Warlpiri

Abstract music. *See* Aesthetic

Additive rhythms. *See* Asymmetrical rhythms

Aerophones, 89, 91, 92, 193–194

Aesthetic: as philosophy, 3, 6, 124; as intrinsic qualities 125–127; as values, 128–132; as sonic design, 132–137; as skill, 137–139; and legitimacy, 139–141; definition of, 124–125; Western views of, 127

Aesthetic locus, 69

Aesthetic (non-referential) meaning, 109, 124–141

Affect, 111, 128–141, 147, 217n.2

Afghanistan: categories of music, 66, 122; motivation for rituals, 152; musicians, roles of, 49; sponsored music, 40–41; views of music, 118–119, 122

Africa: change in music of, 181, 189, 201–202; drumming, 79, 107, 115, 116, 156; Ghana, 78, 162, 180; instruments, 129, 180, 181–182, 194; rhythm, 100, 107, 132; singing, 103, 113, 190; West Africa, 48, 107, 116, 156. *See also* Kpelle; Mbuti; Shona; Tuareg; Venda; Zimbabwe

Age, music and, 44, 48

Agent, 41, 55–56

Altered state of consciousness, 166–168

Analogy, 119, 135

Analysis, 15–16, 36, 41, 112, 118; levels of, 16–17, 24–25, 182–183, 188

Andaman Islands, 23–24, 149, 150

Anderson, Richard L., 51

Animal sounds, 4, 29, 59, 113

Anthropology theory, 20–25, 147–148, 171–174

Anzad. See Tuareg

Apprenticeship, 80

Arnhem Land. *See* Aborigines

Art music, 35, 66, 177–178, 207, 217n.6

Association, 109

Asymmetrical rhythms, 99–100, 197, 216n.(4)1, 216n.(4)2

Audience. *See* Consumer

Aymara: music and society, 63–64, 107, 120–121, 157; performance practice, 52; song identity, 60

Aztec, 32–33, 40

Baggara, 36–38

Bali, 84, 99, 102, 147, 192

Kauffman, Robert A., 104
Kenya, 164
Kenyatta, Jomo, 164
Kimberlin, Cynthia Tse, 50
Kinship, 56
Kirby, Percival R., 190
Kishibe, Shigeo, 51, 62, 72, 94, 97,
  99, 100, 102, 106, 129–130
Kitahara, Michio, 189
Kluckhohn, Clyde and Dorothea
  Leighton, 163, 165–166
Kodály, Zoltán, 18, 66
Kpelle: cues, 118; performance, 18;
  polyrhythm, 107; roles in perfor-
  mance, 52, 54, 55; view of time,
  121
Kroeber, A. L., 152
Kwakiutl, 195, 202–203

Lancy, David F., 151, 152
Language and music: in music in-
  dustry, 200; mutual influence of,
  72–74; similarities between 15,
  17, 27, 112, 115, 116; stress lan-
  guages, 74; tonal languages, 73;
  universal language, 108
Lansing, John S., 147
Leach, E. R., 184
Learning music, 77–81, 153; imita-
  tion, 77–78; institutions, 79–81.
  See also Socialization
Legitimacy, 64–68, 133, 139, 156,
  210, 216 n.(3)1; change in, 67,
  176–179; defined, 64
Li, Charles N. and Sandra A.
  Thompson, 73
Linear form, 102, 120
Locke, David L., 79
Lomax, Alan, 21–23
Long, Tracy, 149
Lutes, 89, 193
Lyres, 89

McAllester, David P., 1, 72
Macedonia: age and music, 48,
  157–158; change, 174, 177, 192;

definition of music, 4; meaning
  of songs, 119, 127; ritual songs,
  70–71, 154
McLean, Mervyn, 84, 98–99, 181
Malm, William P., 100, 103,
  192–193
Malta, 183
Manga, Janos, 178
Maquet, Jacques, 69, 215 n.1,
  215 n.4, 217 n.6
Marcuse, Sibyl, 193–194
Marginal survival, 175–176
Marking, 17–18, 65, 127
Materialism, 207
Matrilineal societies, 47
Mbuti, 30, 41–42, 101, 121, 168
Mead, Margaret, 77
Meaning in music, 108–141;
  change in, 175; types of, 109. See
  also Pragmatic meaning; Sym-
  bolic meaning; Aesthetic
  meaning
Melody, 100–102
Membranophones, 92–94
Merriam, Alan P., 25, 51, 104,
  117–118, 127, 135, 153, 154, 158,
  159, 167, 175, 181, 182, 189,
  215 n.2, 216 n.(3)2, 217 n.5
Merton, Robert, 143
Metaphor, 122–124
Metric rhythm, 99–100
Meyer, Leonard B., 134–135
Mnemonic devices, 79
Mode, 101, 116–117
Moiety, 56, 120
Morgan, Harry T., 123
Motif, 112, 115
Motivation, 139, 142–143,
  147–150, 180–182
Multifunctional, 143–144, 153
Multipart music, 104–107
Multivocalic symbols, 110
Music: as commodity, 207; catego-
  ries of, 5, 35, 59–60, 66–67, 118,
  136; definitions of, 4, 59. See also
  Change in music; Music-making

е

UNIV. OF MD COLLEGE PARK

3 1430 04740458 9

". . . Kaemmer has done an excellent job of summarizing the anthropological concerns of the study of music in and as culture. . . . [The book] will serve as an excellent textbook for general introductory courses on music in world cultures."
—STEPHEN M. SLAWEK, ASSOCIATE PROFESSOR OF MUSIC, UNIVERSITY OF TEXAS AT AUSTIN

Whether for entertainment, ritual, art, or protest, the urge to make music links every human culture. Though the forms and sounds vary widely, music is a feature of all human societies, no matter how much they differ otherwise.

In this comprehensive work, John E. Kaemmer presents an overview of the social and cultural factors involved in music making, as well as an introduction to the unique features of various world music systems. He emphasizes the social sources of music, offering important insights into the human motivations and behaviors that produce music. Organized topically, the book covers four main areas—form, meaning, use, and function of music. Kaemmer draws his examples from both small-scale and modern, complex societies throughout the world.

Music in Human Life will be especially useful to students in musicology and anthropology, as well as ethnomusicology. An accompanying audiotape allows readers to hear the music of the major ethnic groups used as examples in the book.

John E. Kaemmer is a professor emeritus of anthropology at DePauw University.

TEXAS PRESS SOURCEBOOKS IN ANTHROPOLOGY, NO. 17

More on music and culture

MASTERS OF CONTEMPORARY BRAZILIAN SONG
MPB, 1965–1985
By Charles A. Perrone
ISBN 0-292-75102-8

THE MUSIC OF BRAZIL
By David P. Appleby
ISBN 0-292-75111-7, paperback

THE TEXAS-MEXICAN CONJUNTO
History of a Working-Class Music
By Manuel Peña
Mexican American Monographs, No. 9
ISBN 0-292-78068-0
ISBN 0-292-78080-X, paperback

Write for a catalog of books on anthropology.
UNIVERSITY OF TEXAS PRESS
Post Office Box 7819
Austin, Texas 78713-7819

ISBN 0-292-74314-9

90000>

9 780292 743144